The Love of History and the Future of Christianity

Toward a Manifesto for a Next Christianity

By

Gene W. Marshall

Resurgence Publishing Corp.

COPYRIGHT ©2014 Gene W. Marshall

*The Love of History and the Future of Christianity:
Toward a Manifesto for a Next Christianity*

All rights reserved. No part of this book may be used or reproduced in any manner whatsoever without permission, except in the case of brief quotations in critical articles and reviews. Contact Resurgence Publishing Corporation.

Published with Permission: The original materials used in this publication are provided by Gene W. Marshall. All editing of those materials is the responsibility of the editors of this publication and in no way is intended to represent the views or opinions of those who contributed originals or copies of the materials.

Email: Info@ResurgencePublishing.com
URL: www.ResurgencePublishing.com

Cover Art by Lee Sax
Cover Design by Wayne Marshall
ISBN: 978-0-9850458-4-5
Printed in the United States of America

*Presumption upon the past power and glory of Christendom
is perhaps the greatest deterrent to faith's real confession
in our present historical circumstances. Douglas John Hall.*

Contents

Endorsements vii
About the Author xii
Acknowledgments xiii

Foreword 15
Introduction: What is a Manifesto and
        Why do we need a Next Christianity? 19

Part One: The Love-of-History Challenge   21
1. Christianity and the Love of History 23
2. Taking the God of History Personally 41
3. Jesus of Nazareth and the Christ of History 47
4. Paul's Religious Revolution 60
5. The Word of God Controversy 79
6. Christianity and Church History 87
7. The Chalcedonian "Solution" 104

Part Two: Other Big Turning Points
in Western Church History   111
8. Augustine and a Greek/Hebrew Synthesis 113
9. Thomas Aquinas and Aristotelian Worldliness.....................130
10. Luther and the Reform of Authority 139
11. Kierkegaard and the End of Authority 147
12. Kierkegaard's Descendants and the Social Gospel 157

Part Three: A Reconstruction of Christian Practice   175
13. An Existential Trinitarianism 179
14. History and the Age of Spirit 195
15. Post-Christendom Institutionalization 209
16. Christianity as Healing Methods 221
17. Circles, Assemblies, Guilds, and Retreats 240
18. The Eternal Mission to Planet Earth 249

Appendix: The League of Next Christianity Organizers 263
Publisher's Comments 273

Endorsements

Anyone concerned with the life and task of the church may well find this book a refreshing read, either as an individual or as part of a study group. Whether reading Hebrew scriptures or New Testament stories; studying early church councils or key figures of church history; wrestling with post-Kierkegaardian theologians or with current social issues, Gene Marshall offers a 21st century perspective. At every turn of the page, he recasts language born of an ancient worldview into words and images that evoke real-life experiences for our time.
  –*Doris S. Hahn: An organizer and teacher with the Ecumenical Institute and the Institute of Cultural Affairs for twenty-two years*

This book grows out of a decades-long immersion and grappling with the most profound insights from the most original and daring Protestant theologians of the 20th century. No one knows this tradition better than Gene Marshall. Even more, no one has done more to implement this tradition by radically reimagining what the institution and practices of the church are and can become. More than a manifesto, this book is also a how-to guide.
  –*Dr. Jeffrey W. Robbins: Professor and Chair of Religion and Philosophy, Lebanon Valley College, Author of In Search for a Non-Dogmatic Theology*

Gene Marshall captures the essence of active engagement with the texts of Christianity in order to keep it alive and vital for today's and even tomorrow's world. In doing so, he reinvigorates our Judeo-Christian tradition of speaking truth to life, and life to truth. He has written deeply about finding meaning and relevance, guided by the collected wisdom of Hebrew and Christian philosophers, science, reason, history, considerable personal insight and experience and the experiences of some of the great storytellers of all time. You owe it to yourself to be warmed by the glow of the fire that Marshall has kindled. His words are at once personal, intimate, historic, insightful, enthusiastic and perhaps even prophetic.
  –*Caryn Mirriam-Goldberg: Ph.D., Kansas Poet Laureate for 2009-13, bioregional organizer*

Gene Marshall's projection of a "next Christianity" takes into account the entire 3,000 years of Christian history and its turning points, portrayed in the Scripture and tradition of the church, and merges it with the future at the nexus of the present. To validate his claim for the need for a "next Christianity" & the role it will play in the historical continuum, Marshall appeals, not to the authority of the church, but to the authenticity of his own most personal experience. The hope that the author holds out is for the creation of an institutional structure that will nurture, rather than suffocate, the missional dynamic of the movemental church (the "Awed Ones"). The promise of such a hope is not that the church in any of its forms may grow in size and stature, but that a troubled 21st Century Earth may be served through "witnessing, justing and presencing love." One need be neither Christian nor "religious" to find wisdom here for living responsibly and effectively in our challenged and challenging times.

   –Randy Williams: *A community volunteer who promotes sustainable living from the grassroots outward*

In this ambitious work that the author modestly claims is merely an attempt *Toward a Manifesto for a Next Christianity*, Gene Marshall presents a succinct historical overview of the three-thousand year journey of Judeo-Christian practice, emphasizing that a deep love of history is crucial for envisioning a new practice of this religious heritage for the 21st century. Marshall uses strong, often provocative and earthy language to break open new dimensions of thought. He challenges the person of faith to explore an entirely new way of thinking, acting and being, and offers specific healing methods and pioneering social forms to advance such exploration. I found the charts and images particularly helpful reinforcements of the text, and appreciated his passionate call for attention to contemporary social justice issues throughout the book.

   –Marilyn R. Crocker: *BA, MAT, Ed-D, Educational and Organizational Development Consultant*

I want to personally thank Gene Marshall for his enduring love of the Christian tradition. I am especially moved by the idea of a next Christianity. This provocative image should warm our hearts and challenge our minds. It is a must read for Christians and non-Christians alike.

–**Larry Ward**: *Dharma teacher ordained by Thich Nhat Hanh, Coauthor of Love's Garden: A Guide to Mindful Relationships*

If you are seeking to live a 21st century Christian life reconciled with present science and one which begins with authentic human experience and seeks to care deeply for the urgent challenges of our times, then dialogue with Gene Marshall. He will connect your present life experiences and questions to Christian symbols, history and scripture and release your compassion and care.

–*Jeanette Stanfield*: Educator, Editor of The Courage to Lead, by Brian Stanfield 2nd edition, and author of Just Checkin on Ya.

The Love of History and the Future of Christianity exemplifies what Gene Marshall has always done best: express a love for Christianity in very practical terms in a way that does not insult its audience with oversimplification or inaccessible language. Instead, here we have a primer for Christians living in post-Christendom searching for a Christianity that is deeply rooted in history and ready to make the next big historical step for a faith so desperately in need of transformation.

-**Dr. Christopher D. Rodkey**: *Pastor, St. Paul's United Church of Christ, Dallastown, and Instructor, Penn State York, and author of Too Good to Be True*

Gene Marshall does two great things with this book. He brings history alive in a way that enables a person living in the 21st Century to both appreciate and appropriate the journey of consciousness that has been emerging over the centuries of insight by the giants of theological thought. Secondly, for those of us who have despaired at the ability of the historical church to be either relevant or sustaining, Marshall creates a practical vision of how those of us who love this heritage can be newly embodied version of Church. Marshall offers an exciting alternative based on a profound grasp of Reality and communion. A must read for those seeking hope for a new operational form for Those Who Care.

–*Jack Gillis*: Lay scholar of theology, research chemist, Order-Ecumenical member

In this very timely and helpful book, Gene Marshall invites and challenges Christians and potential participants of a Next Christianity to Get Real: real concerning one's understanding of the experience of REALITY or the AWESOME Mystery that scriptures, religions and cultures have called "GOD"; real concerning MYSTERY'S Eternal presence and activity in everyday experience and ongoing history of life; real concerning the inclusiveness and expansiveness of this Next Christianity; real concerning what a realistic life style of trust, love and freedom look like; and real concerning creating a network of intentional, learning communities committed to serving and healing the earth locally and globally.
  –**Ellie Stock**: *Presbyterian clergy, church and community teacher and ecology facilitator*

Death is certain. Experience is certain. In *The Love of History & the Future of Christianity* Gene Marshall takes the reader on a journey into an encounter with Ultimate Reality. It is this encounter we most require today to re-unite our global community with the Real, forsaking the contemporary idols by which we are consuming our selves and the planet on a path to certain destruction. This book represents a necessary first step in abandoning our infatuation with unreality and returning "home" to the One Reality that can restore us.
  –**Michael D. May**: *Teacher, Group Discussion Leader, Curriculum Editor for Interior Mythos Journeys*

Gene Marshall's 'love of history' comes out of the lineage of Isaiah, Jesus, and Kierkegaard. Like all his other books, his theologizing is eventful and personally grounded. He is among those who transpose the 1st century experience of the Trinity into a rigorous existential expression worthy of the 21st century. And, as a prophet in this apocalyptic time, he coined the visionary phrase 'eco-democracy'. For pioneering the next Christianity, this book is a primer for all thoughtful individuals and for adventuresome small groups.
  –**Ken Fisher**: *Regional coordinator of leadnow.ca –for people-powered change to defend our democracy and climate, Realistic Living Research Symposium member*

This masterful pull-together of a radically spiritual understanding of our profound human role in history is all a dedicated group will need: to hear the call, be sustained, and become practically prepared to change history so the "common good" does come on Earth. Gene Marshall has been used mightily with this best one-book source I know for this task.

–*John P. Cock*: *Daily blogger (www.reJourney.blogspot.com) and author of The Transparent Event:Post-modern Christ Images and Our Universal Spirit Journey*

Marshall's Love of History addresses in a single coherent narrative what I have struggled with in my attempt to act as a responsible member of St. James Episcopal Church in Lenoir, North Carolina. His narrative delivers explosive images that can heal the devastating effects of our current societal fragmentation and the resulting experience of living an isolated life. Marshall clears away misconceptions that bar people from "accessing the awe"--the essence of Christianity. In the last section of his book, Marshall completes the narrative with a description of the practices and organizational forms for anyone interested in "accessing the awe" now in this moment and in the moments to come.

–*Don Bushman* *ACloseColleague.com*

About the Author

Gene Wesley Marshall began his education as a mathematician and physicist. In 1953 he decided to leave a mathematics career and attend seminary at Perkins School of Theology in Dallas, Texas. He has served as a local church pastor, a chaplain in the army, and in 1962 joined a religious order of families (the Order: Ecumenical), and traveled across the United States, Canada, Latin America, Europe, and Asia as a teacher and lecturer of religious and social ethics topics. These trips included an in-depth study of world cultures and a vivid sense of the social conditions of the world's peoples. He was an active participant in the civil rights revolution, serving for one year as the Protestant executive of The National Conference on Religion and Race. For six years he served as dean of an eight-week residential academy that trained leadership for religious and social engagement work throughout the world. In 1984 Gene and Joyce Marshall organized a nonprofit educational organization, Realistic Living, and began publishing journals, books, and essays. This book is his seventh book-length project. Gene and Joyce live in Bonham, Texas in a straw-bale house.

Acknowledgments

I am grateful to Joyce Marshall and Alan Richard for continuing help with this book and for years of discussion with me about these topics. Members of the Research Symposium on Christian Resurgence for Century Twenty-One also played a large role in the shaping of the content of this book. And my thanks go to John Epps for his careful reading, editing, and foreword. Thanks also for the editing help of Doris Hahn, Michael May, and Ellie Stock. And my special thanks to George Walters for his editing, layout and publishing labors on this book.

The authors whose insights have gone into this work are many, but prominent among them are Joseph W. Mathews, H. Richard Niebuhr, Rudolf Bultmann, Paul Tillich, Dietrich Bonhoeffer, Rudolf Otto, Susan K. Langer, Richard Feynman, Charlene Spretnak, Mary Daly, A. H. Almaas, and Ken Wilber.

Foreword

January 2014

It's been many years since I've worked closely with Gene Marshall. The invitation to write this Foreword has been a welcome opportunity to see that he has continued to be a master teacher.

The book's title "The Love of History and the Future of Christianity" is an understatement. To be sure, loving history is an underlying theme, but that hardly indicates all of what is to come. This book is a primer in Old Testament, New Testament, Church History, Contemporary Theology, Group Methodology, Environmental Responsibility, and Institutional Design, all presented with clarity and passion, integrity and challenge. While specialists in any of these fields may find points with which to disagree, the basic presentation has a consistency and relevance that is difficult to ignore.

The announced intent of the book is to provide a "manifesto" for what Gene calls "A Next Christianity," what others have referred to as "the shape of the Church to come." As such the book runs through history from Isaiah to Kierkegaard to provide a suitable background and relation to the established Christian tradition. In the historical scan, Marshall de-cyphers the insights of classical doctrines, translating them from their two-story cosmology into language intelligible today. Doing that for the Christological and Trinitarian doctrines of the early Church is a formidable task. Here it is carried out with vigor.

One underlying theme located in the historical scan is the transformation of Authority from an external imposition of power in the early Church to a reliance on Authenticity in post-Kierkegaardian times. Since the Reformation there has been an increasing confidence in the laity, both male and female, to exercise responsibility in organizations of the Church. The capacity for consensual decision-making is a key component of any religious organization of the future. Neither the Bible nor ecclesiastical hierarchy can claim authority in matters of the faith. Only authentic persons (Awed Ones) can do that. Of course this does not mean anomie, and Gene has an interesting section in his description of the future religious organization in which he states that there must be a leadership role ("Enablement Offices") in the new form. And since these organizations still claim the title of "Christian," scripture and tradition continue to have a prominent place.

A second theme of the book is societal responsibility. Faith is not now nor has it ever been for self-aggrandizement. The faithful are to serve society's needs. In this case, protection of the environment assumes prominence as the major issue to be addressed. I was surprised to find it mentioned even in the section on the Prophet Isaiah (as an example of speaking the unwelcome Truth). Readers will be delighted or dismayed with this emphasis, but the focus on environmental responsibility throughout the book will demand that it be taken seriously. Unlike other environmentalists, Marshall grounds his call to action on a New Christian's response to the gift of grace.

The book's section on institutional design draws from the author's experience with the Ecumenical Institute. He advocates weekly circles of 12 and quarterly assemblies of 12 Circles. Then there should be action guilds (temporary groups to carry out particular projects) and occasional retreats. In the section on forming and conducting these groups, the book sets out a list of practical methods for conversing, studying, and engaging in effective action, and provides a list of recommended readings for those who decide to form a Circle. This section is a manual for the implementation of experiments on the new form of the Church.

So who is the audience for this book? Clearly it is meant for those whose interest in Christianity is practical. While there is enough deep theory to challenge the most analytical reader, the book is intended to lead readers to the point of action. If you're one who finds your present Church life satisfying, then this is probably

Foreword

not the book you want to read. If you're interested in theology or understanding the doctrines of the Church, you will find this book both provocative and illuminative. If you're one concerned about practicalities of church renewal, then this can be a manual for action. If you're one of what Gene calls "The Christian Alumni," then you will find the book a welcome homecoming.

John L. Epps, PhD
Author
The Theology of Surprise: Reflections on Life's Mysteries
Resurgence Publishing Corp. 2013

Introduction:

What is a Manifesto and Why do we need a Next Christianity?

A manifesto is an examination of the past and a vision of the future that focuses upon action in the present for a community of actors who are calling themselves and others into being as a historical project of change.

Why is there a need for manifest action to build a Next Christianity? Why do we need a religious practice at all? Why is a Christian religious practice useful for ourselves or for whoever else might choose to join us in such a practice? And how do we ascertain what is for us the essence of a vital Christian practice for living our lives in this troubled and awesome 21st Century – a practice that we want to practice and feel is worth inviting others to practice? What can we learn from the abundance of ways that people have created to practice a religion they call "Christian"? How can we sort out from the history of Christianity what is essential from what is wayward or obsolete?

It is to such questions that a manifesto needs to give answer. At the same time a manifesto needs to be relatively brief and yet long enough to be convincing and clear. These are not easy requirements, for the topics involved can easily consume many books. In fact many very important books have already been written: such writings fill whole libraries. The manifesto I have in mind is a piece of writing that boils down this edge thinking to a tight focus on the core issues needed for a call to action within these 21st Century social conditions and within the redefinition of religion that is taking place in our time. I do not claim that this

Introduction

brief book is that manifesto, but I do claim that it is an attempt to move in that direction.

I am going to take a somewhat indirect approach to dealing with these challenges. I am going to start with a topic that I believe is one of the core blocks to a vital Christian resurgence – a love of history. By "a love of history" I mean a recovery of the past for the sake of anticipating the future in order to live fully in the present. I am assuming that a love of history and a loyal service of that Mysterious Power experienced in the unstoppable flow of time are foundational for a vital resurgence of a Christian-heritage-related religious practice. I am further assuming that such a recovery not only serves those of us who are reaching out for a vital practice of Christianity, but also contributes to our present moment of history a needed revolutionary force that can assist all humans to create a viable future for the human species.

Part One will focus on the basic love of history and especially upon key historical turning points within that period of time in which the writings of the Christian Bible were composed.

Part Two will focus on four key turning points within that period of time we commonly call "Church history."

Part Three will focus on the future, the turning point that we now occupy and the vision of a Next Christianity that is or may be emerging.

Part One:

The Love-of-History Challenge

The story of Christianity is not two thousand years old but three thousand years old. Jesus is a major turning point in this story, but he is also a continuation of the older story. We cannot understand the New Testament without understanding the Old Testament. When Jesus speaks of God, he speaks of the God of Abraham, Isaac, and Jacob, of Moses and the Prophets. Jesus did not see himself as a Christian. Even Paul did not see himself as a Christian. Jesus issued a call to true Judaism, and Paul was a Christ-way Jew. In the lifetimes of Jesus and Paul Christianity and Judaism did not exist as separate religions.

And even after separate religions began to form toward the later portion of the first century, Christianity maintained its ties with the ancient writings, with the old stories, with the Exodus event, the Exile event, and most important of all with the core truth surrounding the word "God." Understanding what that word points to and what trust in God means is a topic that is in serious crisis in both typical Christianity and typical Judaism today.

Christianity maintained ancient Judaism's passion for the importance of Law as a description of the Demand of God. The view of Law that we see in Jesus is a break with the understanding of Law as an objective rule that did not go to the core of the self in that self's relation with God. The view of Law that we see in Paul was a break with Law seen as a means of making oneself righteous in God's sight, a righteousness of which one can boast. For Paul there is no way to be "righteous" through human effort. Only the grace of God and the faith that grace make possible is the route to righteousness. After such a healing of our lives, the Law remains holy and good, an indicator of appropriate behavior in relation to the Demand of God. These Pauline attitudes toward the Jewish Law created flexibility in how obeying the Law was to be practiced. The Spirit of the Law was now more important than the letter of the Law. Tradition was opened up, a fresh creativity for the religious and moral life was initiated from a deeper place than the more objective, authoritative, scribal teachings of right and wrong.

The enigmatic depths of these topics need to be more fully explored. Part One is about a love of history that was well established in the Old Testament period, and about the historical turning points in the history of religion that were initiated by Jesus, Paul, and John.

Chapter 1

Christianity and the Love of History

When I first encountered the topic of history in a high school history course, I was bored to distraction – memorizing dates, learning facts about my nation's origins. It made no contact with me. I loved mathematics. I loved literature. But history, ugh. And I was living within World War II history at the time. I hoped our side would win the war. I knew how to name and identify all the warplanes. But the topic of history did not grab me until I was in college and read an obscure book entitled *Wake Up or Blow Up*. A man named Frank Laubach wrote this book about Hiroshima, Nagasaki, and the nuclear arms race between the US and the USSR. For me, this was an engaging experience with history. Such "history" involved me and my species of life on this planet. It made the meaning of "history" a matter of the future as well as the past.

My love of history reached a sort of peak many years later as I walked the streets of Jackson, Mississippi with Martin Luther King Jr. and went to Washington D.C. to hear him give his "I have a Dream" speech. I knew then that in my small way I was not only living history, I was making history. By that time I was a deeply committed Christian, familiar with the Bible and clear that when Martin Luther King spoke of racial justice as a "promised land," he too was deeply embedded in Biblical imagery. He too knew that the Bible expressed a love of history and that those events of the dim past had meaning for talking about the present and future. I too was able to relate the Promised Land of the Moses story to our own Promised Land of racial justice in the US of A.

History

Sometime later, I had developed, with a lot of help from others, a philosophy of history. I could give a lecture on the three types of history: (1) **scientific history**, the clarification of facts – like who shot Abraham Lincoln, (2) **rational history**, seeing in the mind's eye an organization of the various eras of time – like the stone age, the industrial age, and era of civilization, etc., (3) **existential history**, a swing of memory into the past in order to create a swing of anticipation into the future in order to make relevant decisions in the present. I counted all three of these types of historical thinking as important, but it was existential history that engaged me. It taught me the importance of the past for anticipating the future and making decisions in the present. It also taught me that "history" did not mean inevitable progress or inevitable descent or any other set of determined outcomes. History was open ended and "bendable" through human decisions. The future would be a surprise, but that surprise could be different if humans today choose this rather than that. I was now aware that such existential history was the kind of history that characterized the Bible. In the biblical story, I read with delight sayings like: "Behold I set before you life and death, so chose life and live." Such words as these were framed as the Word of God. If "God" means the Final Reality we are meeting in the events and challenges of history, then God's Word is not specific Hebrew or Greek words magically infused into some Bible writer's mind. Rather, "God's Word" is a revelation to me and others of what confronts us in history.

I knew that Moses, factually speaking, was an obscure person who may have lived in the vicinity of 1290 BCE. But it was his story (much elaborated by later history-loving people) that spoke to me personally. I could identify with: leaving the horrors of slavery in Egypt; escaping into the wilderness; building a new kind of law by which to order a post-Egyptian life; building that new life on the basis of loyalty to that Wild Openness in the nature of history; engaging in possibilities, challenges, and surprises never known by those who stayed back in the patterns of Egyptian civilization. I understood that I too could experience my own Exodus from the familiar patterns that most people took for granted. I too could enter into a wondrous, challenging, and surprising journey of freedom that came with loyalty to the Sovereign Power who spoke to me in the events of history – who called me to action and required me to figure out how to say in relevant language what this Word from the event-speaking God was saying to me and my society.

Christianity

Practicing Christianity in a thoroughgoing way includes a love of history and a responsiveness to the God of history that was worshipped and struggled with for over a thousand years before the life of Jesus. In Christianity, fully appropriated, Spirit and history are melded. This is also true of Judaism. Indeed, Christianity learned this emphasis from its Hebrew roots. Leaving Egypt was about a love of history. Creating stories about ancient legendary ancestors migrating from Ur (Iraq) to Israel was about a love of history. While this love of history was not definitively put to paper until the J-writing in the vicinity of 950 BCE, this love of history was a characteristic of this Hebraic culture reaching back into the very dim past. This history-loving heritage had reached a cultural fullness in the writing of the closing chapters of the book of Isaiah (560 BCE). The book of Isaiah was not written by one person, but by a community of people through several hundred years of history. The early chapters of Isaiah were written by a seer who had the name "Isaiah." He lived at the time of the Assyrian Invasions of Palestine in around 732 BCE. He composed these words, "Ah, Assyria the rod of my Anger." He put these words into the mouth of the God of history. He believed that whatever was happening in history was meaningful as the acts of this Sovereign God. He spelled out this Sovereignty as something Kingly, but not fatalistic. History included the freedom of Isaiah, or any other human, to act this way or that way – to be obedient or disobedient, to be realistic or illusory. Nevertheless, in the course of history there was a KING, beyond all human agency, whose purpose was present in everything that happened. Being a prophet, as Isaiah felt called to be, meant saying what this KING was doing in the history that was happening. Isaiah said that the KING was disciplining Israel and Judea with a cruel rod of discipline. According to Isaiah, the King of Assyria did not know that he was being so used by this Sovereign KING. The King of Assyria was only following his own arrogance, and the KING of history would deal with this arrogant man later on. But for now this arrogant unconscious ruler of a foreign power was a rod, a tool, in the hand of the KING who ruled all history and to whom the Spirit descendants of the Mosaic breakthrough were called to be loyal. Whatever was happening was a Word from the ever-present Eternal Reality. A loyalty to this Reality meant being radically realistic. If your nation is being beaten to death or threatened, this is God speaking to you. You need to wake up and respond.

    Contemporary Christians who are engaged in feminist and democratic commitments often have difficulty with the "KING" imagery used by Isaiah and others, including Jesus. We need to understand that these witnesses lived in an era in which their society never heard of democracy or of a liberation from patriarchy. Social power was invested in a King, and this "kingness" was a metaphor they used for the Almighty, Mysterious Ruler of history. Today, we might prefer another image than "KING" or "Sovereign," but we need to retain the ancient meaning of an All-powerful Force that meets us in our daily, weekly, annual experience of history.

    Isaiah lived a long and eventful life and created within the nation of Judea a strong community who preserved his words and added more words to the scrolls that bear his name. We do not know how many "Isaiahs" authored this book, but the scholars are clear that chapters 40 through 55 were written by one of the most insightful writers in the entire Bible. Scholars call this anonymous writer, Deutero-Isaiah, Second Isaiah. His words were added to the book in the vicinity of 545-540 BCE. He lived during the last years of the Babylonian Exile when the Persian Empire was on the rise and promised new hope for exiled people. Cyrus the Great, the Persian king, conquered Babylon in 539 BCE. One of his first acts was to allow people exiled by the Babylonians (the Jews, among other captive peoples) to return to their respective homes. Back in 598-596 BCE the Babylonians had conquered Judea and carried off some of its people (especially the leadership) into exile in Babylon. Members of the Isaiah community were included. Second Isaiah was speaking to the Judean community in exile, and his words were that the KING of history was doing a new thing. The grand words of this anonymous prophet were adding to the Isaiah scrolls.

> *Comfort, comfort my people*
> *– it is the voice of your God*
> *speak tenderly to Jerusalem*
> *and tell her this,*
> *she has received at the Lord's hand*
> *double measure for all her sins.* (Isaiah 40:1-2)

This prophet continues with a call to return home to Judea and rebuild the ruined land and cities: "clear a highway across the desert for our God." This challenge may not have been appealing to every member of these exiled people. Some had become well-established in Babylon, so making that long trip and doing the hard work of social rebuilding may not have appealed to every hearer of these words. But according to Second Isaiah the opportunity to return was a calling from the Sovereign KING of history. Nowhere in the Bible is the vigorous, inclusive, Sovereignty of the God of History more vigorously stated.

Christianity and the Love of History

Yahweh, the everlasting God, creator of the wide world,
grows neither weary nor faint;
no man can fathom his understanding.
He gives vigor to the weary,
new strength to the exhausted.
Young men may grow weary and faint,
even in their prime they may stumble and fall;
but those who look to the Lord will win new strength,
they will grow wings like eagles;
they will run and not be weary,
they will march on and never grow faint. (Isaiah 40:28-31)

Though we are now clear that all this is poetry, Second Isaiah is interpreting an experience of history. He is articulating a call to be obedient to Reality with a capital "R." He was seeing an opportunity to leave exile, return to their homeland and rebuild their "Reality and history-loving society." If they had not done so, we might never have heard of Judaism, Christianity, or Islam.

We who are choosing to continue this loyalty to the God of history do not need to get distracted into literalistic questions about the existence of a Male Superbeing. At that time in history, a super-realm mythology was the cultural custom. And "male" in that unconsciously patriarchal culture meant "power." For 2nd Isaiah "the everlasting God" meant whatever POWER it IS that we are encountering in the flow of history. History matters. And if history matters to you, you probably learned this from 2nd Isaiah, 1st Isaiah, Moses, and yes, Jesus, Augustine, Luther and their Spirit descendants.

Not every religious practice or philosophy of life has this deep bond with history, but Judaism and Christianity, in their origins, certainly do. If in our churches and synagogues we have lost that love of history, we have lost something essential and precious about this 3000-year-long tradition of religious practice.

Christianity and the Love of History

Jesus

Jesus lived in a time of Hellenistic Judaism, but unlike Paul he did not speak Greek. He was embedded in a rural Galilean village culture that was quite thoroughgoing toward the Hebrew side of this Hebrew/Greek cultural mixture. Jesus may never have heard of Plato and Aristotle, but he had heard of Moses and Isaiah. His language was a language of history that had been created for him since the time of Moses. His "kingdom of God" was something happening in history. "Look, the poor are hearing good news, the sick are healed, the blind see, the lame walk, the dead are rising." This poetry is about history, and so is the following: "Thy kingdom come, thy will be done, on Earth as it is in heaven." This is a prayer about history. Translated into a language for our times this sentence of prayer means: "May the loyalty to that Final Power experienced by us in our history (the Power obeyed by Moses, all the prophets) be realized now on this planet, for such living is the essence of realism."

The birth, life, teaching, doings, and death of Jesus (plus his resurrection in the body of his disciples) are understood as the coming of the long expected Messiah. All this is an event in history that the New Testament writers considered to be the launch of a new era of history. Like the Exodus, this event constituted an agreement with the Sovereign KING of history, The Power that posits all things – their birth, their sustenance, their limitations, their death. This new agreement did not renounce the old agreement; it deepened the old agreement and was an agreement with the same Reality. It constituted an agreement to die to ego, personality, nation, race, humanity, everything and be raised up in absolute obedience to the Sovereign KING of history. We who take on this covenant choose to be born when we are born, to be the gifts and limitations we are given, and to die when we die. We obey the KING. One way to be obedient today is to quit calling Reality "King" or "Queen." New language is needed. "The Power that posits us" will do. "The Mystery that is the final Unknowableness in this somewhat known Reality" might work. "The No-Thing-Ness out of which all things come and to which all things return" might do. And let us not omit "The Every-Thing-Ness in which all things coexist."

We need new poetry; but new words, though essential, are not what ultimately matters. What ultimately matters is our own personal experience of this Mysterious Power that is powering the history of our lives and times. And let us be clear that though we are powerless before this power, we are being given power and honor and freedom by this Power. We are in fact determined by this Power to be our freedom, to make choices that alter the course of history. But this Power does not relinquish to us the ability to fully determine how our choices will work out in history. All final outcomes remain in the control of this Sovereign Power. Whatever we envision, intend, or hope for, the outcomes of history will continually be surprises to us.

Paul

After Jesus and his Galilean followers, the first big shift in the cultural history of Christianity begins with **Paul** (5-67 CE). This shift includes and extends through the writings of Mark, Matthew and Luke/Acts (70 CE or slightly later). Rudolf Bultmann calls this the Hellenistic Judaism period of Christian practice. With Paul Christian practice is adapting to the towns and cities of the Roman Empire. It is in dialogue with the cultural festering of that wider world. Nevertheless, this second stage of Christian practice was being developed within a thoroughgoing Hebraic subculture of the Roman Empire. The "Gentiles" who are involved in this community are the "God fearers" drawn to the devotional and ethical practices of the synagogues. They are thoroughly Hebrew-ized even though uncircumcised. They know and worship the Hebraic God of history. They accept the teachings of Paul, Mark, Matthew, and Luke as enrichments of what it means to worship the

Sovereign of history that was worshiped by Moses and the prophets.

John

The next big shift in the cultural history of Christianity begins with the writings of the Fourth Gospel and the three letters ascribed to the pseudonym "John" (90-100 CE). In these writings the Christian impetus is being communicated to people who are not familiar with Hellenistic Judaism or with the Hebraic historical story. Christianity is now beginning a thoroughgoing adaptation to Greco-Roman culture. John maintains his Hebrew roots by making it clear within the Greek worldview that the Word of God is not words in Greek or Hebrew, but an event in history, especially a particular body of flesh and blood encountered and "eaten" in a historical setting.

To be a competent practitioner of an up-to-date Christian practice in the 21st Century we need to be aware of at least this much detail about the early history of Christian practice. We cannot properly grasp the writings of the New Testament without a sense of this historical story. It is not necessary that every Christian practitioner be an expert on the intricate details of New Testament formation. What is needful is that we each have a sense of this basic story and the awareness that this historical story about Christian practice is an essential part of the Next Christian practice, if that practice is to be fully adequate as a continuation of a Christian mode of religious practice.

The Old Covenant

The first four-fifths of the Christian Bible contain understandings about the God of history that preceded Jesus. Those who have suggested that Jesus worshiped a different God than Moses and the prophets do not understand a single word of the New Testament. Even the term "New Testament" is meaningless until we see that this term points to a New Covenant with the same Reality that was covenanted with by Moses and friends in the Exodus. We have no understanding of the Old Testament until we understand that the words for God used in the Old Testament writings are devotional words for Reality – the plain and simple Reality confronting us in the course of history, my personal history, my nation's history, my planet's history, and the history of the cosmos. And "history" in this context does not mean a dead past. History means something happening now. History means something anticipated in the future. And only within a present and future understanding of history does the history of the past come alive for us.

Also, let those of us who practice Christianity understand this New Covenant as a dynamic in both Christianity and Judaism rather than as an evolutionary advance for Christians over Jews. The New Covenanting dynamic began with Joshua at the Jordan River. Jeremiah spoke of a New Covenant when his nation was being conquered and exiled. Jeremiah was not predicting Christianity, but seeing the Mosaic covenant written anew on the hearts of his people, now without a nation. So when Christians spoke of the Jesus events as a New Covenant, they were reenacting an old understanding. And both contemporary Jews and Christians can and need to embrace Jesus' rejection of nit-picking moralism and ethical hypocrisy. New covenanting with Final Reality is a dynamic in the whole of human history, not a special virtue of Christian-identified practitioners. The New Testament does indeed witness to a new covenanting of long lasting meaning, but it is also a thoroughgoing affirmation of the old covenant of the Exodus and of the Old Testament writings included in the Christian Bible.

Also, it is important to note that the writings of the prophets of the Old Testament are themselves happenings in history in which the Hebraic roots blossomed into full flower. These major sages – Amos, Hosea, Isaiah, Jeremiah, Ezekiel, Second Isaiah – are comparable with other sages across the planet who lived in the same time gap (750 - 540 BCE), the Buddha, Lao Tzu, Zoroaster, and a number of others. The oldest of the Upanishads were slightly earlier. The Socrates, Plato, Aristotle upheaval was slightly later

(450 - 322 BCE). The Old Testament prophets must be understood if we are to fully understand Jesus and the Christian sages that followed after Jesus. I will illustrate the relevance of this prophetic heritage with some further reflection on one of those prophets.

The Prophet Isaiah

"Prophet," by the way, is a word that needs translation. Here is its meaning in language that we 21st Century humans might be able to absorb: A prophet is a visionary who sees what is happening in history more clearly than what is being seen by most of the people who are the companions of this awakening person. A prophet sees the future more clearly, not in the sense of a prediction of what is going to happen, but as clarity about the options for human action that can be taken NOW and the probable outcomes of those actions or inactions. So, with that in mind let us decode First Isaiah's own story (Isaiah 6) of his calling to be a prophet.

> *In the year of King Uzziah's death I saw the Lord seated on a throne, high and exalted, and the skirt of his robe filled the temple. About him were attendant seraphim, and each had six wings; one pair covered his face and one pair his feet, and one pair spread in flight.*

This Divine King whose train filled the temple was not seen with biological eyes: it was seen in dream imagery; and even in this dream imagery only six-winged angels were seen. The KING was hidden behind these wings of flapping Awe.

In this trance that Isaiah was having in the temple, the super-angels were "calling ceaselessly to one another,"

> *Holy, Holy, Holy is the Lord of Hosts*
> *the whole Earth is full of his glory.*

In his book *The Idea of the Holy*, Rudolf Otto defines "holy" as an experience of a "tremendous mysteriousness" that produces dread and fascination and requires courage to sustain. "Awe" is another word for this experience. So I can imagine that the cry of these angels had a rather harsh tone like the caw of crows.

AWE, AWE, AWE
the whole Earth is filled with this cawing.

This seems to be pretty close to how Isaiah says he experienced it:

And as each one called, the threshold shook to its foundations, while the house was filled with smoke. Then I cried,

Woe is me! I am lost,
for I am a man of unclean lips
and I dwell among a people of unclean lips;
yet with these eyes I have seen the King, the LORD of Hosts.

Isaiah is talking about a "tremendous mysteriousness" that is undoing his entire religion, convicting him of lying and of dwelling among liars who do not speak the truth. Isaiah's "unclean lips" does not mean jam on them or four-letter words coming out of them. Isaiah was a preacher and his words had been false. His lips are dirty because of the words that he had been speaking were lies, and he was telling these lies among a people who are also lying. Apparently, part of this lying had to do with not being willing to face that nation's vulnerability to the Assyrian conquests, their trusting in weak allies, and their general delusory attitude toward historical developments. I can certainly see such lying in my own society today.

We also need to unpack some of the other symbols Isaiah uses. The house that was filled with smoke was Isaiah's temple of worship. Whatever had gone on there had become cloudy. And the threshold that shook to its foundations was that same temple, that same worship that Isaiah and his nation practiced. Isaiah's religion was being shaken to its foundations by the death of King Uzziah and whatever other happenings had audited the religious inadequacies that Isaiah practiced. As we see from Isaiah's further writings, he was dealing with the rise of Assyrian power and the danger his nation faced in the light of that history. His companions in the worship of the God of Israel were unenlightened about what that loyalty to the God of history meant in those historical circumstances.

Interiorly, Isaiah felt his whole sense of self being undone, yet he saw himself staring at WHAT rules the cosmos. "King" is a symbol for being ruled, not a description of that indescribable Final Reality. The Final Reality Isaiah sees is not seen with the descriptive mind. It is seen with the image-making consciousness of Isaiah. Isaiah uses the poetry of his time to share his experience, but in order for us to hear Isaiah rightly, we need to hear that Isaiah's King of history is a "tremendous mysteriousness" mediated to us by experiences of Awe flapping between us and that Final Majesty.

"LORD of Hosts" might be translated as "YAHWEH, the GREAT I AM THAT I AM, the Source of all angels – all experiences of Awe." And "YAHWEH" is a historically rich term that reaches back in Isaiah's memory to the Exodus from slavery in Egypt and to the adventures in Awe-filled living told of Abraham, Isaac, and Jacob.

So, Isaiah sees something in his history, something important, however cryptic it may seem to us in the way Isaiah tells about it. It has to do with the impending conquests of the Assyrians, and perhaps with the death of Uzziah, a fairly competent King. Anyhow, Isaiah's story of his call continues:

Then one of the seraphim flew to me carrying in his hand a glowing coal that he had taken from the altar with a pair of tongs. He touched my mouth with it and said,

> *See, this has touched your lips;*
> *your iniquity is removed,*
> *and your sin is wiped away.*

Christianity and the Love of History

This forgiveness or fresh start for Isaiah is pictured as a hot experience. Lying lips are seared, burned clean with a hot truth that has been suppressed by Isaiah's frequently spoken untruths. What a wonderful teaching about forgiveness this is: forgiveness is not an indulgence of our falseness, but a welcome home to our reality. Being forgiven by The Final Reality means the burning of our false approaches to living and an opening to that mode of living that we are made for, the real historical situation to which we must respond.

I imagine that Isaiah is more or less stunned, but with eyes and ears open to see and hear something fresh about the way life is. And what Isaiah says he hears is YAHWEH discussing something with his angels as if Isaiah were not even there.

Then I heard the LORD saying, "Whom shall we send? Who will go for us?"

I imagine there was a bit of pause in the drama at this point, before Isaiah points out that he is listening and that he is ready to be the one who is sent.

And I answered, "Here am I; send me."

Then the King, the LORD of Hosts says in effect, "GO and tell this people THE TRUTH."

The "Divine Voice" explains further that the people are not going to listen. So Isaiah asks, "How long do I have to endure saying what no one hears?" And the substance of the answer he got was this: "As long as it takes."

So what does it mean for us to be prophetic in our moment of history. <u>Here is an obvious example of a prophetic truth we might proclaim:</u>

<u>Burning fossil fuels is a "crime" of massive destruction against the planet and all its life forms, including humanity</u>.

Christianity and the Love of History

If any of us are going to take up the Hebrew and Christian style of "prophet" in our historical setting, we will need to proclaim this truth for "as long as it takes" for humanity to hear it and live it. Global warming deniers are rejecting this truth because it calls into question almost everything they believe, as well as entailing a serious challenge to the self-interests that are protected by disbelieving this truth of the impending climate catastrophe. Their supposed "selves" are being called in question by this truth. That is why their resistance is so strong.

And so a prophet speaking to our times will need to continue to enrich his or her poetry: "The Seas will rise, the hurricanes and tornadoes will become stronger and stronger. Eastern Seaboard cities of the US will become uninhabitable, washed to their deaths by so many floods that rebuilding is futile. Currently inhabited low-lying islands will disappear entirely. Rich agricultural land will become deserts. Previously dry places will become lakes. Floods and droughts will appear where never experienced before." Perhaps such poetry will get and is getting many people's attention. But more is required. The case needs to be made that lying is taking place in denying global warming; in denying the extent of its consequences; in denying that human agency is causing the CO_2 buildup; in denying that burning fossil fuels is a crime against humanity, the Earth, and plain honesty. That these denials and their consequences are not yet a crime with regard to the laws of a society is not a justification for denial, but a challenge to change the laws.

Furthermore, this truthful, contemporary prophet will need to take on the moderate liberal in his or her halfway responding. "Even those of us who do believe the truth of global warming and its consequences and who are willing to act upon these realizations need to confess that we are nevertheless guilty of the crime of burning fossil fuels whenever we switch on a light or press the starter on our automobile. Even if we drive a Prius and opt for an electric bill that presupposes Green energy production, we only moderate the evil in which we participate. There is no escape from participation in this criminal society in which we are embedded.

Believing the truth of global warming means that for us to be persons of integrity, we must confess our guilt in supporting solutions to this crisis that are trivial. We are being called to upgrade our thought and action to a more serious level: namely, dismantling (rather than repairing) this entire social fabric and building an alternative way for all of us to live.

And that means: Starting wherever we can best start. For example, the unneeded industry of tar-sands oil that is just starting up can be resisted totally – stopped in its tracks no matter what the costs of doing so, no matter what our Presidents and Congress persons are not willing to do. We prophets must make plain to a blurry-minded population that burning the tar-sand energy source may be the end of life on earth for our species, at least a set of catastrophes so immense that we do not want to even think about it.

Secondly, we can support a moratorium on all new coal-fired power plants. Coal was making a comeback when it was cheaper than oil or natural gas, but as natural gas becomes cheaper, coal is not even needed for the transition away from fossil-fuel burning. Furthermore, we now have the technology to move toward an electro-hydrogen infrastructure energized mainly by solar and wind energy sources. We have to accept a period of transition from oil and natural gas to solar and wind, but we do not have to accept the lie that we cannot prosper without expanding our fossil fuel use.

Furthermore, we 21st Century prophets will need to call out our culture for minimizing the possibilities of an alternative energy system. The cost of solar and wind energy production has already come down to the same level as fossil fuels and is still falling. It is already the cheapest and least destructive way to go. People who claim that these technologies have not yet achieved the readiness needed for energizing our society are like the people who said the automobile was not ready because there were so few smooth roads for it, and it scared the horses. Yes, a new infrastructure for solar and wind energy must be constructed; but however big this task may be, the facts of our situation simply do not support the foot-dragging pessimism that tells us that this transition cannot be accomplished at a quick-time pace. The sophisticated lies of oil-company-financed think tanks can now be laughed off our TV screens and ripped out of our news magazines.

As history unfolds the above account may need to be changed in some details and expanded further, but it illustrates the style of the 21st Century prophet on this and many other issues. Getting people to listen to Reality is the prophetic task, but we prophets are called to speak the truth whether people listen or not. And we are called by the KING of history to continue telling the truth for *as long as it takes* for everyone to hear it.

* * * * * * * * *

These honest detailed words about climate crisis call to our attention the meaning of a "Word" from the Sovereign KING of history. A 21st Century prophet is called to speak words to our illusion-ridden and lying society that are the WORD of REALITY. Such speaking is part of what it means to love history. Such speaking is part of what it means to practice a Next Christianity or a Next Judaism. Such speaking is also part of what it means to be a contemporary devotee of Allah and to renew the deep heritage of Islam. Such speaking is part of what it means to be an engaged Buddhist or a Gandhi-inspired Hindu. Judaism and Christianity have pioneered this deep love of history, this deep love of speaking for the God of history. But even the avowed atheist who sees the truth of global warming and acts upon this truth as a *call* from history to be a realistic person is thereby more Jewish and more Christian than he or she may want to claim.

Such an understanding within our historical times with regard to Isaiah's witness within his historical times is an example of the process of decoding any part of the Biblical witness. Such a manner of dealing with Christian scripture is a necessary part of creating a

Christianity and the Love of History

Next Christian practice that speaks to those of us who are choosing a Christian practice for our nurture. Such an interpretation of Scripture also informs our witness as Christians to our human companions who experience with us the history of our times and the Final or Eternal Reality that we all confront within that history.

Chapter 2

Taking the God of History Personally

As noted in the previous chapter history is not simply a study of the past but a study of the present and future. As we anticipate being a Christian in our present time and in our future, we find that the very idea of "God" is in crisis. This has been the case for many decades. Many of us, perhaps most of us if we are honest, have serious doubts about the reality of a second-story realm occupied by God, angels, devils, gods, goddesses, or the souls of our grandparents. So faith in God is in crisis in our contemporary culture. Some don't care. Some are glad to see all that strange talk disappear. Some intuit that all this strange talk was mythology and that such myth was pointing to something serious. But even those of us who like a good myth find decoding the myths of the Bible a challenge. Finding personal meaning in these ancient stories requires help not commonly found in most Christian communities.

The biblical scholar and theologian Rudolf Bultmann, living in the mid-20th Century, wrote an essay entitled "The Crisis of Faith."[1] He understood that we needed a means of personally understanding how we experience or can experience whatever it was that the biblical writers were pointing to with "faith in God." Following is a summary of his way of introducing us to the

---

[1] Bultmann, Rudolf; *Interpreting Faith for the Modern Era* (edited by Roger A. Johnson, Fortress Press: 1991) "The Crisis of Faith" page 240

meaning of the word "God," when that word is taken seriously – that is, when it means something in our experience.

Bultmann begins by pointing out that we all have deep cares given with our existence. We care about our security. We care about having true and beautiful "up" experiences and wanting them to last. We care about having persons who love us and whom we love. We care about finding knowledge. We care about accomplishing something that lasts. And we care about having a good image of ourselves. We care. We just do care. We can't help but care. Yet all these cares meet disappointments, limits, and stone walls of termination. Bultmann examines these cares one by one and in the process shows us how the word "God" can point to real experiences that we have every day.

First of all, we all care about being secure. We store food for meals today, tomorrow, and the next day. We want to keep clothes on our bodies, a roof over our head, and a good bath ever so often. We put away money for our impending retirement and old age. We make friends who may help us in our times of need. We conduct good health practices to secure a longer, healthier life. We care about all of this. If it were up to us, we would be secure in these and other ways forever.

Yet we know that we cannot make our lives absolutely secure. No matter how much money we have, we could die next week. Tomorrow we could step on an unexpected ice slick on our back porch, hit our head on a stone, and die. Then what benefit to our security would all that money be. Or we might come down with a dread disease. A stock market crash might wipe out our hard earned retirement. The electricity might go off and spoil tomorrow's dinner. We are not secure. The course of history, the cosmos, our real life is not set up in such a way that we can be as secure as we would be if it were entirely up to us. Some mysterious ongoingness, some "power" in the way history is constructed interrupts our quest for security with the insecurity that is always part of our lives. That mysterious power that we all experience or can experience is, according to Bultmann, the God of

Taking the God of History Personally

biblical faith. This God is not a supernatural being, a big person, a being of any sort. This God is the Source of our being, the sustainer of our being, the limiter of our being, and the tomb of our non-being. However unconscious we may like to be of this mysterious Power, we are zero distance from this God in every moment of our personal history.

Bultmann continues showing us other ways that we confront this God. We care for pleasant times. We are in constant quest for true and beautiful "up" moments, and we hold on to such moments for as long as we can. Perhaps we recall moments with a lover in some beautiful place. Perhaps we recall great times with our children before they morphed into teenagers. Perhaps we recall great times with our teenagers. Perhaps we recall times when the work we were doing was intensely satisfying. Whatever the "up" moments that we have, here again we meet a grim truth: we cannot control time. Time is controlled by some other Power than our will. Time is unstoppable by us. Our "up" moments end, perhaps turn "down" into moments we want to end sooner than they do. We confront a power that is in charge, not us, of the flow of time. That power is or can be personally experienced at any time in our lives. That power, Bultmann says, is an experience of "God."

We also care about being loved by others and feeling loving toward others. We want acknowledgment and acceptance from others. But our lives turn out to be more than living like two lovebirds that can never separate. We experience being catapulted into solitude. As Martin Luther put it, we all do our own dying as well as our own trust in God. Indeed, we are alone in all the big decisions – whom shall I marry, what shall I do with my one life? We may even like solitude sometimes, but we also find that we desire to be in some nest of love. And in relation to this desire for love, we often resist times of absolute solitude: we rush to find friends to be with us. We find that it is some Mysterious Almighty Power, not us, that is forcing solitude upon us. This power is an experience of God. We cannot escape it. This power is not a supernatural being, not a being of any sort. This power is the

Ground of all Being. Paul Tillich called this power the mystery, depth, and greatness of our existence. Solitude is part of that greatness, but as Søren Kierkegaard noted about solitude:

> *In the constant sociability of our age people shudder at solitude to such a degree that they know no other use to put it to but (oh, admirable epigram!) as a punishment for criminals. But after all it is a fact that in our age it is a crime to have spirit, so it is natural that such people, the lovers of solitude, are included in the same class with criminals.*[2]

Bultmann continues by pointing out that our care for knowledge also meets its limits. Just when we get Newtonian physics well in mind, perhaps we learn how Einstein improved things. Perhaps we resonate with the scientist who said with some astonishment, "The more we know about nature the more we know we don't know." I entered my first marriage thinking I knew what it meant to be married. Within months I did not know. In my second marriage, I am still learning. A similar experience is met in our life of doing. Our accomplishments are seldom as much as we want, and what we do accomplish seldom stays done. I made some great changes in that first church I pastored, but the next pastor undid them all. They say that even the great pyramids of Egypt are wearing down. One day they will just be more sand in the desert. Our accomplishments like our knowledge are limited. A Mysterious Power *"sets a terminus to our knowing and doing."* This power, Bultmann says, is God.

And finally, Bultmann described the limitation we call "guilt." In whatever ways we seek to think well of ourselves, we find that these very quests set the stage for still another type of limitation. Bultmann's description of these limitations is devastating: our existence he says, *"knows the call of conscience which summons to duty, and recalls from thoughtlessness and aberration to everyday things, and pronounces the verdict "Guilty" on wasted time and lost opportunity,*

---

[2] Kierkegaard, Søren; *The Sickness Unto Death*, (Water Lowrie translation, Princeton University Press: 1953) page 198

impure thoughts, and mean actions." We live in a cosmos in which we are constantly shown our failures to master ourselves. In spite of our "good" efforts, we also get to experience *"our pettiness, incompleteness, and wretchedness."* These experiences of limits to our quest to think well of ourselves are also experiences of that mysterious Power that Bultmann insists on calling "God."

Then, Bultmann notes that this same mysterious power that is limiting our cares is also putting us into our finite lives in which we do care for security, long for beautiful moments, desire love, seek knowledge and meaningful action, and strive to think well of ourselves. *Having all these cares* is an experience of God, as well as the limitation of these same cares. The same mysterious power *puts us* as well as *limits us*. But why, Bultmann asks, call this mysterious power "God"?

> *"Why give this enigma, this mystery which drives us this way and that and hedges us in any other name than simply 'the enigma' or 'fate'? Does the name 'God' not gloss over the fact that we are in the dark and are at the mercy of fate? Or, if there must be a name, why not equally well that of the devil? Does not this power play a cruel game with us, destroying and annihilating? Is not unfulfillment the mark of every life? Is not death, nothingness, the end?"*[3]

"God," as this word appears in our Bibles, is a devotional word. Faith in God is the courage to designate that dark enigma, that sovereign power as my devotion, my loyalty, my cause, my God. Such faith is a "nevertheless" of trusting that such loyalty to what is fundamentally real is the best-case scenario for our lives. <u>Trust in God is trust in the trustworthiness of Reality</u>. It is trust in the goodness of my realistic responses within whatever moments are confronting me. In order to actually do such realistic living, it is essential that you or I understand what Jesus and Paul never tire of pointing out to us: that this enigmatic power is our friend,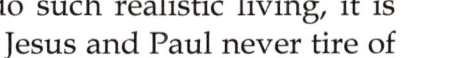

---

[3] Bultmann, Rudolf; *Interpreting Faith for the Modern Era* (edited by Roger A. Johnson, Fortress Press: 1991) "The Crisis of Faith" page 244

welcoming us home to Reality, accepting us in spite of all our shortcomings and estrangement from Reality, providing us the opportunity for a fresh start in the realistic living of our lives.

Whether or not you or I can accept this direction for understanding what it means to "trust God," it remains true that Bultmann has provided us with a way of understanding what we are pointing to with the word "God." He has not reverted to asking us to believe in some otherworldly myth about a Big Person hovering over us. He does not ask us to believe in a supernatural being. He agrees with Paul Tillich who insists over and over again that God is not *a being* alongside other beings, like humans or angels. God is the mysterious Ground of all Being. God is that power of Being that posits whatever comes to be. That same Ground is also the Grave into which all beings return. This Ground of Being is the Mysterious Void, the No-thing-ness out of which all things come and into which all things return. This Ground of Being is also the Mysterious Every-thing-ness within which all things coexist in community with each other. Clearly this understanding of God is a sort of atheism, for it refuses to believe in or trust in the "gods" that most people claim for their devotion. At the same time this understanding of God recovers for us, in a gripping and personal way, what the biblical literature was pointing to with its "God talk."

The biblical God of history can be our God in our own present and future history. We each are meeting, and can consciously meet, the God of history in our own personal history every day.

Chapter 3

Jesus of Nazareth and the Christ of History

I have become convinced that everyone who wants to practice a Next Christianity needs to have a relatively accurate historical portrait of Jesus of Nazareth. But the truth is, all historical knowledge is approximate and more improvement of it is always possible. This is especially true about Jesus, for whom so few uncontested historical facts are gleanable from the abundant reference to him we find in the New Testament. This is the first lesson we need to learn in order to read the four Gospels of the New Testament: THEY ARE NOT FOUR RECONCILABLE BIOGRAPHIES OF JESUS. Whatever our Sunday school teachers implied and our pastors lied about, the Gospels are works of theological insight employing an amazingly exaggerated sort of fiction. We have four pictures of Jesus not one, and these pictures are significantly different. In spite of the overlaps among the first three gospels, each of them is a wildly different and fictional portrait of Jesus. To say that the historical Jesus gets lost in all the furor over him is an understatement. It has seemed plausible to some scholars to test the hypothesis that Jesus never existed at all, that he is pure fiction.

Jesus of Nazareth and the Christ of History

I reject the no-real-Jesus hypothesis. My grounds for doing so are not based on anything the historical scientist can prove or disprove. It is simply my view that this much furor cannot be made over nothing. Some sort of historical event happened that involved a real human being of Buddha-like stature, and this human event (this human being) deserves the attention of any serious student of the history of world religions.

The Historical Jesus

When the dust settles, the scholars, though differing, have provided me with a picture of Jesus that I can accept as approximate, but plausible. I am not going to attempt to paint that picture in its entirety, but here are some references that may help you create your own plausible picture. My first choice is Albert Nolan's *Jesus Before Christianity*. Nolan is excellent on using small facts like Jesus joining the John the Baptist movement to imply things about Jesus' thinking and passion. I also find many interesting factual discussions about the historical Jesus in John Dominic Crossan's *Jesus a Revolutionary Biography*. Both of these works reveal how Jesus was a response to his historical times and what a profound social revolutionary he was. I also treasure Rudolf Bultmann's original 1934 work *Jesus and the Word* in which the results of form criticism were first pushed to the raw edges of this ongoing research. Bultmann showed us something that recent scholars have sometimes neglected: that any picture of the historical Jesus is highly improbable if the resulting "Jesus" did not understand the word "God" in the ancient Hebraic sense – that is, as the God of history described in the last two chapters.

Jesus did not invent a new God, a better God, a more loving God. Rather, Jesus showed us how to love that same old Hebraic God of history. And even this was not entirely new, for the older biblical books also spoke of our loving God with all our heart, soul, strength and mind. Jesus showed us what loving God looks like in a fully radical manner that illuminates not only Jesus' own

48

life, but the lives of Moses and the prophets and our lives as well. Jesus showed us what loving God looks like in the living Now of experience, and he called forth that depth of love in others. He initiated a timeless or "eschatological" community that can witness relevantly in any time and place about what it means to love God/Reality and how loving this Eternal Actor transforms our temporal living. I realize that such statements need illustration, which I will attempt to provide in the rest of this and following chapters.

The Ethical Teaching of Jesus

Almost all the teachings that have a high priority of being authentic teachings of the historical Jesus are ethical teachings. Jesus lived in an ethics-emphasizing culture. He deeply subscribed to the Law of Moses and its radicalization by the prophets. His critique of the moral "experts" of his day was that they did not interpret the law deeply enough. On "Thou shalt not kill," he pushed for his companions to see that our inner attitudes of fury with people are a form of murder. Implied here is that every person is a gift of God to us, a neighbor whom we are to love as we would love ourselves. His teaching about adultery is similar. The inner attitude of lust for love affairs that are not appropriate for us means indulging in a form of adultery. He is not implying here that sexual desire is evil or that we have absolute control over what we desire. But he is certainly implying an attitude similar to the one described in the Garden of Gethsemane story: "Not my will (my desire), but what the Almighty wills (desires of us)" is the overarching guideline for living. All Jesus ethical teachings are anchored in that first commandant: loving God totally. If we interpret loving Reality as a "desire" for truthfulness, we need to notice the tension between the desire for truth and many of our other desires.

Jesus of Nazareth and the Christ of History

This total love of God was not something Jesus' society had never heard of, but Jesus pushed it to places people were reluctant to go. Here is a good example:

> *Then one of the experts in the Law stood up to test him and asked, "Master, what must I do to be sure of eternal life?"*
> *What does the Law say and what has your reading taught you?" said Jesus.*
> *"The Law says, 'Thou shalt love the Lord they God with all they heart and with all thy soul and with all thy strength and with all thy mind – and thy neighbor as thyself.' he replied.*
> *"Quite right, " said Jesus, "Do that and you will live."*
> *But the man wanting to justify himself, continued.*
> *"But who is my 'neighbor'?"*

Jesus tells the expert in the law the story about the Samaritan man who helped a man in need.[4] The Samaritan was a member of a group of "next-door" persons disrespected in a manner similar to the Texas nativists' attitude toward undocumented Mexicans. So here is a modernization of this bit of Jesus' educational fiction:

A man ran out of gas and waved down another vehicle that turns out to be thieves who stole his money, took his car, beat him up, and left him by the road dying. A Baptist Clergyman in his Cadillac drove on by. A Catholic priest in his Mercedes drove on by. Then an undocumented Mexican in his Chevy stopped, gave the man first aid, put his bloody body in the back seat of this car, drove him to a Motel, paid for a room, left him in their care, and promised to pay for any additional expenses on his way back.

---

[4] Luke 10: 25-37 – Scholars tend to agree that this story dates back to Jesus. The words surrounding it are likely somewhat elaborated by the Gospel writer, but even these words reflect the setting in which Jesus taught.

Jesus of Nazareth and the Christ of History

Jesus concludes his story by asking,

"Which of these three seems to you to have been a neighbor to the bandits' victim?"
"The man who gave him practical sympathy,' he replied.
"Then you go and give the same," returned Jesus.

This story implies that any person in need who enters into our scope of action is a neighbor, given to us by God and making a claim upon us for "practical sympathy." Jesus is convicting his whole society of estrangement from the elemental instruction of their traditional ethical teachings. Jesus is also convicting our society and each of us personally of estrangement from the God of history, our neighbors, and our own true selves.

The impact of Jesus' teachings becomes clearer when we know more about the society in which he lived. About 85 percent of that society were literally destitute: that is, they struggled each day for food and other needs. Many of them were sick, blind beggars, lame, deaf, and perhaps stricken with leprosy, an illness so feared that no one wanted even to touch them. These are the people Jesus hung out with. He ate meals with them. He rescued them from the disrespect in which they were held by the more established parts of their society. "Blessed are the destitute, Jesus said, for they are open to the arriving 'new deal' of the Kingdom of God." "Blessed are the vulnerable (i.e. open to everything), for the entire Earth will be given to them."

The more "respectable" people took offense at Jesus' associations with these "riffraff;" they expected a real prophet to hang out with the "better" people.

In that culture there were many groups of "better" people. (1) The wealthy elite: the Kings, royalty, and Temple leaders called "Sadducees." These people had made their peace with the Romans, secured their wealth and status by doing so, and were perhaps shrewd in realizing that the Roman power was invincible in their day. (2) Deeply opposed to these "compromisers" were the Zealots who were the nationalists of that day. They wanted to throw off the Roman yoke by violent means and make Israel an independent and righteous society. They tried this, unsuccessfully, several times, and they keep on trying until Roman strength wiped out the nation entirely in about 70 CE. (3) The scribes and Pharisees were a third group who opposed the Sadducees for their compromises and the Zealots for their political naivety. They set about to preserve the treasured heritage through forms of ethical practice that Jesus found to be less than fully serious. (4) Then there were the Essenes who found the entire social situation intolerable and left it for an ascetic and mystical existence removed from participation in this dismal state of affairs. They hoped for a Messiah of a more cosmic quality to come in some all-powerful way and rescue them from this whole mess.

Jesus identified with none of these groups. He joined instead the John the Baptist movement. John engaged the then existing society head on. He embodied a strong message of judgment and a warning that this people, so deeply estranged from their heritage, were headed for total ruin. Jesus was baptized by John. Whether Jesus began his own ministry immediately after Baptism or later after John's death may not be clear, but what is clear is that he abandoned John's ascetic style and ate and drank and celebrated an arriving "Divine Kingdom" with a joy that John had yet to experience. Jesus revered John, but moved beyond him. Like John, his core message included the estrangement and doom of the nation, but in addition he announced the arrival, in the here and now, of the Kingdom of Eternity that was overcoming Satan's kingdom of estrangement from Reality. Forgiveness, a fresh start, and a new life were his themes. People responded and experienced that new life.

Jesus was not a mild suburban moralist: he was a revolutionary within his society. From his first sermon to his last "march" to Jerusalem, he was challenging everyone in his society with precisely those truths about themselves and their world that they were denying.

Jesus of Nazareth and the Christ of History

In conclusion, in spite of the limitations of our raw data about the historical Jesus, we can tease out a plausible picture. Our historical scholarship will surely get more fine-tuned, and we can be relaxed about this or that detail, for it does not infinitely matter. What does matter is seeing Jesus within his times operating not with universal principles, but living day-by-day before what he was encountering from the God of history. His teachings are time and space specific, not easily transferred rationally to the next or the next age. But what is applicable to any age is his underlying attitude toward life. We can glimpse this partly through our hard-won historical facts, but also through the further imaginings about him by those who viewed themselves as his resurrected body.

Interpreting Jesus

Whatever we conclude to be true about the historical Jesus of Nazareth, we are still faced with interpreting this raw historical data for a meaning that can make sense of interpreting him as the Christ (The Messiah). We also need to interpret the raw data about Jesus in a way that illuminates the flourishing community that emerged after his death, the furiously effective ministry of Paul, and the elaborate soul-addressing fictions of the Gospel writers.

Christianity is born out of a furious response to Jesus and the interpretations of him that expressed that response. I accept the conclusions of many historians that the historical Jesus never heard of Christianity and probably did not even claim to be the Christ. Everything about his being "the Christ" can be true about his real significance without assuming that Jesus himself was doing anything more amazing than living his life fully in obedience to the Reality that he faced. He did not have to believe that he was the Christ to be qualified for this exalted interpretation. He demonstrated what "saved" from "estrangement" looks like, and was therefore seen as the Christ by those who had eyes to see this.

Jesus of Nazareth and the Christ of History

For Christian theologians of the 21st century, it is of foremost importance that we grasp the following understanding: seeing Jesus as the Christ and sharing in his resurrection mean the same thing. The disciple-composed-flesh-and-blood Body-of-Christ was the resurrection, not some magical appearance of the corpse of Jesus that the grand poetry of the Gospel writers seems to depict to our literalistic minds. The resurrected Body of Christ is simply the flesh-and-blood bodies of those who saw Jesus as the Christ. They became "in Christ" by seeing Jesus for what he was. They looked into the eyes of one another and they saw Jesus-the-Christ living right there in the bodies of each other. This was a revolutionary event so deep that it could not be told about in everyday scientifically literal, factual language.

The wonder of this event had to be told about with Virgin Births, walking on Water, and rising from the dead. We 21st Century followers and potential followers of Jesus need to be clear about what was probably the literal facts and how these deep interior realizations required such extreme means of communication. Take the Virgin Birth as an example. There are two different stories about this, one in Matthew about kingly visitors and one in Luke about surprised shepherds who were tending their flocks by night. Mark has no Virgin Birth story unless you count Jesus' baptism in which God speaks from a cloud saying, "This is my Beloved Son." And in John's gospel the imagery of Virgin Birth is applied not to Jesus but to those of us who receive him. What we need to learn from this weird literature is that we do not understand Jesus' Virgin Birth unless we understand how we ourselves may have the same Virgin Birth. The fact that a literal virgin birth is impossible is part of the point of this poetry. This radical second-level birth is impossible for humans to accomplish through human means. Nevertheless, all things are possible for God: including our Virgin Birth, our own walking-on-the-water of our own wind-blown, stormy lives, and our own resurrection from the dead of eating our own egoism rather than eating the food that Jesus gave us. The radical "giving" of Jesus' own body and blood proclaimed both: (1) our hopeless estrangement and (2) our forgiveness and acceptance for a fresh start in the realistic living of our true lives.

We have no understanding of Jesus' resurrection until we understand our own resurrection. We have no understanding of Jesus' walking on water until we, along with Peter, also walk on water. We have no understanding of these joined words "Jesus Christ" until we understand what it means for us to be "in Jesus Christ." The term "Jesus Christ" became a symbol in the ongoing Christian practice for the perfection of life. Theologians from Paul forward were clear that we were all hopelessly estranged from this perfection, but that we could be reconciled to it, participate in it, and move toward the full stature of it. "Jesus Christ" means our true nature. Indeed, it means everyone's true nature, no matter what religion they practice or what religious formations they disbelieve. "Jesus Christ" means the essential human, our profound humanness.

"Jesus Christ" also means the *event* through which we move from our estranged condition into this perfection. "Be ye perfect even as God is perfect" is not a meaningless phrase. I like to put it this way: The Awesome Perfection has come to us, rendering us the perfect Awed Ones who live in an Awe not of our own making. This Awe given through the events of Reality crashing into our unreality is the Spirit of Christ that is also the Holy Spirit of the Almightyness that has "created" and is "creating" us, as well as the entire cosmos. I will explore the meaning of this further as we proceed through the historical unfoldment of this historical Body of Christ that has also been called the "communion of saints." Also I will point out that this communion of saints is not synonymous with the practitioners of a Christian religion. Rather, this Jesus Christ Presence is a dynamic in history. This Presence is the called-out portion of the human species that is leading all humanity toward their true profoundness.

Jesus of Nazareth and the Christ of History

The Meaning of "Christ" in the Culture of Jesus and Paul

The common understanding of the expected Messiah in the culture in which Jesus lived did not square with Jesus, a man who was crucified as a common criminal. Most people at that time hoped for a leader who would do something remarkable like delivering them from the Roman oppression. Some pictured this in more general terms like the defeat of the world of evil and the coming of a world of good. In term of such expectations, Jesus was a flop; that is, he was a failure to be the long-expected Messiah.

Joe Mathews in his essay "The Christ of History" makes the point that we all have expectations that are similar to those of Jesus' contemporaries. Mathews calls these expectations the "Everyman Christ," a term he distinguished from the "Jesus Christ." In the 21st Century we must no longer use "man" to mean both men and women, but I will quote Mathews as he originally wrote it.

> *This Messianic hope of EVERYMAN is born out of his experience of the limitations of existence. His encounter with the unknowns, ambiguities, sufferings, and deaths of this world discloses his insecurity. This primordial anxiety breeds the Messiah image. Watch him, as he is thrown up against his finitude, become a seeker after some truth which will overcome the unbearable incomprehensibles of life. Watch him search, however subtly, for the justification which will alleviate his sense of insignificance. Watch him relentlessly strive for a peace which will somehow blot out this lucid awareness of the tragic dimension of life. One senses in the spectacle a creature vainly striving to rise above his creaturely limits. Finding his givenness burdensome beyond bearing, he dreams of discovering some other kind of a world. Indeed he already has a different world, for he literally exists in his present hopes about the future. Thereby he escapes his actual life in the Now. His very meaning is his anticipation that some tomorrow will render his situation quite different. On that day the ultimate key will come clear: the final excuse for his existence will emerge and true*

contentment will bathe his being. Then shall he truly live, so he imagines, delivered from this present world of uncertainty, unfulfillment, and anxiety. Such a life-quest is an experience, I submit, that all of us are quite privy to. People dwell sometimes very explicitly, most times quite vaguely, in great expectations of what will relieve them of the necessity of living their given life in the present situation. This great hope, whatever its form, is the CHRIST OF EVERYMAN.[5]

Not only did naming Jesus as the Christ contradict this Everyperson expectation, it also included the offense that becoming a follower of Jesus Christ meant being rejected by a world that is still trapped in the Everyperson expectations. This awareness gives concrete meaning to the phrase "Take up your cross and follow me." What is the value of following such a Jesus-Christ style of living? It is the truth. Every other life walk, though it may seem true, is a falsification of some sort or another. And in being the Truth, the Jesus walk is a powerful and contagious sort of living. It is indeed Messianic in the sense that the evil world of lies is overcome and a new life of truthfulness has begun. Such a transformation is indeed a resurrection from the dead.

A Closer Look at Biblical Resurrection

Many people have had difficulty believing that the Biblical stories about resurrection have anything to do with our being resurrected in our currently lived lives. The story told in the 24th chapter of the Gospel of Luke is most helpful in revealing the personal nature of resurrection. We read here of two disciples who have a resurrection experience. After the crucifixion they leave Jerusalem on a seven-mile walk to the village of Emmaus. Jesus is walking with them, but they do not recognize him. Here is my interpretation of that line of fiction: Our profound humanness

---

[5] See *Bending History: Talks of Joseph Wesley Mathews* (General Editor: John L. Epps; Resurgence Publishing: 2005) page 43

Jesus of Nazareth and the Christ of History

is always walking with us, even though we do not recognize it. Jesus (profound humanness) speaks to them:

> *"What is all this discussion that you are having on your walk?" They stopped, their faces drawn with misery, and the one called Cleopas replied, "You must be the only stranger in Jerusalem who hasn't heard all the things that have happened there recently." "What things?" asked Jesus. "Oh, all about Jesus, from Nazareth. There was a man – a prophet strong in what he did and what he said, in God's eyes as well as the people's. Haven't you heard how our chief priests and rulers handed him over for execution, and had him crucified? But we were hoping he was the one who was to come and set Israel free. (24:17-21 J. B. Phillips Translation)*

That last sentence is surely one of the strongest expressions of despair in the whole of human literature. The story does not say exactly what these two disciples were expecting, but clearly the crucifixion of Jesus was not it. They were fleeing the city of death in which their hopes had been totally dashed. If we wish to personally feel this part of the story we might try to remember times in which our hopeful expectations turned out to be completely out of touch with reality. Then in Luke's story, Jesus provides some theological education:

> *"Aren't you failing to understand, and slow to believe in all that the prophets have said? Was it not inevitable that Christ should suffer like that and so find his glory." (24:26)*

I take this to mean that all prophetic persons suffer the rejection and hostility of the deluded. When they arrived at Emmaus, these two disciples sit down to eat supper with Jesus, but they still do not recognize who he is.

> *Then it happened! While he was sitting at table with them he took the loaf, gave thanks, broke it and passed it to them. Their eyes opened wide and they knew him! But he vanished from their sight. (24:30-31)*

Jesus of Nazareth and the Christ of History

So what happened? They got a new view of how Jesus was the Messiah. The horrific event of losing their mentor in such a cruel, stupid, and tragic way was as it should be. This is what a Messiah looks like. This is what happens to authentic persons under the conditions of our actual world. Was it not always so? Understanding the Christ in that way proved to be a transformative vision. They had just walked seven miles before supper, and before they even finished eating, they rose from the table and walked seven miles back to the city of death, to the tomb that Jerusalem had become for them. The despairing events they had fled became the glory they returned to live. This transformation is the resurrection!

Until this sort of thing happens in your or my internal life, we have not experienced the resurrection. It remains an enigma at best, and more likely a superstition that we have to dismiss. So here is the next personal question: "Have I experienced resurrection in a manner that it is not just accepting a belief that someone told me to believe, but an event that has actually happened to me, an event that has affected my whole body, including my legs and feet so that they could walk seven miles back to the "worst" experiences of my life and find them good?" Is that word "good" too much? Yes, it is certainly extremely much, for this transformation is an Infinite shift. So let us face that question in all its radicality: When has some truly grim, delusion-smashing Friday become Good Friday for you or me?

Chapter 4

Paul's Religious Revolution

Among the facts that are clear about the apostle Paul is that he was both a revolutionary in the life of the new Christian community and a revolutionary in the life of the Roman Empire. Because Paul is so early and so determinative in the development of the Christian religion, it is difficult to separate him from all the interpretations that theologians through the ages have made of him. Like Jesus, David, Moses, Lao Tzu, and the Buddha, Paul, the original historical person, gets lost in the things said about him by others. John Dominic Crossan in his book *In Search of Paul*[6] points out that even within the New Testament itself, we have at least three different answers to the question, "Who was Paul?"

(1) There is the picture of Paul that can be gleaned from the letters most scholars now consistently identify as letters actually written by Paul – here they are listed in the order of their approximate dates: 1 Thessalonians (51), Philippians (52-54), Philemon (53-54), 1 Corinthians (53-54), Galatians (55), 2 Corinthians (55-56), and Romans (55-58)

---

[6] Crossan, John Dominic and Reed, Johnathan L. *In Search of Paul* (HarperSanFrancisco: 2004)

(2) There is the picture of Paul drawn by Luke in the book of Acts. (Acts was written after Paul's death, perhaps as early as the late 60s, perhaps later.)

(3) There is the picture of Paul we can glean from the letters written in his name after his death: Ephesians, Colossians, and 2nd Thessalonians; the pastoral letters 1st and 2nd Timothy and Titus; and Hebrews, the most different of all the books in this list.

When I use the word "Paul" in this chapter, I will mean the person who wrote that first list of letters. The Book of Romans is Paul's master pull together. Rather than focusing on specific issues arising in specific places, Romans is a somewhat systematic organization of Paul's entire thoughtfulness about the revelation that came to him through the witness of that community who first interpreted Jesus as the Christ. It is interesting to me that Paul calls this revelation an experience of the resurrection to a "come-lately" like him. I find this encouraging to me in my notion that we much later adherents of this heritage can also experience the resurrection and join with the original witnesses in this transforming event that enabled them and enables us to be "in Christ" as Paul frequently calls this "revelation."

So I am going to attempt to untangle some of the webs of confusion that have settled around Paul. I will do this by decoding for our times some specific passages from Paul's letters. I will begin with what Paul says about the God of history in the opening chapter of Romans.

Everybody Knows God!

The following passage from Paul's letter to Rome deals directly with what Paul means by the word "God." In Paul's text I will use an "X" as a substitute for the word "God." I then propose to solve this portion of Paul's letter for the meaning of "God" as Paul used that word. (I am using J.B. Phillips translation of Romans 1:18-24, and for clarity I am adding a few parenthetical phrases.)

Paul's Religious Revolution

Now the holy anger (awesome fury) of X is disclosed from Heaven (the realm of Mystery) against the godlessness and evil of those persons who render truth dumb and inoperative by their wickedness. It is not that they do not know the truth about X; indeed X has made it quite plain to them. For since the beginning of the world the invisible attributes of X, e.g. X's eternal power and divinity, have been plainly discernible through things which X has made and which are commonly seen and known, thus leaving these persons without a rag of excuse. They knew all the time that there is X, yet they refused to acknowledge X as such, or to thank X for what X is and does. Thus they became fatuous in their argumentations, and plunged their silly minds still further into the dark. Behind a façade of "wisdom" they became just fools, fools who would exchange the glory (awesomeness) of the immortal X for an imitation image of a mortal human, or of creatures that run or fly or crawl. They gave up X: and therefore X gave them up to be the playthings of their own foul desires ...

So, what content for X does Paul's text assume? If we assume that God is an idea in a human head that makes sense of everything (or at least many things), we can see that such a substitution does not fit the text. "X" is clearly an active power not an idea. Furthermore, any idea of God that humans create illustrates what Paul is pointing to with his phrase "an imitation image of a mortal human." Any image, model, or art piece that humans have created is not X. X is not created by humans. X is the Power that is creating humans and the possibility of all human creations.

Why can Paul say that humans already know X? This is so because what Paul means by "X" encounters us as the Eternal (i.e. boundless) power that is "discernible" in all the things that are commonly seen and known. Paul also claims that something called the "divinity" of X is "discernible" in all the things that are commonly seen and known. By "divinity" he means some sort of commonly experienced glory, majesty, or awesomeness that goes with the enormous power already mentioned. X is "invisible" but the effects of X are not invisible. Everything that has the power of being is empowered by X. Humans cannot get their minds around X, but their "deep inner beings" discern the presence of X. Clearly, X is the Awesome Mysteriousness that is creating, supporting, and ending every visible thing. The failure of humanity is not a lack of experience of X, but the refusal to come to terms with X and to worship X as their life meaning. Such worship means nothing more nor less than being realistic, for X is Reality with a capital R. Such capitalization is symbolic of a boundless and inescapable Power not created by human hands and minds. X is not "a reality" created by humans to fit their preferences. X is *the* Reality that undermines every reality created by humans. X is the Infinite Truth that judges all our finite efforts toward truthfulness as well as all our overt lies.

Paul uses the word "heaven." This is a key word in Paul's metaphorical system of thinking about profound experience. In fact it is a key word for Jesus and all the other teachers and authors in the biblical collection. But "heaven" is not part of our metaphorical vocabulary today. "Heaven" has died as a useful metaphor. We now know that there is no transcendent space in a literal sense – no angels, no devils, no gods and goddesses, no Big Person up there to take care of us. We no longer live in a double-deck universe. Furthermore, we can no longer helpfully use the double-deck metaphor as a metaphor for talking about Ultimate Reality. We need to use other metaphors, and millions of us already do so.

Nevertheless, many if not most of us today have difficulty understanding how those who lived in past eras could talk about their primal experiences using the double-deck mode of talking. Most people think that those ancestors took supernatural space literally, as contemporary fundamentalists attempt to do. But the ancients were not taken up with our modern categories of "literal" and "non-literal." They lived quite comfortably in their double-deck universe. There was ordinary space and there was "divine" space. They may or may not have noticed that this double-deck picture was merely a metaphor created by the human mind. In any case, the metaphor served them well as a way to talk about the profound matters of their existence. It may be hard for contemporary people to grasp that Luther, Thomas Aquinas and Augustine were not literalists, but "existentialists" who knew (in their own way) that the double-deck metaphor was a metaphor. Jesus was also this kind of existentialist. When Jesus prayed "Our Father who art in heaven" he was saying in his culture what it would mean for us to say in our culture, "Like a good parent to us are You, Oh Awesome Mysteriousness shining through every rock, hair, and leaf of nature." The great saints of the past were not dumber than us: they simply used a different metaphorical language.

When we clearly understand this shift in metaphorical language, we can translate Paul's text into twenty-first century talk without losing what Paul was pointing to in his own life and without requiring ourselves to pretend that we can use his metaphorical language. With our own language we can point in our own lives to the very same dynamics of existence that Paul was expressing.

Today as then, everybody knows X, the same X that Paul was talking about. But few of us acknowledge X and worship X as the core meaning of our lives. It is still true that the masses of our age have given up X and therefore X has given them up to be the playthings of their own foul desires. "Foul desires" covers more than our drug addictions and our sex addictions. Our core foulness has to do with our desire to be the creator of our own reality, rather than allowing our true lives be given to us by X.

And what is X? X is the Reality for which we are making a substitution when we create our own reality. Birds do not try to create their own reality. Squirrels do not try to create their own reality. They perceive and interpret their experience with mental products we might call "multi-sensory reruns." They do not use the type of mental products we call "symbols." For example, four is a symbol used by humans to see a common quality between four clouds, four days, and four dogs. Humans (using the symbols of mathematics, language, art, and religious forms) have the capacity to put together a mental picture that can be substituted for reality. Our ability to do this is a great and useful gift, but it also presents us with a temptation not faced by birds and squirrels. The temptation is to live in terms of the pictures we have created rather than the Reality we are attempting to picture. Our yielding to this temptation makes us the most dangerous species on the planet. Our yielding to this temptation means that we worship our own creations, a state of living that Paul interprets as rebellion against Reality, the Reality for which we have built a substitute. While it may seem almost inevitable that humans confuse their own pictures of reality with Reality, Paul is saying that there is no excuse for it. Furthermore, Reality "responds" to our unrealistic substitutions with the consequences that derive from our trusting in those substitutes. We don't get rid of Reality or the Power of Reality by building our substitutes for it. Since we have given up Reality for substitutions, Reality gives us up to the consequences of our living with substitutes. Paul sees this substitution process as the primal root of the corruption of the human species. In this text he calls it "foolishness." In other places he simply calls it "sin." Let us hear Paul's words again:

> *Behind a façade of "wisdom" they became just fools, fools who would exchange the glory (Awesomeness) of the immortal X for an imitation image of a mortal human, or of creatures that run or fly or crawl. They gave up X: and therefore X gave them up to be the playthings of their own foul desires ...*

So when we see humanity waging wars in defense of their religious creations, we are seeing humanity in the state of having been given up by X to be the playthings of their own foul desires. When we see humanity abusing and belittling persons who do not fit into their cult-group of beliefs and morals, we are seeing humanity in the state of having been given up by X to be the playthings of their own foul desires. When we see humanity destroying the planet in the name of free enterprise, economic growth, a still bigger population of humans, a style of wastefulness and consumer obsession, and other substitutes for sober realism, we are seeing humanity in the state of having been given up by X to be the playthings of their own foul desires. When we see humanity killing the truth tellers of their times rather than listening to them and changing their ways, we are seeing humanity in the state of having been given up by X to be the playthings of their own foul desires.

In other words, this is the core problem of humanity: having given up Reality for substitutes, and thus being stuck with the substitutes that we have created. The consequence of this is that Reality has given us up to be the plaything of our substitutes, that is, our unrealism. And, according to Paul, there is no excuse for this. Here are Paul's words on excuses:

> *It is not that they do not know the truth about X; indeed X has made it quite plain to them. For since the beginning of the world the invisible attributes of X, e.g. X's eternal power and divinity, have been plainly discernible through things which X has made and which are commonly seen and known, thus leaving these persons without a rag of excuse.*

Reality is mysterious to the finite human mind, yet our elemental consciousness can experience this Mysteriousness. Though this Absolutely Mysterious Reality is beyond our mental reach, this Mysteriousness is discernible. It is commonly seen and known. Mysterious Reality is not an *idea* that we have thought up or have not yet thought up. Mysterious Reality is not a mere *idea*; it is more like a truck crashing into the side of our car. Mysterious Reality reaches us through some snake biting our toe, some cancer growing in our bowels. Mysterious Reality reaches us through a large host of pleasant things as well. Reality encounters us in the "miracle" of having been born at all. Reality comes to us through the gift of our amazing body and its intricate functioning. Reality is the entire Mystery of empowered "actualities" that we cannot avoid. There is no excuse for making substitutes for Reality and then (1) forgetting that they are substitutes and thereby entering into the illusion that these substitutes are Reality or (2) using these substitutes as our ground for fighting against Reality.

By "fighting against Reality" is meant viewing Reality as our enemy because Reality does not operate by our values. Violent destruction is as much a part of Reality as surprising creation. A mega-star violently explodes. A volcano, flood, storm, or fire destroys a whole town or city. A cheetah runs down an antelope and eats it. A band of humans slaughter another band of humans. People often protest that any Reality that empowers or permits such violence cannot be "good" enough (by our standards) to deserve our worship. So we create some other "being" to be our "good," our "God," our "worship." Perhaps we imagine that this self-created "being" is real enough and powerful enough to interfere with the course of nature on our behalf. Paul wants us to know that these gods of our own creation do not even exist. There is no divine being coming to rescue us from Reality. Our fight with Reality is far worse than useless. Reality always wins. Fighting against Reality is a hopeless way to live. As Søren Kierkegaard so intricately describes, fighting Reality results in despair. There are many forms of despair: unconscious despair; painfully conscious secret despair; restless plunging into sensuality or noble work; suicide; defiantly creating and defending a fake self; defiantly becoming a living proof to ourselves that Reality is no damned good. All of these states of despair are needless; and the alternative is close at hand – namely, humbling ourselves before Reality in trust that the Reality that is actually confronting us is providing for us the best-case scenario for our lives. According to Paul this is the "faith" that saves us from the despair (hell) we have been cast into because we have worshiped our creations rather than that Final Creative Force from which we cannot escape.

So what is "God" in the texts of Paul? It is that Mysterious, Awesome, Unrelenting, Inescapable Reality that has posited us, sustains us, and will inevitably eliminate us from the course of history. This X, this God, is a daily confrontation that everyone knows who is willing to know what they know. But is this "knowing" not a belief in some alien Big Other that takes away our freedom and responsibility? No, it is not a belief at all. It is just a conscious noticing of the WAY LIFE IS. We can simply notice that the Reality that is actually confronting us is putting us in being with our freedom and our responsibility. Our primal act of freedom is choosing to be free rather than vegetating in all our excuses and withdrawals and compulsions. Our primal act of freedom is choosing whether or not we will be our freedom, choosing and assuming responsibility for our choosing among our real options (possibilities) toward the future. This freedom is part of our obedience to Reality. To serve Reality is not acquiescence to the status quo. The status of our lives is never "quo." Our options are limited and the consequences of our actions are not completely predictable, but we do have options and we do choose among those options, either in responsible freedom or in flight from that freedom.

The inexcusable "sin" of which Paul is accusing us is our rebellion against the true limits and possibilities of our lives in favor of some substitute, some unreality that we have created to match our preference for a life that is different from the one that we cannot escape. This self-created attitude results in bondage, not freedom. When we are in our freedom, we are free to rebel against Reality, but this rebellion creates bondage. When we use our freedom to rebel against Reality, our freedom is spent: we are delivered to an unfreedom, a bondage, a life of being the plaything of our own foul desires. As strange as all this may sound to our simplicity-loving minds, a devotion to the Final Determining Power liberates us to be our full freedom. Being "determined" to be free does not mean that we are a tale already told, just waiting to unfold. No, our freedom will create part of the tale. The Determining Power is determining us to be freedom. When we rebel against this Power we create for ourselves some sort of box in which we live, separated from Reality and from the reality of our Freedom. And this box is an alive state of living – a compulsive, defensive, destructive slavery from which we will have to be rescued or we will end up in the hell of despair.

Some will complain that this "God" of Paul's is not personal. This is not true. It is very personal for Paul. It is his devotion, his papa/mama, his cause, his drive, his life, his personal worship even unto and during death. The vision of a big Person in some parallel universe that assists us to rebel against Paul's X is a sheer illusion not held by Paul. In terms of the most common beliefs in God, Paul is an atheist. He does not trust in the gods that humans create. He only trusts the UNCREATED SOURCE of his and our lives.

If we define "existing" as emerging or "showing up" out of nothingness, then Paul's God does not exist. Paul's God is the Source of all existing things, processes, events, happenings, possibilities, pasts, futures, as well as our freedom to share in the unfoldment of these existing things. Paul's God is that Void, that No-Thing-Ness, out of which all existing "things" "show up," have their day, and then pass away. And it is not just Christians who have worshiped this God. All humans face this Finality that "jealously" opposes our primal devotion to anything less. The Old Testament texts are not understandable without this understanding of God. And Paul, like Jesus, is a thoroughgoing disciple of Moses and the prophets.

Reconciled and Reconciling Others

What does it mean for "God to be in Christ reconciling the world to Himself." (2nd Corinthians 5: 19) This saying of Paul's has been much preached upon, but clarity about the meaning of this formula has been much confused.

Let us assume that by "God" in this sentence Paul means what we just explored in the last section. He is saying that the inescapable Eternal Mystery that we persist in trying to escape was in Christ reconciling the world of humanity to that Eternal Mystery that is positing the world and humanity. Paul does not say that the

Eternal Mystery became Jesus, a historical figure. To say that "incarnation" means that the Eternal became a finite person is superstition. The incarnation means something else. Jesus was God only in the sense that the Eternal became Present in this flesh and blood person in a way that was healing to humanity. *If we do not understand what it means for one of us to be the place where the Eternal becomes Present in a way that is healing to humanity, then we do not understand how this was true for Jesus.*

When Jesus dies upon the cross, this is not the dying of the Eternal Mystery. The cross is the outpouring of the life of Jesus in obedience to the Almighty aspect of the three-faced experience we call "The Trinity." Jesus, as he is pictured in the story of the Garden of Gethsemane, is quite clear about this. "Not my will, but thy will be done."

So what does it mean for the Almighty to be in Christ reconciling the fallen world to the Almighty? It is clear that Paul associates the man Jesus with the title Christ, but "Christ" has a wider meaning when Paul says that the community of those who accept Jesus as the Christ are "in Christ." Further, to be "in Christ" means that we share in his crucifixion and in his resurrection. How is that so? What is crucified and what is resurrected in the ongoing drama in which all of us can participate?

We can begin by saying that our crucifixion means that our expectations for a Messiah who would save us from the terrors of Almighty God was rudely slain by the God who is God. Jesus was and still is a disappointment in terms of being a Messiah who would rescue us from the tyranny of the Roman Empire, or from the British Empire, or from the U.S. Empire, or from racist society, or from civilization's momentum toward ecological doom. In terms of such expectations, Jesus was and is a failed Messiah. His death (as well as his life and teachings) killed our expectations of the arrival of someone (or some event) that would rescue us from the grim and grimy tasks of resolving our own earthly affairs. Furthermore, those among us who have given up our expectation for a false messiah are going to be swimming upstream, for the fallen world is taken up with false expectations of many sorts. Here are some: When I get a new job, then I will be really living. When I find a proper mate, then I will be really living. When my children finally leave home, then I will have life at last. When my health returns to normal, then ----. When some pill, doctor, or faith healer cures my most troubling pain, then ----. There is no such Messiah on the way. For Jesus to be your Messiah means you have renounced all such messianic expectations. With a Jesus sort of Messiah, there is just NOW with its possibilities and responsibilities. There is just us who, like Jesus, face the challenging demands of the Almighty God to expend our lives for something worth expending it for, and to do so before our life simply expends itself. Jesus in his teachings again and again explained that clinging on to whatever we think our life needs to be, has been, or is hoped for, will mean the loss of our true Life. We who are "in Christ" move from clinging to flinging. We who are "in Christ" are flung and are flinging ourselves into experiencing the resurrection of the Full Life that was in Christ Jesus. And this Life takes place, not tomorrow nor yesterday, but Now.

So being "in Christ" means flinging our life into the Now of our own times. This means flinging ourselves into the ecological crisis or whatever else calls us in our moment of living on this Earth. For Jesus it meant questioning the moralistic use of the Mosaic Law. Jesus called people to simply fling themselves into a forgiveness that was universally present. It did not matter how messy was the past: Now the kingdom of God was being offered to us as our true home – the entry into which means flinging ourselves into an ever-forgiving fresh start that is present in each and every living Now in which we are being posited by the Ever-Present, Eternal, Almighty, Mysteriousness.

Here is the New English translation of 2nd Corinthian 5:19-20 in which Paul spells out his vision about being in Christ:

Paul's Religious Revolution

What I mean is, that God was in Christ reconciling the world to himself, no longer holding men's misdeeds against them, and that he has entrusted us with the message of reconciliation. We come therefore as Christ's ambassadors. It is as if God were appealing to you through us: in Christ's name we implore you, be reconciled to God!

Paul is saying that we who have been reconciled are now called to be the reconcilers. This means taking God's side (Reality's side) in the ongoing conflict with humanity's complaints against Reality. Taking God's side is seen as compassion for the complainers. It means seeing that the true Life of the complainers depends upon the complainers being reconciled to God. Reality is not going to change to please the complainers. The complainers have to do the changing. (1) Step one of this change is not stopping our complaining, it is simply admitting that we want to substitute something for our real lives. We are basically and deeply complainers. We can pray prayers of complaining if we like. Many Psalm writers certainly did. But the completion of step one means seeing that our complaining against the Enigmatic Power shining through nature and history is an estrangement from our own reality, the reality of others, as well as from the Final, Overall, Mystery, Depth, and Greatness of Being. For reconciliation to occur, this understanding of our "fallenness" or "corruption" needs to be confessed. (2) Step two in our reconciliation to X (to Reality) is realizing that Reality welcomes us home to Reality in spite of our lifetime of complaining against Reality and acting out our complaints in various forms of malice toward others and ourselves. (3) Step three in our reconciliation is surrendering our complaining and instead flinging our lives into a Life of reconciliation with Reality – making Reality our God. Only after this reconciliation (this shift from Reality our enemy to Reality our friend) can we begin to understand the love Reality has for us. Reality loves us by insisting upon our realism and welcoming us home to a fresh start in realism as opposed to carrying on in a lifetime of futile fight with

Reality and thus living in the despair, hopelessness, malice, and slavery to obsessions that a fight with Reality includes.

When Reality is in us reconciling the fallen world to Reality, we are going to encounter the same rejection from most of humanity that Jesus encountered. In the Gospel of John, John's fictitious Jesus explains to his disciples that the disciple is not above his master. If humankind rejected and persecuted the master, they will do the same to the disciple. This arrangement of things is Reality's (God's) forgiveness toward the fallen world of complainers against Reality. As followers of Jesus we get to be Reality's forgiveness through our weakness of being vulnerable to the rejection of humanity, a humanity that hates Reality and prefers malice and murder and even their own despair to being reconciled with Reality. Some portion of humanity will, nevertheless, respond to the reconcilers. Some will repent and join the "Kingdom of God." They will become reconciled and reconcilers. They will take their place in the Reign of Reality, picking up their own measure of suffering (i.e. their own cross) which will be worked out by "Reality" as their lot in being part of the reconciling body of Christ. They will pray with Jesus, "Not my will, but Thy will be done."

Martin Luther King, Jr. provides us an example and some understanding of what it means to reconcile humans to the Almighty, to Reality, to God. We may have had difficulty sorting out what it means for Jesus to have died for our sins. But clearly Martin Luther King, Jr. died for our sins, for our racial estrangement. Whether we citizens of the United States were conscious or unconscious bigots who oppressed a portion of our citizenry, or whether we were among those who allowed ourselves to be outwardly and/or inwardly oppressed, King died for our sins. If we were willing we were "born of Martin's Spirit and washed in his blood." King knew that he was risking his life. He knew he might be killed. He did not know when or how or whether, but he was aware that he might not enter the promised land. Nevertheless, he was willing to lay down his life that others might enter that land. The exact same dynamic applies to Jesus.

We, humanity (not Jews, not Romans, but humanity) killed the best of what humanity could be. The characteristic sin of that time was not racism toward African Americans, but a type of ingrown arrogance with regard to law and moralism. Jesus challenged his times to the core, and he delivered many to new life. That part of Jesus' times that was not willing to accept his challenge, shed his blood. That blood was shed for us. The Almighty Reality was in Christ reconciling fallen humanity to the Almighty Reality. The Almighty was in Martin King reconciling fallen humanity to the Almighty. The Almighty was in the Muslim, Malcolm X, reconciling fallen humanity to the Almighty. The Almighty was in the Hindu, Gandhi, reconciling fallen humanity to the Almighty. We need to add to this list women like Harriet Tubman, Susan B. Anthony, and many others who flung their lives into the estrangement of their times. The Almighty Reality can be in any one of us reconciling fallen humanity to Almighty Reality. We are exploring here a universal dynamic of history, not a mere Christian dogma.

> Blessed Assurance Martin is mine, Susan is mine, Jesus is mine!
> Oh what a foretaste of glory divine!
> Heir of salvation, purchase of God,
> Born of his Spirit, washed in his blood.

> This is my story, this is my song,
> Praising my Jesus, Martin, Susan, Malcolm, Harriet,
> my Paul, my _____
> all the day long.
> This is my story, this is my song,
> Praising my Healers all the day long.

The Ethical Teachings of Paul

Like Jesus' ethical teachings, Paul's ethical teachings were rooted in his love of the Forgiving Reality to which Paul was reconciled by the proclamation to him of Jesus as the Christ. Like

Paul's Religious Revolution

Jesus, Paul is a devoted member of a Hebraic culture that emphasizes ethical teachings. And like Jesus, Paul's ethical teachings were space and time specific. Paul's teachings are different from those of Jesus because they are specific to a different time and space. While the time span is only about 27 years between the death of Jesus and Paul's first letter, the difference in location is more distant. Paul is ministering to the Hellenistic/Hebraic synagogues of the Roman Mediterranean, while Jesus was a rural Galilean for whom travel to Jerusalem was a big trip. Paul was a citizen of the Roman empire, spoke and wrote Greek, was significantly educated in not only the Hebrew scriptures but in wider affairs of the Roman world. Jesus did not live in that "social space." His mission was to the "lost children of Israel." Only indirectly was Jesus' mission an attack on the whole Roman world. Paul, on the other hand, was setting in motion a movement of human beings moving westward with a reversal of values almost directly opposite to the values that were moving eastward from Caesar Augustus' Rome. Perhaps Paul would have gone on to Spain had he lived to do so.

In such a context Paul was building a network of communities. Any of us who have done or attempted such things know how difficult that is. Paul possessed a powerful message relevant to many people and Paul was a tireless and capable champion of his cause. And Paul had a sense of urgency about his work. As Jesus had seen before him, Paul saw that Eternal life (the Kingdom of God) was breaking in upon us through the astonishing healing of the lives of people in the present. Paul also saw that the general culture and patterning of the Roman dominated world was based on lies and was therefore under judgment by the God of history. Rome was indeed doomed by Reality, though not quite as soon as Paul imagined. Nevertheless, Paul had respect for the laws of the Roman world and saw such order as the gift of God for the present. He could not and did not call for an explicit social revolution. But he did call for an inner transformation and a style of communal living that were revolutionary within those specific circumstances and, over the long haul, made a huge difference.

Paul has been criticized by modern feminists for continuing a number of patriarchal customs, but the inner heart of Paul's community work actually gave great honor to women. Women were among his most important coworkers, and he did not tolerate disrespect toward them from their husbands. Indeed, he taught that a husband should see his wife as worthy of the same sacrificial and abounding love that Christ has for his Church. And Paul was not an ascetic, though for himself he gave up marriage for the sake of his urgent task. The sexual rules he recommended for these new communities can be viewed as conservative by modern standards, but in his situation a workable order for those fragile communities was the overriding value.

Paul has also been criticized for not being stronger in opposition to slavery, but here again, within his world his heart was amazingly compassionate on this topic. He could not undo the institutions of slavery in the Roman world. But he could encourage Christians to free a slave or for slaves and masters to express faithful love toward one another. These steps would not have been adequate for the United States of the 1870s or 1960s, but to understand Paul we need to try to view his heart operating within his circumstances.

But, on the topic of not requiring male Gentile converts to be circumcised in order to be full members of the Body of Christ, Paul was firm to the point of risking his life. Paul was clearly committed to the notion that within the family of true service of the Living God, all humans are equally treasured. *This universalism is a revolutionary element of Paul's attitude.* And it is upon such foundations, initiated by Paul, that we have seen in recent times the emergence of the abolition of slavery, the civil rights revolution, women's empowerment, and, yes, even some equality and respect for gay and lesbian persons. Paul was indeed confused about this last group, but it is nevertheless true that the Pauline attitude of universal respect played its part in gay and lesbian liberation.

Paul's Religious Revolution

Mostly, Paul's ethical teachings center around the down-to-Earth practical issues of maintaining good working order among his emerging communities of still healing human beings. That he succeeded with this and inspired many others to continue such work has resulted in great benefit, including benefit to our current controversies with regard to the current hangovers of patriarchal and hierarchical patterns in Christian practice. It is our job, not Paul's, to complete these ethical implications of the Christian breakthrough.

The Pauline Century

Paul was important for the rest of the first century. The writings of Mark, Matthew, and Luke-Acts were extensions of the Pauline revolution in religion. Mark can be credited with inventing the Gospel, a new form of biblical literature. This was a literary work of theological intent, not a biography, not a random collection of older tradition. Mark put together a story with a theme. Basically, his story hangs together around this much repeated question: "Who is Jesus?" In the center of Mark's Gospel, Peter suggests that Jesus is the Christ, but Peter does not know what this means. Peter does not understand how it could be that the Christ should suffer and die at the hands of the establishment. In Mark's story the wonder of calling Jesus the Christ unfolds to the very end in which a "resurrection" happening frightens a group of women who are struck speechless about this overwhelming experience. Also, Mark has Jesus call 12 disciples and heal 12 sick Israelites including a 12-year-old girl and a woman with a 12-year flow of blood. Clearly, Mark is creating a metaphorical story about the birth of a new Israel, a new 12. Mark is creating a work of art not a scientific biography of Jesus.

Matthew puts together a longer work of art that deals with problems that are appearing among the more law-loving Judaea wing of the Christian movement. Luke puts together another long version plus a second volume, "The Acts of the Apostles." Luke has a different style than Matthew or Mark. He is addressing the more skeptical, Gentile wing of the Christian movement.

The writings of Paul, Mark, Matthew, and Luke all witness to the richness, the many layers, and the broad diversity that characterized the second historical stage of the movement that came to be called "Christian." A third historical stage begins with the writing and publishing of the letters and Gospel according to "John." We will explore this turning point in the next chapter.

Chapter 5

The Word of God Controversy

As mentioned in the previous chapter, the ministry and letters of Paul provided a turning point in Christian thought from the deeply Hebraic, rural, Galilean culture to the Hellenistic Judaism of Eastern Mediterranean urban settings. Toward the end of the first century a second big turning point began with the writings of the Gospel of John and its accompanying letters. In the Johannine writings we see the Hebraic love of history making an impact upon the more spatial and metaphysical motifs of Greek thought. This important quality of the Johannine writings has been hidden from view by the notion that these writings were written by John, the disciple of Jesus. This view would put these writings in a much earlier setting, and thus cloud the true meaning and profound significance of them. What we have in the Gospel of John is a sort of stage play in which John, the disciple, is a character, and Jesus is also a character. The entire composition is a piece of historical fiction designed to communicate with a different cultural audience in a different historical setting than the one addressed by Paul, Mark, Matthew, and Luke.

The religious genius who composed the Johannine writings was speaking to people who were not conversant with Hebraic customs and history. They needed to hear the Good News of the Christian breakthrough in their own language and metaphors. One proof of this is that the text includes explanations of obvious Judean practices that would have been well known to the earlier audiences. For Example in John 4:9 a Samaritan woman says to Jesus, *"What you, a Judean, ask a drink of me, a Samaritan woman."* And then the Johannine author adds, *"(Judeans and Samaritans, it should be noted, do not use vessels in common.)"* The people being addressed by the earlier New Testament writings would not have needed that parenthetic explanation.

The opening verses of John's Gospel join together the ancient Hebraic image of the Word of God as speech from the Universal-Creator with the Greek concept of "logos." Our English translations typically translate "logos" as "Word," so we tend to miss the full genius of this innovation. The Greek meaning of "logos" did not carry an association with the image of *speech* that we find in the Hebraic phrase "the Word of Yahweh." "Logos" was a secular and "mystical" term for "the inclusive meaning of the fullness of Reality." So the Johannine Gospel is joining together the Greek notion of "the meaning of it all" with "the Speech of Yahweh who created all things." For the Johannine author the Hebrew "God" still speaks through historical events of every kind.

Let us listen to the opening words of the Gospel of John inserting this strange word "Logos" in place of the usual "Word."

> *When all things began the Logos already was. The Logos dwelt with the Creator and what the Creator was, the Logos was. The Logos, then, was with the Creator at the beginning and through the Logos all things came to be; no single thing was created without the Logos. All that came to be was alive with the life of the Logos, and that life was the light of humanity. The light shines in the dark, and the darkness has never overcome it.*

So far those verses might grab the mind of the Greek listener, but down the page a short ways we find a sentence that would be absolutely paradoxical within that Greek mindset.

> *So, the Logos became flesh (that is, physical, biological, down-to-Earth history); the Logos came to dwell among us, and we saw the glory of the*

The Word of God Controversy

Logos, the Creator's only Offspring, full of healing for us and truth to live by.

Today we are still asking the same "64-billion-dollar question" that the original hearers of this Gospel surely asked: **"How can the Eternal Meaning of everything take on historical flesh?"** And this was probably asked in an even more offended manner, "How could such a magnificent event occur in an obscure man of peasant stock in some out of the way province of little civilizational significance."

The following sentence is even more shocking both to early hearers and to contemporary hearers as well (I have added a few words for clarification):

To all who received this Logos-manifestation-in-history and yielded their allegiance to this humanly walking, talking Logos gave them the path to become, like the Logos himself, offspring of the Creator, not born of any human stock or by the fleshly desire of a human father, but the offspring of the Creator of all that does or will exist.

This sentence might be called "a Gospel-of-John version of the Virgin Birth topic." In the above sentence, it is not Jesus alone, but also other ordinary humans who are being Virgin Born. In other words, we who see the healing power of this Absolute Truth confronting us in this fleshly, down-to-Earth history of Jesus (understood as the Christ) find ourselves born (or we might say reborn) with an Eternal quality of life, clearly distinguishable from the quality of life that originates from our parents. This does not imply contempt for our biological life or for our parents. Indeed, this profound life takes place in our biological life, and in the space-time coordinate in which we are born and live and die. It is pure flesh and pure Eternity present together in the same historical time and place and person. The event of Jesus as the Christ becomes reduplicated in the lives of other humans.

This fresh set of Johannine images set off a flurry of theological controversies that erupted into quarrel after quarrel for the next three and half centuries. Indeed, these controversies are still going on in the life of the Church today. Today, however, they go on differently. In those early centuries of that Greek-thought-based culture, Christians and prospective Christians found the fleshly historical pole of this paradox the hardest part to accept. Today we are more secular-minded, and therefore we find it more difficult to accept the Eternal pole of this paradox. Indeed, I must ask myself, "Do I experience anything Eternal that I can identify as true in my life?" If so, what is it? It can seem to most people today that we are only "once born." Being among the "twice born" is so cryptic to us, that we either dismiss this idea altogether or we twist it into a superstition about "purchasing" a positive otherworldly destiny through submitting to forced belief in a set of unbelievable doctrines.

So if you, like me, are a typical, Earth-bound, 21st-century human who wants to trust in what you can know with your own consciousness through your own experience, *what on Earth are we talking about with this second birth?* A new poetry is needed to access the Eternal as a real daily experience for any of us living in the 21st century. Here are two of my efforts to share my experience of the Eternal through what I have called "teaching poems."

The Infinite Silence Speaks

The Infinite Silence Speaks
through every rustle of tree leaves,
through every singing bird,
through every sound of any kind,
and through the silent spaces between the sounds.

The Infinite Silence is Void and Darkness
but also Fullness, a dazzling backlight that shines through
every gleaming tree, every shimmering squirrel
and surrounds every human being
with a halo.

The Word of God Controversy

This poem indicates a massively important direction for 21st century religious thought. We can no longer think about the Eternal in terms of a transcendent space – that is, of a Divine Being "existing" in a transcendent "place." Instead we have only one "place" – here and now in our ordinary bird and squirrel, life and death existence. The Eternal can only be spoken about as shining through our Earthly historical encounters. Our second birth only happens when our historical place/time moment turns transparent to the Eternal. Here is a more elaborate poem about this cultural shift from transcendence to transparency.

The Reappearance of God

Sometime last century, or was it the century before,
    all Supreme Beings died.
The whole realm of super-ordinary goings-on died.
Only the ordinary lived on.

But human beings,
uncomfortable with changes of this magnitude,
reinvented Supreme Beings,
knowing that they did so,
knowing that Supreme Beings
    were a human invention.

Unconsciously, as unconsciously as possible,
human beings knew they were worshiping
their own inventions,
but they did not care.
Human beings wanted to worship themselves anyhow.

Meanwhile, GOD, who is not a Supreme Being,
who is not a human invention,
who is not human in any way whatsoever,
who is not even known or knowable by human beings.
became known again by human beings,
known as the unknown,

The Word of God Controversy

the real unknown,
the UNKNOWN, UNKNOWN.

GOD, not standing above, but shining through
every natural being,
every space-time event,
every cosmological transformation,
every personal transformation,
every social transformation,
GOD became visible once again.

Visible but not known.
Seen but not understood.
Present but not controlled.
Unavoidable but not named.

Humanity, those who faced this fully,
found themselves affirmed by this,
ennobled by this,
healed by this,
refreshed by this,
enabled to be themselves by this.

Humanity was
Oh Yes,
brought down
    but brought down from an uncomfortable
        high horse
    brought down
    to be a completely ordinary organism--
    vulnerable, dependent, passing--
and yet,
nevertheless,
conscious
of the SHINING THROUGH
of GOD.

The Word of God Controversy

For the future of Christian theology, "God" must be clarified as a very special word that both points to our ongoing experience of the Eternal that shines through every event and also includes these meanings: "devotion" "loyalty" "worship" "calling" "center of value." The word "God" is a devotional word that means loyalty to, obedience to an inclusive center of value in terms of which all other centers of value are evaluated.

Only when such theological clarification is in place, can we understand rightly the Word-of-God controversy that characterized that period of Church history between the Gospel of John (90 CE) and the Chalcedonian Creed (451 CE)

I will deal with that Chalcedonian Creed in a later chapter, but first we need a rough picture of the history that led up to it. Origen (184-154 CE) was a truly great philosopher and Christian theologian who set in motion many directions of clarity for his time; nevertheless, he created an adaptation of Christianity to Greek thought that became intensely controversial. He followed the philosopher Plotinus' view that Reality had rings of manifestation that move outward from a core of Full Eternity to an outer ring of material manifestation. In Origen's scheme of theological thought, the Father Almighty, the Mysterious Void and Source of all things was the core of Full Eternity. In the next ring out was the Logos, which was also divine but subordinate to God's full "substance" of illuminating Light. Still further out was the material world, which included the flesh of Jesus, an ordinary human in which the Logos fully dwelled.

The emerging "orthodox" "Church" ultimately found this way of explaining these primal verities heretical. Jesus they claimed was to be understood as the full presence of God in all God's fullness, not rings away from that fullness. They said that the Logos was also God himself not a creation of God. The Logos that was also God was what walked among us in Jesus in order that we might participate, like Jesus, in the fullness of Eternity. However cryptic this furious argument may sound to modern ears, we can begin to understand it in this manner. Origen was making adaptations to the Greek world of spatial thinking that did not square with the temporal historical metaphors of the Hebraic view of God (Creator of the entire cosmos) and with the ongoing communications of this Creator with humanity throughout each and every event of history. In the Hebraic mode of theological thought, God, Yahweh, the Ultimate Reality, was met in the ongoing events of history and nowhere else (Even the deepest interior being of our lives is part of history). Therefore, what had been met in the history of Jesus and the resurrection of his historical Body (the Church) was Yahweh himself, not some creature of Yahweh. The We-Thou relation set up by the Exodus event had been transformed into a new We-Thou relation set up through the historical event of Jesus' birth, life, teachings, actions, death, and fleshly reappearance among his followers.

Among these "resurrected people," historical organizations emerged to organize, nurture, and witness to the Truth revealed to this flesh and blood, we-Thou community. According to the slowly emerging consensus of that body of people, Origen plus a number of other "quasi-Christian" thinkers were found "wrong," because they encouraged a departure from the core revelation that defined Christianity. In this down-to-Earth, controversial manner, a Christian orthodoxy was being invented.

What does all this mean? How do we translate the meaning of this for people today? Before engaging in further clarification of these "God-Logos-human" issues, I will explore the meaning of the concept "Church." I especially want to explore the tension between the Church as a "Spirit" people (a communion of saints) and the Church as a series of historical religious institutions. In the end, I want to envision how these obscure matters inform us today – those of us who wish to belong to a Next Christianity that deeply loves history and who loves the history of this communion of saints living here on Earth through ever-changing circumstances, responses, and Christian practices.

Chapter 6

Christianity and Church History

The Christian love of history does not end with a love of Biblical history. It continues on into what is typically called "Church history." Church history might be said to begin with the "resurrection of the disciples" from their despair over the untimely death of Jesus. But more frequently Church history means the ongoing life of this basic movement of Christian practice beyond the New Testament formation period. Both of these definitions of Church history are useful. Clearly the New Testament writings, especially the later ones, include a great deal of attention to the community of Christian practitioners. But especially among some Protestants, we often find a neglect of interest in the history of the Christian religion from the time of **John's gospel (90 CE)** until **Martin Luther (1483-1546 CE).** Obviously, the glory of what was explored in the previous chapter about "Christianity and the Love of History" did not end with the end of the first century. Our love of history as builders of a Next Christianity needs to include a love of the entire History of the Church. In fact we need to expand our view of the term "Church history" so that it begins with the Exodus (and earlier) and extends into an unknown future whose shape with regard to Christian practice I am examining in this book.

I already introduced in Chapter 1 examples of how history is not only about the past but also about the present and future. Indeed, it cannot be said often enough that we simply do not have a profound love of history if our probing of the past is not being related to our present circumstances and our decisions relative to possible outcomes for our emerging future.

Most Protestants and many Catholics too, know very little about Church history and even less about translating the meaning of that history into our current historical challenges, including the challenges with regard to building a Next Christian practice that is adequate to these times and for our emerging future. In this chapter I will explore some of the turning points in the post-New-Testament history of Christian practice and how Christians in those times were dealing with their history and what their dealings tell us about dealing with our historical challenges. I want to focus especially on the meaning of the term "Church" and how their struggle with the meaning of "Church" informs those of us who are choosing to create and do a Next Christian practice for this century.

The meaning of the word "Church," as a religious institution serving a neighborhood of geography did not come into full flower until after the Emperor Constantine's edict in 313 CE allowed Christianity to be an authorized religion of the empire. Until then, Christianity was a widely diverse and creative outpouring from that enigmatic but powerful breakthrough in human understanding that Jesus, his first disciples, Paul, and the Gospel writers put into history. That movement's basic understanding of itself was to manifest a community of people called out from the nations to be a communion of saints who as Christians needed no place of status in this world. After Constantine that image changed.

Whether Constantine was a true Christian or merely a shrewd politician may never be completely agreed upon. Perhaps he did hope to unite his empire with help from this fairly well-organized movement of popular strength and enthusiasm. But the Christian movement at this time was still small compared to all the other religious practices going on. Constantine did not ask for everyone to become a Christian. In fact, he forbade the rich elite from becoming clergy. Constantine viewed the Christian leaders as ministers to the poor, and he did not want to divert the wealth of the elite from supporting the Imperial court. Mostly, what Constantine did was to protect the Christian movement from persecution and provide its leaders with the status needed to do extended work. So perhaps Constantine did have a deep love for this movement. However that may be, the Christians who accepted the challenge of being befriended by the Emperor faced a new problem: *What was validly Christian and what was not?* Also, how were they to remain true to their integrity as a vital movement loyal only to Reality and yet remain a useful and appropriate body of religious practice to this friendly emperor. Surely this entailed a temptation to lean too far into the imperial customs of thinking. Some Christians did. But in the main Christians remained a scrappy group who were dedicated to a vision of Reality that is infinitely beyond the canopy of reality typically accepted in that Roman civilization.

Constantine may have been surprised that this religious movement, that he hoped would help bring unity to his empire, was already embroiled in a furious division caused by the spread of a vigorous movement in the Eastern part of the empire called Arianism, after its charismatic founder Arius. So serious was this challenge that in 325 Constantine called together, paid for, and facilitated the first empire-wide council of the Christian movement. More local councils had been held, but this, the Council of Nicea, was the first of several empire-wide councils to iron out what was the Christianity that the Emperor was supporting, and what was not. After a whole month of furious debate, the Arians turned out to be the losers in this meeting. And this was a serious matter for them, because it meant a loss of support from the Emperor, a replacement of leaders in their home areas, and a vulnerability to persecution by the winning forces. All these consequences did occur, but the Arian movement did not go away. Several more councils moderated somewhat their defeat and went on to other controversial issues. Nevertheless, a serious gap of vision with regard to what Christianity was persisted and eventually the

Eastern churches separated from the Western churches over the issue of having a pope in Rome. But the deeper reason for the separation was that these Eastern areas were pursuing a somewhat different religion. But I am getting ahead of my story. Let us examine the struggle with being "the Church" that was going on before and during the reign of Constantine the First.

The issue of what was the "authoritative" Christian faith was a raging debate in Paul's letters. By the second century each local gathering (ecclesia) of Christians had evolved a bishop whose role had become that of settling in the theological battles of the time. Mostly, the institutionalization of a bishopric came into being to resist Gnostic views. Marcion of Sinope (85-160), a typical Gnostic Christian leader, distinguished a "good" God, from the "crass" Demiurge (the source or creator of chaotic material substance and its tragic history). He rejected the goodness of nature.

In order to meet such "departures from the faith," the Bishop acted as a sort of theological bouncer, whose job was to cast out of his community those who did not see that the appropriate worship included devotion to "the creator of heaven and earth." In other words, for this emerging "orthodoxy" the so-called Demiurge was also the Christian God. Their "appropriate" worship was the God of history revered by Moses, the prophets, Jesus, Paul, and so forth. Years later, we see this reflected in the first line of the still famous Apostle's Creed that stated that this Gnostic dualism was not Christian faith: "We *credo* in God, the Father almighty, creator of heaven and earth." The significance of this anti-Gnostic direction is still deep for us today. It means a full affirmation of the goodness of our own bodies (their birth, their sexuality, their variety as both men and women, their limitations, and their death). It also means a full affirmation of the natural planet (the other-than-human forms of life, the mountains, the trees, the grasses, the breezes and storms, the earthquakes and floods, etc.). These early Christians did not have our current understandings of ecosystems and ecological responsibility, but this ancient fight for devotion to the Divine Source of the material world undergirds current Christian passion

Christianity and Church History

for ecological responsibility. The gnostic teachings do not do that. We find a form of Gnosticism present in many forms of contemporary Christian practice – for example, those that emphasize escape to an otherworldly destiny and a consequent devaluing of the human body, sex, animal life, the Earth, and history. In order for these bishops and their followers to win this fight against gnostic forms of Christian understanding, a movement was begun toward defining an authoritative Christian faith and establishing an authoritative organization of Christian community to maintain that important emphasis.

Although this trend toward an authoritative Christianity was underway long before the Constantine's edict, it took on a new urgency after 313. As already mentioned above the Council of Nicea in 325 was a big fight and a big step with respect to clarifying the boundaries of an authoritative Christianity, which included defining the boundaries of "the Church" as an institution under the protection of the Emperor. The issue at Nicea was different than the earlier Gnostic struggle, but the deep conflict between the Greek and the Hebrew heritage was still part of the background of this new fight. In the forefront of the fight was the issue of the relation of Jesus Christ to God the Almighty Father. It had already been more or less settled that the Gnostic rejection of the goodness of the material creation was a Christian heresy. There was no argument over Jesus being a real human being who was born and died as a biological person. But what was the "divinity" that characterized Jesus Christ as divine as well as human? That question is still being asked today. When Christians today claim that Jesus was God walking this Earth, what on Earth do they mean?

In order to understand this fight, we 21st Century Earth walkers have to get our minds into the philosophical framework in which these Christian ancestors were operating. "Jesus Christ" had become a symbol for a mode of being that preceded the creation of the world. "Jesus Christ" was a symbol identified with the "logos" which we might translate as "the meaning of it all." So it was "the meaning it all" that was incarnate in the flesh of the ordinary Galilean human, name of Jesus. Also, those who were being healed, saved, made righteous, joined with the family of the Eternal, and all such big transformations were said to be "in Christ." This need not mean perfectly "in Christ." It was understood that Christians were still growing up into the full stature of Jesus Christ. But this being "in Christ" was real enough as an experience in personal life that it is quite accurate to say that everything the Council of Nicea was saying about Jesus Christ was also being said about those of us who were "in Jesus Christ" – that is, were the true Church of Jesus Christ. If all this background is not understood, it remains incomprehensible why these Christians at Nicea were so passionate about a single word, indeed a single letter in a short piece of official Credo.

So what was this Nicean controversy about in terms of human existence, our human existence, everyone's human existence? This is the question we must ask about every word of Christian heritage for the last 3000 years. The original Nicean Creed ended with the following footnote that was dropped in later editions of this long Creedal fight: "But those who say: 'There was a time when he (Jesus Christ) was not;' and 'He was not before he was made;' and 'He was made out of nothing,' or 'He is of another substance' or 'essence,' or 'The Son of God is created,' or 'changeable,' or 'alterable' – they are condemned by the holy catholic and apostolic Church."

Of course "those who say" such things were the Arian members of the Council. What were they saying? They were saying that the "Eternal logos" that was incarnated in Jesus was first created by God, the Almighty. The Arians were saying that the Son of God essence of Jesus was one step removed from God himself. In other words we were not meeting the fullness of God in Jesus but a creation of God whose creation preceded the creation of the cosmos. Now, what was wrong with this, and why did they care? In the ancient Hebrew thinking about the God of history, there was no problem meeting the fullness of the Almighty in a bush, or an ass, or a prophet, or a whirlwind or an earthquake or a small still voice inside one's own consciousness. So it was entirely plausible to the anti-Arian crowd that the fullness of the Almighty could be met in Jesus. Furthermore, this side believed that properly understanding their salvation depended upon Jesus being the full encounter with God in order that their life "in Christ" could be understood as participating in an incarnation of the Fullness of the Almighty. They felt that to say of themselves they were merely the incarnation of a halfway God, a creature of God, was appalling. So they went out of their way to make plain that the Jesus-Christ logos was not less than God, but was of one substance with God. It was indeed God and not some creature of God who had saved us and was saving us. Arius, we might intuit, was trying to make the gospel a bit more appealing to his own Greek mind and to the Greek mind that still shaped the sensibilities of many people. Is it not still true that we 21st Century Earth-walkers also find it difficult to see Jesus and ourselves as the walk of the Infinite mystery upon this Earth? Perhaps most of us are somewhat Arian, rather than orthodox Christian as defined by the anti-Arians. So let us keep asking ourselves, "What is the Truth of our own existence that made the Nicene Creed fight necessary?" Paul Tillich raised this companion question, "Would Western Civilization have been more vulnerable to becoming Muslim instead of Christian had the anti-Arians lost their fight? And here is our even deeper question: did humanity actually encounter the full majesty of Reality in the flesh and blood of Jesus poured out for our illumination? Have we indeed been reconciled to Reality, adoption into the living body of profound humanness, "new-risen, resurrected, starved from the tomb, starved from a life of devouring always myself"?[7]

---

[7] This imagery is taken from the D.H. Lawrence's poem: "New Heaven and New Earth."

Christianity and Church History

The Enigma of the Church

While the Nicene Creed may not be the clearest expression of the Christian good news, it was a piece of clarity about being the Church. The Church is a scrappy bunch of saintly/sinners and sinner/saints who concern themselves with the course of history. Jesus, Paul, and the Gospel writers all understood the communities they were building as a communion of saints who were also sinners growing toward a full flowering of sainthood, and who were active in rescuing others from their delusory worlds of fallen humanity.

The communion of saints understanding was never entirely lost, but from the Nicene Council on, the understanding of the "Church" as a religious institution become more and more a basic theological topic. As a communion of saints, the boundaries of the Church are invisible, "known only to God." But the boundaries of the Church as a religious institution are defined, known and written down, and its cultural, political and economic processes spelled out. The 136 years from the Council of Nicea (325) to the Council of Chalcedon (451) included a series of creedal statements that were definitive of what the institutional Church was, and what it was not. These creedal statements were not literal rational beliefs, as we often take them to be. These statements were a sort of mystical-mythic-poetry about cosmic powers of being. In the next chapter I will attempt to decode the Chalcedonian Creed. But in this chapter I want to follow the thread of an authoritarian Christianity on down into our times.

Augustine of Hippo

Augustine (354-430) is the philosopher/theologian who pulled together a three-century long ferment of Christian theologizing within and for the Greek/Roman cultural world. His synthesis of Greek and Hebraic themes enabled a certain stability of thought and practice for the next 800 years of the Western practice of Christianity. Something different happened in the Eastern practice of Christianity, but we who have been nurtured or misnurtured by

Christianity and Church History

some form of Roman Catholicism or Protestantism need to first understand the Western story, so I am focusing there. Augustine in his *Confessions* introduced a style of biography that honored the Hebraic love of history. This love of history also appears in his *City of God* reflections. He provides a strong encouragement for sustaining a historically successful institutional Church.

Augustine was a seeker who came to Christianity after a number of breakthroughs that included astronomy and the Plato-leaning philosophy of Plotinus. In other words he mastered the Greco-Roman wisdom of his day that was available to him. He was also inspired by the teachings of the, by then, quite sophisticated and widespread Christian Church. Augustine did not find his mastery of Greek philosophical thinking adequate to affirm the "truth value" he found in this rich Hebraic/Christian heritage which dated all the way back to Moses. So Augustine held that the truth-value of this heritage assembled in the Western Church be seen as an **authority** to be taken on faith quite beyond any possibility of proving it through the powers of Greek thought.

But the source of Augustine's own willingness to embrace this authority was that it spoke to something missing in his own life – that is, it opened his awareness of his own inauthenticity and his own consciousness of his own profound humanness. In this sense Augustine was an existentialist rather than a doctrinalist in the contemporary security-hungry and bigoted sense. It is important to see him this way in order to properly honor him today. And yet his support for an authoritative attitude toward Church heritage we now need to reject as we move forward into a vital Next Christianity. I will say more about this in the following chapters.

Out of the Augustinian pull-together (and earlier) grew the pattern of Church expansion that has dominated Christianity until our day. Here is a sketch of that pattern: take the best authoritarian doctrinal system so far created by the saints, theologians, and dignitaries of the "Church" and impose it on every village that a band of priests, nuns, monks, lay thinkers, and lay-financiers can reach. Those who do this bold task know that the children and untutored peasants will not understand what is being imposed upon them and ritualized for them every week. But these Christian cultural warriors do this in the hope that at least some of these masses will one day in their lives catch on to the truth contained in this imposed "authoritarian" system. However objectionable this crass telling of that process may seem to many of us today, we need to also notice that this method worked. Some people did catch on. Throughout the Middle Ages, wave after wave of "saintly" living did arise.

Thomas Aquinas

The life of **Thomas Aquinas (1225-1274 CE)** is associated with a next huge shift in Christian practice. There were precursors to Aquinas, but his pull-together was determinative. This turning point is taking place at the high point of the Middle Ages in terms of massively elaborated and stable social structures. But cracks were appearing. It is hard for us who are living on this side of Thomas Aquinas to imagine what it was like to live in a society that had so thoroughly emphasized the Platonic side of Greek heritage and so fully neglected the Aristotelian side of Greek Heritage. We now live in a society dominated by natural science, which has been a development of the Aristotelian emphasis on a type of truth that arrives from our observations of the external and material world. Thomas Aquinas, who has become such an establishmentarian figure within Catholicism, was in his lifetime a maverick, a revolutionary who, along with his Dominican Order, was recovering the wisdom of Aristotle that was being communicated to Europe from the Muslim side of the Mediterranean. Aristotelian wisdom was obviously helpful for conducting a vast and complex social system. In Thomas's mind it needed to be adopted as far as it could go. Since it did not go far enough to encompass the wisdom of the authoritative Church, Aquinas resolved his overview of truth by stacking the wisdom of the Church on top of the wisdom of Aristotle. These two layers (natural and supernatural) became more distinctly separated than was the case earlier. The exploration of nature was set loose to follow its own lights. The continuing clarification of Church heritage also had its role. Thomas assumed that there was no fundamental contradiction between the wisdom of nature and the supernatural wisdom of the Church. Both reflected Truth from the same God. The hierarchical ordering of the two seemed to work quite well for a time. But as we have seen, the explosion of the nature-based wisdom of the sciences began to cast doubts on the Church side of this partnership, or at least on the ways that the Church side of the partnership was being communicated. The Church way of communication was still the same authoritarian way that was initiated by Augustine and earlier theologians – that is, having Church workers impose a highly developed set of doctrines upon a population and waiting for them to catch on to their interior meaning. Modern science included a method that was almost the opposite to this – namely, approaching all current thought with doubt and being open to explain our experience with new ways of looking at things.

Today, no matter how well crafted a doctrine may be, the communication style of imposing doctrine is inherently problematical. Though an imposed doctrine has been refined by many fierce battles among careful thinkers, no doctrine will hold for everyone the Spirit that generated the doctrine. No belief in rational statements can substitute for the direct personal experience of profound humanness.

Furthermore, the inherited doctrinal system of Medieval Christendom was vulnerable to perversion, both the sort of misunderstandings that can so easily arise over time as well as the direct misuse of the enlarged authoritarian power by the Church's top authorities for less than noble purposes.

Martin Luther

In the late Middle Ages it became clear to wave after wave of would-be reformers that the Christian hierarchy from the Pope on down had become crazy-making. **Martin Luther (1483-1546 CE)**, an Augustinian monk, broke with the authority of the Church and succeeded in establishing an alternative Christian practice that was based more on the authority of the Bible than on the authority of the current Catholic (that is, supposedly universal) Church. This was a huge break, a break based on Luther's own existential discoveries about the radicality of personal faith or trust in Reality. Upon that basis he was criticizing both the established Church and many portions of the Bible. Nevertheless the Reformation was not a break with the authority mode of theological thinking: it was a reform, not a replacement for authority thinking. Luther reconstructed an authoritarian Church with a significantly new doctrine and practice. Other reformers did likewise. The authority-mode of theological thought and religious practice, with its usefulness and its vulnerabilities, has dominated Christian thinking and organizing to this day. When we hear such questions as "What do Methodists believe?" we are hearing authoritarian thinking.

A valid Christian practice is not about what my church group believes; it is about personally entering into the history-illuminating event called Jesus Christ and thereby being enabled to participate in our own profound humanness. Many contemporary Protestants (and Catholics too) have come to expect a personally grounded truth, but the church organizations to which these awakening persons belong (or once belonged) still tend to operate with the Medieval model of imposing a set of beliefs or doctrines that people are expected to catch on to by simply living with them and practicing them on a regular basis.

The Protestant Reformation did not resolve this paradox of using the term "Church" to refer to both an authentic communion of saints and an authoritative religious institution. We still struggle with this topic. Any Next Christianity that is a daily, weekly, yearly religious practice will also face the paradox of an invisible communion of saints in tension with a visible community of the people who have a specific religious culture, polity, and economics.

Kierkegaard

However enduring this Medieval model of Christian practice still is, a thoroughgoing authenticity mode of theological thinking and religious practice is now at least a couple of centuries in the making. We can date its beginnings with **Søren Kierkegaard (1813-1855)** – with roots somewhat earlier. In Kierkegaard's wake we see this mode of theological thinking and practicing being fleshed out and taught broadly, by luminaries like Rudolf Bultmann, Paul Tillich, Dietrich Bonhoeffer, H. Richard Niebuhr, Reinhold Niebuhr, as well as the more orthodox-styled Karl Barth. Many other names could be added. Simone Weil is a woman writer on Christian topics that I would add to this core group. And there is a much longer list of women authors, from Suzanne de Dietrich to Mary Daly who also breathe the Kierkegaardian air. This Kierkegaardian beginning has also been manifest in a number of influential Catholic theologians such as Karl Rahner, Jacques Maritain, and Catholic writers such as Thomas Merton, Pierre Teilhard de Chardin and Thomas Berry. Whatever be the gifts, limitations, and disagreements among these many voices, *authenticity*, as a mode of Christian thought and practice, is in history and is not likely to go away. A strong movement of ordinary Christians, as well as scholars, still live, witness, and explore being a Christian in the "post-Kierkegaardian era."

Nevertheless, we who wish to promote a vital Next Christian practice based on this authenticity breakthrough, still have work to do sorting out authenticity thinking from the hangovers of authority thinking that remain in our culture, in our Christian practices, and in our own "gizzards."

For example, in order to appropriately guide the development of a vital "Next" Christian practice, we will be called upon to distinguish authenticity thinking from the many side-trips being taken into forms of relativism. The typical relativist tends to view authenticity thinking as another form of authority thinking. As important as it is to learn to mistrust the authority of the Church, the authority of the Bible, the authority of Pastor Smothers, or the authority of Pope Perfectas, it is just as important not to "fall off the other side of the road" into an "absolute relativism." I use the term "absolute relativism" to distinguish extreme relativism from our clarity that all cultural creations, including all religious creations, are indeed relative. No religious teaching is an absolute teaching dropped down from a presupposed heaven. Nevertheless, the truth of authenticity exists and this truth judges our various creations as more or less valid.

"Absolute relativism" can be defined as an unwitting escape into another form of authority – namely, "believing" that there is no such thing as an *authenticity experience* that can render one religious practice or insight more valid than another. Absolute relativism tends to be a psychological re-stimulation in the lives of people who have been hurt by some form of authoritarianism and thereby react negatively to any sort of claim to "certainty." Absolute relativism can also be a deep rebellion against all meaningful discipline – a type of inner bondage similar to spending one's whole life kicking the shins of a brutal or controlling father.

We who are flowing in the wake of this post-Kierkegaardian awakening are in the process of constructing a Next Christianity based upon the experience of authenticity – not authority, and not relativity. The departure from authority means giving up entirely any further dealing with a set of correct beliefs that can be imposed on a body of people or an entire society by some elite body of theologians, bishops, and cardinals, or any collection of the centuries of writings by apostles, saints, and heroes of Christian loyalty. On the other hand, with respect to the relativity swamp, a vital Next Christianity needs to produce a set of religious methods that enable practitioners to discover in their own inner beings the living Truth of the historical breakthrough that occasioned the surge and spread of Christianity as an expression of profound humanness. Profound humanness is not a set of concepts or virtues; it is an experience, an inner certainty about the "real me" that arises as each specific estrangement from that profoundness is acknowledged, forgiven, and abandoned.

The above summary statements require more thought in order for the deep wonder and truthfulness of the Kierkegaardian transformation be fully seen. I am going to suggest that it is a turning point in Christian understanding more basic than the Reformation. The Reformation was a reform of Christendom, but as I will develop more fully in later chapters, the "Kierkegaardian Era" in Christian renewal is more than a reform of Christendom. As Kierkegaard himself dubbed his work: it is an "Attack on Christendom." I am noting this in order to begin shaking our minds out of the authority rut in which most Christian practice is still stuck.

Here is a verse of scripture that enables us to view Jesus himself as a champion of authenticity over authority.

> *And when Jesus finished these sayings, the crowds were astonished at his teaching. For he taught them as one who had authority, and not as their scribes. (Matthew 7:28-29, J. B. Phillips translation)*

I understand this verse to mean that Jesus operated with an *authority of authenticity* rather than the *authority of tradition*. The scribes were using a scholarly proof texting. During the time in which Jesus and his first followers lived, the scribes were respected religious teachers. Many scribes were sincere persons, but they based their teachings on the written words of the heritage. The meaning of the above passage is that Jesus spoke with an inward type of authority, unlike the scribes who spoke with the objective authority of the traditions. I would say that Jesus spoke with the authority of authenticity while the scribes spoke with the authority of their scriptures. A similar scribal authority is manifest when contemporary Christians speak with the authority of their religious groups, their "pastors," their "Pope," their Scriptures, their favorite theologians, their favorite philosophy teachers, or some other mentor, parent, or friend, whom they are allowing to take the place of speaking from the heart of their own experience.

I will develop further details on this topic in later chapters, but for now, I will focus on the historical significance of the authenticity mode of teaching and practicing a Next Christianity. In making authenticity rather than authority the core approach for our Christian understanding of "Truth," we have entered a new era of Christian practice. This turning point in Church history is surely as vast as any of the other turning points mentioned. Of course, whatever major turning point a person is now experiencing can seem like the most radical turning in all of history. But at least we must say to ourselves that this turning point is huge, not trivial.

Living this turning point from authority to authenticity means taking a new look at Augustine, Thomas Aquinas, Luther, and others. All these luminaries lived in an era of Christian thought and practice in which authority was the taken-for-granted mode of thought and practice. We need to notice this context of their lives in order to be appropriately critical of these writers and not fall back into some fresh invention of authoritarian doctrinalism. At the same time we need to notice that these were great men precisely because they dealt with their authority-breathing times in a manner that expressed their own experiences of authenticity. They were able to be creative with the existing authoritarian structuring of their religion precisely because they were operating from a fresh experience of authenticity. In order to show the truth of these assertions to reason-loving and authority-hating readers, I am going to write an entire chapter on each of the above three turning point figures: Augustine, Aquinas, and Luther.

Also, much more needs to be said about how we practice a Next Christianity in which authenticity, not authority, is the foundational motif. The following core difficulty will come up: any sort of historically ongoing Christian practice entails the creation and learning of a set of practices that actually access the authenticity of our profound humanness. Such practices will be relative historical structures. Along with these relative practices go the equally relative theoretical explanations or theological efforts that I am doing right now. All this amounts to creating historical structures – cultural commonality we might call it. In order to have a historical community of Christian practice using the authenticity mode, we will need to fashion some sort of cultural commonality, political organization, and economic disciplines that organize and support the Christian practice. So, we will have created a new version of the historical, institutional church, whose boundaries will not be the same as the invisible boundaries of the communion of authenticity saints. So how do we create such an institution without reverting to some new form of authoritarianism? How do we explain to ourselves that the structures established for our commonality of culture, politics, and economics are expressive of the Spirit of authenticity that we claim to base our institutionalization upon? How do we create a form of institutionalized commonality that discourages both authoritarianism and relativism? If you think this will be easy, you certainly need to read the rest of this book. If you already sense the difficulty of these issues, then you may want to read on.

Chapter 7

The Chalcedonian Solution

In order to appropriate the history of Christian thought and living, we 21st Century Christians have to criticize all attempts to understand the Trinity as a picture of heavenly persons. This mystical reasoning was done within what is now a strange, ancient two-story manner of thinking. Such heavenly talk has come to an end as a viable symbology for a Next Christianity. To communicate anything meaningful today, we must begin with our own human experience. Thinking in that way, the Trinity can be described as a threefold-shining-through within our temporal experience of our realization of the Eternal. This can be done in a way that will illuminate the meaning of the struggles of the second to fourth century Church with the twofold nature of Jesus Christ and with the threefold nature of the overall Godhead. Without a huge transformation in our thinking about these primal matters, the stormy Church councils of those early centuries are cryptic beyond all bounds of understanding with our current sensibilities.

Here is a shorthand version of how these triune dynamics can be seen from the perspective of our everyday human experience. Instead of imagining three persons or faces of God in a heavenly place, we can describe these three dynamics as three faces of one experience here on Earth: (1) Face one is our experience of the Awesome Ultimate Mystery, the Void out of which all things come and all things return (the Father Almighty). (2) Face two is that

The Chalcedonian Solution

part of humanity who is having this Awe experience (the fleshly Offspring of the Ultimate – the Body of Christ) (3) Face three is the various states of Awe taking place within the Awed community that is beholding the Eternal Awesomeness (that is, the Holy Spirit of Trust, Love, and Freedom, also described as the courageous heart of hope, the peace beyond understanding, the joy unspeakable, and other qualities).

For three and a half centuries these dynamics were described and intensely argued about within that now obsolete mythical-heavenly fashion that was derived from both ancient Hebrew and ancient Greek origins. Finally, in 451 CE these arguments were more or less resolved in a creed that was adopted at the Fourth Ecumenical Council, held at Chalcedon, located in what is now Turkey. Below is a literal English version of that creed. Followed each section of the creed is my 21st Century translations into an experiential language appropriate for our times.

> We, then, following the holy Fathers, all with one consent, teach men to confess one and the same Son, our Lord Jesus Christ, the same perfect in Godhead and also perfect in manhood; truly God and truly man,

As a reality that can be experienced by us, "The Son our Lord Jesus Christ" means the community of those who manifest profound humanness. We who access our profound humanness are the Body of Christ. "Jesus Christ" means a community of human beings, not merely a first century Galilean with a big title. Jesus was an ordinary man in human history, a man who became viewed as Christ by a community of ordinary men and women who saw themselves as the resurrected Body of Christ. They were the resurrection of Jesus, so everything that they said about Jesus, they were saying about themselves (that is the true aspect of themselves that went along with their sin of separation from that essential humanness). They did not claim perfection in their manifestation of the Christ essence, but they did claim some experience of that perfection.

The Chalcedonian Solution

We who comprise today this community of the Christ Body (by whatever religious means or lack of one) participate with Jesus, the Christ, in this perfect humanness and perfect Eternalness. And it is through this participation that we are able to say what is so about Jesus Christ. In our essence we are, like Jesus, a mysterious being – as mysterious as the Wholeness of Being is mysterious. In accessing our true being, we share in the true mysteriousness of that Every-thing-ness in which all things mysteriously coexist. Again, this does not mean that we manifest this profound humanness perfectly. We do not even know historically if Jesus of Nazareth manifested this profound humanness perfectly. Nevertheless, we can say that this profound humanness, to whatever extent it is manifest, is perfect in humanness and perfect in Eternalness as the Creed says.

> *of a reasonable [rational] soul and body; consubstantial [co-essential] with the Father according to the Godhead, and consubstantial with us according to the Manhood;*

Experiencing our profound humanness does not do away with also experiencing the presence of our body, a mind, a consciousness, a personality, or a self-image. We are not two persons. Rather these temporal dynamics coexist with our Awesome Holiness of Trust, Love, Freedom, Peace, Joy, Courage, that cannot be accounted for within the physical-biological-social scope of things. We are both a biological evolvement on this planet and a citizen of that Mysterious "Land" that is the "Source" and "Tomb" of all finite things.

> *in all things like unto us, without sin; begotten before all ages of the Father according to the Godhead, and in these latter days, for us and for our salvation,*

Profound humanness is without estrangement (sin), and in that sense profound humanness is perfection, a perfection that no particular human being can fully claim. The Jesus Christ image is a

The Chalcedonian Solution

picture of our own humanness in its perfection. I repeat we cannot know whether or not Jesus, the individual human, ever reached such perfection or never departed from it. There can be no historical knowledge about such a topic, but "Jesus Christ" means more than a historical person. "Jesus Christ" is a symbol, a sort of fiction about profound humanness, about a mysterious dynamic of the cosmos. The earliest Christians claimed to have seen this perfection manifested in Jesus, and drew from that experience the "Jesus Christ" image of perfection that is viewed to picture the true being of every human. This perfection, so the Johannine story goes, preceded the creation of the cosmos. In that sense, profound humanness precedes our birth, precedes the evolution of our species, and even precedes the Big Bang. Profound humanness is an Eternal dynamic that is, nevertheless, given to us to participate in the here and now. If that seems paradoxical, it is because it IS. Nevertheless, it IS the truth of Christian experience.

And this perfection is not something we individual humans need to create or achieve. This perfection is the "true me" which appears when my estrangement from the "true me" is evaporated. So Jesus, as the appearance of that perfection among us, operates as our healer (our salvation) awakening us to that perfection, establishing in us that perfection, and calling us to the task of awakening the perfection of true humanness in others. If we are going to use language like "perfection" and "true humanness" we must remain clear that this perfection is not a human accomplishment, nor something to be possessed and bragged about. It is a moment-by-moment rescue from our self-inflicted estrangements by that Almighty Realty in relation to "whom" that perfection exists.

born of the Virgin Mary, the Mother of God, according to the Manhood;

This means that when we enter our profound humanness, we too are Virgin born of Final Reality. Profound humanness was given with our birth; our mother is also the Mother of God. We might even add that our Father is the Father of God according to our manhood or womanhood. Such a heretical sounding statement need not contradict the deeper truth of the Virgin Birth myth that Final Reality is the Father and Mother of our Virgin birth, provided of course that we have indeed experienced a birth into our "divinely" posited profound humanness.

> *one and the same Christ, Son, Lord, only begotten, to be acknowledged in two natures, inconfusedly, unchangeably, indivisibly, inseparably; the distinction of natures being by no means taken away by the union, but rather the property of each nature being preserved, and concurring in one Person and one Subsistence, not parted or divided into two persons, but one and the same Son, and only begotten, God the Word, the Lord Jesus Christ; as the prophets from the beginning [have declared] concerning Him, and the Lord Jesus Christ Himself has taught us, and the Creed of the holy Fathers has handed down to us.*

All these many rejections of what is not true about profound humanness can be summed up in this single sentence: *When we enter our profound humanness we lose nothing of our ordinary humanness.* We do not become two persons in one body. We become our true person who is both fully ordinary and fully extraordinary at the same time. Furthermore, the "extraordinariness" is nothing more than our true ordinariness with which we are created. So we might even say that it is our fall into estrangement that is the truly "extraordinary" state – a grim addition to our created norm, or a tragic subtraction from our glorious authenticity.

These considerations are not a mere theory, (that is, one opinion as opposed to other opinions); rather the Christian claim was then and needs to continue being that we can experience this profound humanness – that it is being experienced by humans in every part of planet and within every time period of the past, present, or future. We can become now, today, both God and human, both Final Reality's Offspring and the offspring of this historical, temporal, blood-drenched biological process that goes back to single-celled life popping into play on planet Earth.

The Chalcedonian Solution

And it is important for us to remain clear that becoming "Godly" as participants in the authentic Christ Body does not mean that our finite personhood becomes the Power that posits, sustains, limits, and ends all temporal beings. It does mean, however, that being a participant in both finitude and Eternity, we become a family member with that invincible Power that is our God. We share in the Final Truth of that Final Mysteriousness, manifested in our lives as a Final Certainty, a Final Freedom, a Final Healing that can unravel all that ails our deeply depraved state of humanity. It is this kind of truth that was at stake in the early Church Councils.

In our era of Post-Platonic, Post-Aristotelian, existential experience, we can understand anew the Christian Trinity with some astonishing simplicity – three faces of one experience. Here is a minimalist summation of what those three faces are:

FACE ONE: The Awesome as the Enigmatic Almightyness within Historical Encounter

FACE TWO: The Awed Ones as the Enigmatic Wonder of Human Historical Response

FACE THREE: The Awe Itself as the Enigmatic Spirit of Timeless Presence in Time

I will illustrate these three Faces of the Eternity experience in Chapter 13 with a thoroughgoing existential (i.e. personal) exposition. But before I do that, I will continue an overview of some key turning points in the history of Christianity. I will examine four of those turning points, each associated with a key person: Augustine, Thomas Aquinas, Martin Luther, and Søren Kierkegaard. These turning points were accomplished by more than one person. There was much build up before each of these named persons lived, and there was much follow-up after them. Nevertheless, these four creative persons are appropriate symbols for these turning points.

Also, we can discern dozens of other turning points in the history of Christianity, but these four are massive in nature, and they teach us important lessons for a viable future for Christian practice. Christianity is a religious tradition and practice that has undergone massive turning points before; so we need not be surprised to find ourselves in another of those massive turning points now.

Part Two:

Other Big Turning Points in Western Church History

Christianity is now a tangle of many threads that have gone in many directions: Eastern Orthodox, Roman Catholic, Protestant, and many versions of each. Each of these threads contain valuable lessons for all of us, but each person who claims a Christian practice as his or her religion is living in and choosing to continue to live within one of these many threads. The thread I will discuss in Part Two reaches through four major turning points in Western Christian history.

As already mentioned in Part One, these turning points are associated with the illuminating work of these four very creative persons: Augustine, Thomas Aquinas, Martin Luther, and Søren Kierkegaard. It will not be my aim to add to the basic scholarship about these persons and their times, but merely to tell a story about a thread of history that has brought me, and others, to our current place of envisioning a Next Christianity. The Next Christianity I have in mind is a pull together of the vast current turning point in which I (and many others) now see our sector of Western Church History deeply embroiled.

Chapter 8

Augustine and a Greek/Hebrew Synthesis

In this chapter I am not going to do a full examination of Augustine's writings or of the historical situation to which Augustine was addressing himself. This has been done and needs to be done, but I will attempt a much more limited task in this chapter.

I am going suggest that Augustine's work was a pull together of several centuries of intense theological discussion that was also a pull together of many of the key gifts from two quite different cultures: the Greco-Roman inheritance and the Hebrew cultural ferment that most characterized the Christian Scriptures. Indeed Augustine's work was a synthesis of truth for living that was powerful enough to guide Christian thinking and living for the next 800 years.

Augustine is also interesting as a personal story, a story that is well told in his own *Confessions* and in the many books and sermons written and delivered over a long public career. He was a determined seeker for "truth to live by," and he lived by the truth he found. He was both a Greek style mystic and a Hebrew style servant of history. He was both a monastic who renounces private property for himself and a Bishop and politician who defended private property for others as long as that wealth was viewed as a gift from God and was given generously as alms for the poor and support for the work of the church. He saw the depth of Christian community as a palpably intimate communion of saints, and he saw Christianity as an institution of religion that contained only sinners who were being provided daily, weekly means of grace for their Spirit journey. He was both an authoritarian church-person who honored fully the inherited traditions and yet was also capable of a remarkable freedom to enact creative thought and action. I find it impossible to know this man deeply without identifying with him strongly, and yet I also find ways in which I am impelled to disagree with him.

I will sketch some of these powerful themes. What I hope to contribute with this chapter is a method for appropriating the greatness of Augustine for our times. Secondly, I want to indicate three places where Augustine's Christian thought needs to be significantly corrected: (1) the mingling of his thinking about sex with his thinking about sin, (2) his use of the idea of predestination to undergird the experience of dependence on God's grace for our restoration from sin, and most important (3) his use of the concept of authority to establish the validity of the teachings of the Church. With regard to this last point it is interesting to note that Martin Luther was an Augustinian monk who pioneered a reform of our Christian understanding of authority. But Luther was also an authoritarian in ways that current Christian renewal is moving beyond. Nevertheless, in our dialogue with Augustine we need to notice that his authoritarianism, like Luther's, had a personal-experience basis to it that today is often missing in both conservative Catholic and Protestant practices.

Following is my simplified tour through these overwhelming themes.

The Hebrew Augustine

As a Hebrew heritage lover, Augustine provided to his times and ours a keen sense of history and of the God of history. We can see this in his *Confessions*, his personally intimate story of his own life journey. We also see his sense of history in *The City of God* books in which he examines how history is made by the interaction of the Eternal City with the Earthly cities of humanity. Augustine knew that his writings were making history, and he intended them to do so. His forceful quarrels with Donatism and Pelagianism indicate a passionate concern for the future of Christianity and for humankind as a whole. Augustine knew that the Empire of Rome was corrupt, yet he also saw within it great gifts capable of transformation and useful for his project.

The Greek Augustine

Augustine was open to the secular culture of his era, even though he always viewed himself as some sort of Christian and maintained a deep communion with his remarkably Christian mother. He was for seven years deeply involved in the Manichian view of good and evil: that the evil in this world could be understood as the result of an evil force in the cosmos that fought with another cosmic force for good. This took the form of a deep intellectual fellowship with fellow seekers who found in this Christianized Zoroastrianism both a realistic view of the tragic evil of the world as well as a path to participation in the "Eternal light" of good. His conversion or return to a more orthodox form of Christianity included the Hebraic understanding that the force of Reality is entirely good, that evil is but a hole in the good, a perversion of the good that does not do away with the good but instead makes the participant in evil vulnerable to an all-powerful good that is driving evil to despair. Augustine was also a student of Greek astronomy that gave him the sense of a cosmos of great order. This may also have assisted him in his doubt of the Manichean view of an evil that was built into the structure of the cosmos. He was also a student of Plotinus, a powerful current development of the Platonic side Greek philosophy. Plotinus' mystical depth was a significantly deepening force in Augustine's journey. The practical social thought of Cicero was also important to him. Augustine was not privileged to know everything about Classical Greek heritage, but what he learned from the available Latinized Roman versions of this ancient heritage was very deeply appropriated and applied. The "force for truth" within these powerful gifts from Greek heritage were as much a part of his writings as his Hebraic influence. But it was the truth he found in the teachings of the by then well-established Christian Church and its Bible that become central for his more settled adult life. Without Augustine's synthesis of these two vast spheres of truth and his skillful communication, the Western world would have been deeply impoverished.

The Enigma of Original Sin

One aspect of Augustine's lean toward the Hebrew side of his Greek and Hebrew influences found expression in his thinking about sin. The Greek mind was comparatively optimistic about human nature. Though seeing humanity as tragically flawed, Greek heritage also viewed humanity as capable of greatness, a greatness that the human mind and will could achieve. Augustine found this typical Greek-based attitude to be less than fully true. In terms of the *good* that is described by a full obedience to the Hebrew God of history, (that is to mysterious Reality with a capital R), the story of humanity was a history-long, oft-repeated fall into deep estrangement from what is fully true. Augustine saw this estrangement as so deep that the human mind and will did not have the power to counter this condition.

Augustine described this estrangement as **pride**, not the psychological pride that is the opposite of self-depreciation, but a *hubris*, as Paul Tillich prefers to call it. Hubris is an unrealistic view of self, a self-promotion that is out of touch with realism, a defense of the indefensible, a *megalomania* of the inner being.   Both Augustine and Tillich saw self-depreciation as a depreciation of God's creation, and thus also as a form of hubris.

Augustine and a Greek/Hebrew Synthesis

Augustine also analyzed how a human who is enthralled in this hubris has lost control of the body. The human body becomes trapped a power of *concupiscence*, a desire to be infinitely fulfilled, a desire that can never be fulfilled and that is therefore restlessness and vulnerable to despair. We have seen a similar analysis take place by contemporary psychologists who point out how humanity is driven by out-of-control desires that render one permanently dissatisfied – so much so that a person can experience a desire for death rather than continuing in this troubling state of unpeace. Freud, we may recall, made comments on this topic – his so-called "death instinct."

Augustine viewed the essence of these complex states of estrangement (sin) as a "bondage-of-will." The will of the human person is bound in an inability to live otherwise. The will is not free as the Greek mindset tended to claim. The will is trapped in a tragic state from which it does not have the power to extricate itself. A liberation must come from outside – the inside having become lost in bondage. Augustine was not talking about our capacity to decide this over that, or our capacity to make history, change the course of things, make a difference, and so forth. He was talking about how all our choices are set in a pattern determined by the bondage of our will to some form of hubris, megalomania, concupiscence, addiction, unrealism, ideology, crass foolishness, denial of truth, etc. As long as this estranged devotion has captivated us, we cannot perform the good of loving Reality and living realistically.

Augustine conducted much of his discussion on this topic through an elaboration of the Adam and Eve myth. Adam, he claimed, was in full possession of his God-given freedom before the fall, as was Eve. There was no reason for this fall; Adam had everything he needed for a full life, but he (he and Eve) found themselves capable of envisioning a step up into hubris, of substituting human creations of reality for the given true Reality. This misplaced stepping-up toward a knowledge of good and evil turns out to be a step down or away from the GOOD of GOD.

Augustine and a Greek/Hebrew Synthesis

Augustine did not have our sophisticated cultural anthropology for explaining how our estrangement from the GOOD is passed on from one generation to the next in a cultural way. He gave a biological explanation to the continuation of estrangement from one generation to the next. This explanation tends to imply that the goodness of sex and the goodness of the human body have been lost in the fall, rather than remaining good and powerful forces that still exist as a challenge to our "fallen" sexual and bodily addictions and other estrangements from the enduring good of our created nature. Augustine was correct, however, that humanity's estrangement affects everything, and that the general state of humanity is a lostness from our true being, including the true being of our body and its sexuality.

The essence of this enduring estrangement is, I believe, best described today as a result of the temptation that is present within our greatest gift, our ability to think – our ability to create and believe in the reality of a fabricated world that we prefer to the real world that is being given to us. We prefer our own *finite knowledge* of good and evil to any sort of *Eternal Truth* that characterizes the cosmos, rules the course of history, and undergirds everything that takes place in our lives. Such an *Eternal Truth* judges or undermines our *finite knowledge* of good and evil.

A Historical Method for Reading Augustine

The writings of Augustine are difficult for contemporary readers because he was operating within the two-realm metaphor of heaven and earth that was dominant in his time. I will illustrate how we can translate his thinking for our era. I will use one small piece of his writing to illustrate a method I call "metaphorical translation." Following are my comments upon this famous opening line of his *Confessions*:

> "Our hearts are restless until they rest in Thee, Oh God."

Augustine and a Greek/Hebrew Synthesis

To understand this phrase we need to know in our own life experience what Augustine was pointing in his life experience with the word "God." Similarly, we must translate into our experience the words "hearts" "restlessness" and "rest."

Hearts: Luther, the ex-Augustinian monk, provides us a clue to the meaning of "heart," as this term was commonly used in Medieval Christian theological thought. Here is a quote from Luther that I have found illuminating: "Trust and faith of the heart alone make both God and idol . . . for the two, faith and God, hold close together. Whatever then thy heart clings to . . . and relies upon, that is properly thy God."

"Heart," in both Luther and Augustine, means the seat of our basic devotion, our primal passion. It is to the heart, not to the mind, that we must look for the personal meaning of both God and idol. To what are we devoted? To what does our heart cling? What is the worship of our heart?

God: In the above prayerful cry, Augustine is saying that our worship of any "god" different than the biblical God (The Ultimate Reality manifest in history) renders our hearts restless. To find "Rest" in our hearts we must cling in passionate worship to this awesome, mysterious "God." We must be devoted to "God" to find "Rest." Augustine means the same "God" experienced in Isaiah's foundation-shaking temple vision, in Second Isaiah's world history lessons, in Paul's eternal power and divinity that are plainly discernible through things which are commonly seen and known, as well as in Psalm 90's Almighty Limiter of our finite lives. In a full 21st Century experiential language, "God" is that Mysterious Power we experience in the unstoppable flow of time and in all the events that encounter us in our planetary and solitary history.

Restlessness: The restlessness that Augustine has in mind is a restlessness that characterizes our heart's devotion to some finite object of life meaning. Sex additions and drug addictions teach us something about restlessness. But the restlessness to which Augustine is pointing is more far-reaching than the much-discussed topics of sex and drug addiction. Anytime we reject the fullness of Reality as it is manifest in this moment and hope for something else, we are thereby trapped in a desire that cannot be satisfied. We are restless, seeking what can never be.

We all tend to be addicted (or have been addicted) to some sort of "someday." Someday I will have enough money to be happy. Someday I will find the right partner to make me happy. Someday my current partner will die so I can find another. Someday I will have children. Someday these children will finally leave home. Someday I will find the work I like. Someday I will finish my education so I can begin my life. Someday my health will improve. Someday I will be less busy. Someday I will get around to tending to my deeper life and become restful and happy.

Someday never comes. It is always and only today. It is always Now. Yes, things change – sometimes for more pleasant days, sometimes for less pleasant days. But the many changes we will experience are not in themselves the advent of that Rest that overcomes all restlessness. If we get what we want, we may discover it is not what we want. Of if we get what we want, we then become restless that we will lose it. If we do not get what we want, we remain restless to get it. And if we give up getting what we want, but still want it, we are restless as well. Restlessness is the action of our consciousness toward some other moment than this moment.

This lesson on restlessness is an especially hard lesson for those of us who have experienced or do experience serious oppression. Of course we want to be liberated from that oppression. We may be hard at work to bring about a social someday in which oppression is no more. "Free at last, free at last, thank God Almighty we are free at last." If some of us are members of a racial minority in a bigoted culture, of course we want to live in a culture that treats us with the respect that our humanity deserves. If some of us are women in a patriarchal culture, of course we want to live in a culture that treats women with the respect that our humanity deserves. If we are gay or lesbian in a culture that misunderstands, mistreats, and despises such persons, of course we want to live in a culture that treats us with the respect that our humanity deserves. We may be hard at work to bring about that cultural someday, that promised land of social freedom. And that work is noble compassion for others and for ourselves.

But even with regard to these deep and valid longings for a non-oppressive someday, we can notice that someday is not today. The issue of Rest or restlessness is about today. Whatever be the set of cultural oppressions that oppress us, we can find Rest today in the Rest of which Augustine speaks. We do not need to wait until that someday when our oppressive culture is healed. Even if or when such a someday comes, we will find other oppressions about which to be restless for some other someday. If we are the oppressor, we are oppressed by our participation in that oppression, and we have our own "somedays" to which we escape and thereby escape confessing our mistreatment of others and the "Demand" to correct our living

Many of us have experienced the oppression for being a religious person, coming from a religion-ignoring or religion-hating culture. Indeed, the most hated person of all is often the one that has realized human authenticity to such an extent that he or she does not fit into the existing culture. Let Jesus be our illustration. Yet in spite of his ongoing oppression, Jesus surely experienced the Rest of which Augustine spoke.

Rest: So what is this Rest that overcomes all our restlessness, or at least exists in our lives alongside the many forms of restlessness that threaten to swamp us? It is Rest in the fullness of Reality pointed to with the word, "God." This God of Augustine and Luther, as well as Jesus and Paul, does not exist in terms of what we normally mean by "existence." The biblical words for God (Yahweh, Lord, Father, Mother, Friend of Abraham, Rock, Shepherd, Foundation) all point to the Ground of all that exists. This Ground does not exist in the common sense of the word "exist": that is, this Ground does not come into being or go out of being. This Ground is not a being alongside other beings, like angels or humans. God is the Ground of all "coming into being."

Augustine and a Greek/Hebrew Synthesis

And God is also the cosmic grave of all "going out of being." Just as the Earth is both Ground and Grave, that inclusive Reality that includes the Earth is Ground and Grave of the Earth as well as everything of which the Earth is also Ground and Grave.

This everlasting Ground and Grave is the experience pointed to by the worshipful word "God" by Jesus, Paul, Augustine, Luther, and millions of others. This Ground and Grave is the "abba" or "papa" of whom Jesus spoke. And this Ground and Grave of all existing beings is experienced by these exemplars as benevolent toward us, as the bestower of Rest in our hearts.

This papa-mama-friend benevolence of God is only experienced by those who are willing to be content with being Grounded into being and Graved out of being – that is, being content with limits and possibilities, living and dying, coming into being and going out of being. We lack the stillness of Jesus, of Paul, of Augustine, of Luther until we Rest in our present moment, renouncing all rejection of that moment, renouncing all hope for a different moment, and thus having no desire to have the unhaveable – that is, some other moment than the moment we have.

No other time than Now is the moment of Rest, of stillness, of life before God. The moment before God is not some imagined moment in the future. This Now is the moment before God. "Now" is the only time for Rest. Rest takes place Now, not someday. It is this moment, however tragic or fortunate, that contains the "final arrival," the heaven promised to us by Jesus and his many witnesses.

Yes, Jesus was a strange Messiah. He did not bring us what we wanted – the end of ruthless rulers, the reward for our religious excellence, the prosperity we think we have to have, the knowledge that ends all need for learning, and so on and so on and so on. He brought us back to something far more important – he brought us to ourselves, to our true lives, to our Rest in being who and what we are – not yesterday, not someday, but Now.

And in this living Now, whatever it is in temporal, historical terms, we have the capacity to discover Augustine's Rest. We can

Augustine and a Greek/Hebrew Synthesis

look and see for ourselves. We can notice for ourselves those things that we have been unwilling to notice. We can notice how committed we are to those somedays that make us restless. We can notice how resistant we are to being who we are in the current circumstances of our lives. We can notice that this "me" who resists today and longs for some other day is just a figment of our own invention. My "restless me" lives only by my own insistence. We can notice that it can become within our capability to give up being the "restless me." The "me" who is restless is not the true me. If we give up the false me, we will notice that we are already the one that is not restless. We are forgiven for all our departures and delays in finding this Rest. We are welcome home to the family of Reality of which we are part. We can find ourselves enchanted with Being, singularly compassionate, fearlessly confident, meditatively brilliant, prayerfully initiative, detached, engaged, audacious, and at peace – yes, at Rest. Such Spirit gifts may not all be manifest in each and every moment, but they are all there ready to come forward as needed. We can take our Rest!

Not every sentence of Augustine needs this much commentary to bring it into our understanding, but the entire scope of his witness does. In his 10-book work called "*The City of God*, he builds upon the "Rest" theme with the word "Peace." He speaks of how our Peace with God brings peace into family relations, into communal life, into the wide-world relations. He spells out how "The City of God" is a presence in the midst of the City of Humankind that has become separated from God. He sees the then well-established institutional Church as a sphere within which the City of God dwells. From this City of God Presence on Earth, greater Peace can come to the world. He also sees that the Church is an institution composed of many humans whose lives are very far from Peace with God. Nevertheless, even a faithless priest who performs the Church's sacramental graces brings healing Peace to the world. Almost every topic of life is engaged by this theologian, and he vigorously engages every misunderstanding that rears its head against his City-of-God realism, Peace, and Rest

The Ongoing Conflict with Pelagianism

Augustine waged one of the most memorable conflicts in Christian theological history with Pelagius and his followers. Pelagius was a brilliant and dedicated Christian theologian, but he did not grasp how the will of a human being can be bound by estrangements that the unassisted will cannot break. Pelagius was a proponent of free will. He emphasized that it is up to each human to do good and to not do evil. Augustine also emphasized the will rather than the reason as the core dynamic in human life, but he sees that the will, having rejected Reality (i.e. God), has thereby become bound within this rejection in a manner that can only be broken from the outside by events of Reality's action (grace) upon us. This controversy still rages in contemporary theology, and Augustine's view still proves itself the deeper vision. The healing of our addictions, rages, or malice requires a Word of judgment that reveals to us the tragedy of this despair-characterized state of living. We also require for the freeing of our will the gift of the Word of forgiveness that welcomes us home to the Reality for which we are made.

Pelagius was a perfectionist and an optimist. He was a monk and an ascetic; he opposed private property and asked rich people to give up their property and join his radicalism. Such acts he believed humans could and needed to do. His view was, "It is up to us to be good." Pelagius, in a less extreme form, would fit into many of our contemporary liberal Churches. "It's simply up to me to be good" is an oft-heard message, but it is not the good news clarified by Augustine. Many of us today suspect that the world is more tragic and more mired in difficulties than a Pelagian or semi-Pelagian view can encompass.

Augustine's view of a tragic world in hopeless restlessness is a realistic vision that is also profoundly optimistic. Augustine does find within himself the experience of Rest in God. He is an activist bringing Peace on Earth. Augustine knows, however, that such transformation of human life does not take place by a mere act of human will. Our healing requires an act of God. It takes a power beyond our self-willed illusory worldview to crash into that closed circle of estrangement and welcome us home to Reality.

Augustine's View of the Church

Augustine resonated with the sense of the Church as a society of the Holy Spirit, a communion of saints, a comradeship of love of self, God, and neighbor. He sought to manifest that sort of community in his own monastic order. But he also uses the word "Church" to indicate the empire-wide religious institution that had by his day become a cultural, economic, and political force. That social power was relatively small in a still largely pagan world of Roman form. But Augustine was intent on increasing that social power and creating an historical religious institution that deserved to have the social power it was acquiring. He worked with his fellow bishops to fight off Pelagianism and other teachings and practices he found wanting. He saw the religious institutions of Christianity to be carrying a deep gift that gave it a sacramental power even if that power was administered by flawed, deeply estranged, and unbelieving priests. He fought with the Donatist Christians who held that baptism or marriage by a defrocked priest was invalid. Augustine's view was that such a rule was unenforceable because only "God knows" for sure who are the unfaithful priests. He also claimed that if these rituals were performed correctly, they had the same nurturing effect no matter who performed them. Augustine understood that the views of the Donatists were a form of perfectionism that ought not be applied to the historical Church. At the same time Augustine fought to move the visible, historical Church toward the sort of effective religious institution it needed to be to do the good it needed to do in the world of its time.

His use of the authority imagery made Augustine's perspective a strong proponent of tradition even though he was a very innovative person himself. He argued for the authority of the heritage and based his programs for Church improvement on the authority of the Scriptures and the Church Fathers. He saw himself and the fellowship of bishops with whom he worked as an extension of that authority and as an historical group deserving of an obedience that seemed arbitrary and needlessly stubborn to the free-minded Greek influenced rationalists of his time, and also of our time. But as we study Augustine's life closely, we can see that his intent in all his scrappy orthodoxy was to sustain, proclaim, and extend the ministry that he had experienced healing to himself and the many people that he served. Some of Augustine's fights have never been entirely won within the wide-range of Christian practice. Indeed, some of his positions can now stand some correction. But we need to honor this man and his friends in mission for delivering to the succeeding centuries a more vital and realistic form of Christianity than we might have had without him.

Corrections to Augustine's Vision that 21st Century Christians can See More Clearly

Three aspects of Augustine's vision now stand out to me and many others as in need of correction: (1) his way of mingling his thinking about *sex* with his thinking about sin, (2) his use of the idea of *predestination* to undergird the experience of dependence on God's grace for our restoration from sin, and most important (3) his use of the concept of *authority* to establish the validity of the teachings of the Church.

Sex: Augustine may have been helped by the Christian witness to overcome his own sexual addictions. This may have been one source for his certainty about the existence of the bound will. But some Medieval theologians and many Modern theologians have criticized his view that sex and birth is the means of the transmission of estrangement from Adam and Eve to the following generations of humans. It was an overkill for Augustine to suggest that Adam before the fall only had erections when he chose to have them, implying that our more out-of-control experience is a sign of the fall. It is more consistent and nature-affirming to view sex, with all its controllable and uncontrollable features, as merely part of our biological nature, part of our created Christ-innocence, not a factor of our estrangement. Estrangement comes into being through our erroneous relationships with sex and other features of our finite lives, and these estrangements are transferred to following generations through cultural rather than biological means. Though concupiscence is a real experience, Augustine's biological overkill had far reaching consequences for Christian living – an overemphasis on celibacy and asceticism with regard to sex, giving a needless second-rate status to married life, and worst of all encouraging a diminished status and honor toward women. Further, such views tend to deny us the redemptive role of women in the lives of men as well as the redemptive role of men in the lives of women. And all the above creates suffering for the gay and lesbian persons in our populations.

Predestination: The experience that it is God's grace, not our own action that restores us to our authenticity was a positive contribution of Augustine as well as of Luther, Calvin, Wickliff, and others. But it has been another overkill to buttress the grace experience with the notion that our "liberation" from the swamp of estrangement was predestined from the foundations of creation. It is perhaps true that it does feel that way when one realizes the comfort of total dependence upon God (Reality) for our authenticity. We do not have to achieve this authenticity, we only have to surrender to it. But to spell this out as a predestination has consequences that need to be questioned. John Wesley insisted against a decayed Calvinist predestinarianism that "faith is 100% God's gift and 100% my choice." I find this to be strange mathematics but, nevertheless, true to my experience. As Paul Tillich spelled this out, the grace happening is incomplete without its third aspect: my acceptance of God's acceptance of me for a fresh start in spite of my many estrangements. This trusting of God is my doing even though it is a surrender, a sort of non-doing, an effortless-letting-be of "God's reign of forgiveness," rather than an accomplishment of which I can boast.

Authority: Augustine's view of the authority of the Church had a mystical or existential element to it that the post-Aquinas era lost to a large extent. So when Protestants criticized the overreaching authority of the Church, they were criticizing an authoritarianism that was a decayed form of the Augustinian view of authority. For Augustine the authority of the Church meant obedience to a received body of teachings, creeds, and practices that had a very personal or mystical meaning. Augustine surrendered to these inherited traditions because he experienced their healing power. The "grace" of these traditions seemed to him like a fluid substance that flowed from this authoritarian inheritance into the souls of those being healed of sin. Whether this heritage was the letters of Paul or the elements of the Eucharist, such tradition was felt to have healing power, making it an authority for Augustine. But as the history of Christianity unfolded after Aquinas, a more objective view of the authority of the Pope and the Church become customary and that development became deadly to our trust in our own experience as well as our trust in the deep reasonings of the heart of faith. In the post-Lutheran and post-Kierkegaardian eras, a new view concerning the authority of the Church has become a crucial theological and practical issue. Today, we can admit that the inherited tradition contains teachings and practices that can be healing, but we can also be clear that all these humanly-invented contents are just methods that sometimes work of our healing and sometimes do not. The story of our healing needs to be told in a more accurate way than a surrender to Church authority. Not only can the Pope of Roman Catholicism be wrong on matters of faith and practice, but the "popery" of Protestant denominations can also be validly questioned. It is my intent in this book to paint the possibility of a vital Next Christianity that rests upon the supporting ground of authenticity, rather than on a subservience to the authority of any institutions of Christian heritage, including those institutions that I myself might invent. I understand this to

Augustine and a Greek/Hebrew Synthesis

be a theological and practical improvement of the thinking of Augustine, Aquinas, Luther, and many others. The move toward authenticity over authority does not mean that we cannot learn from all the vast variety of Christian formations, but we can also say our "yes's" and "no's" to these sources from a fresh viewpoint that trusts the "Holy Spirit" operating in our own personal depths of consciousness. We deeply need to trust that Spirit over any former attempt to describe that Spirit and its implications.

Chapter 9

Thomas Aquinas and Aristotelian Worldliness

When I suggest that Thomas Aquinas is in the center of the next huge turning point in Church history, I do not deny that many significant events took place between the fourth and fifth century Augustine and the thirteenth century Aquinas. One of the most significant of those events was a development in Christian monasticism. Christian monasticism predated Augustine. Augustine himself was a monastic and the founder of the Augustinian order. Nevertheless, the work of Benedict (480-543 CE) in redesigning Western monasticism can be viewed as a major event in Church history. Benedict combined labor, prayer, contemplation, thoughtfulness, and communal stability into concrete practices that are still amazingly provocative. In spite of his important innovations, Benedict was a worker in the Augustinian wake. He did not contradict or change the basic Augustinian pull together. Theologically Benedict was an Augustinian.

And there are many other events before Aquinas that might be counted as major: Hildegard of Bingen (1098-1178) was a Benedictine abbess of remarkable creativity in terms of her love of nature. Francis of Assisi (1182-1226) and Claire (1194-1253) also supported a deepening of the love of nature. And all three of these persons can be viewed as Augustinians in their basic theology.

Thomas Aquinas and Aristotelian Worldliness

However, the turning point I am associating with Thomas Aquinas (1225-1274) is a fundamentally new approach of the Church to a much changed world, a world under many influences – a world that is due to change even more. The more mystical and metaphysical emphasis of the Augustinian heritage was in need of an upgrade in the scientific realm of living. The Church would have been left with a weakened relevance if the Aquinas' revolution had not been accepted.

With Aquinas we are dealing with a radically competent response to the Aristotelian thought that was being imported from the south Mediterranean Islamic world. A much-changed response for the Church was already underway through a development of Aristotelian thinking within the Dominican order of which Aquinas was a member.

While Aristotelian thought had some influence on Plotinus who was Augustine's philosophical mentor, both Plotinus and Augustine leaned heavily toward the Plato side of the ancient Plato-Aristotle polarity in philosophical thought. The extent to which the thought of Aristotle had been neglected during the eight centuries between Augustine and Aquinas is remarkable. There was a lack of serious interest in what we today call "the natural sciences" – that is, with how the particulars of "material" nature affect our overviews of thought. Today in the West we are so embedded in a post-Aquinas culture of scientific emphasis that it is hard for us to imagine that such was not the case in those earlier centuries.

Aquinas was a revolutionary in his time. His writings were strongly opposed by the Augustinians in the Franciscan order and elsewhere. The Franciscan movement was another important development within the Augustinian wake. In Aquinas' day the Franciscan Bonaventura (1221-1274), born Giovanni di Fidanza, was an Italian medieval scholastic theologian of formidable power and a strong opponent of Aquinas' innovations. In spite of this and other strong opposition, we can suppose that Aquinas finally won his place in Church thinking because the power of his thought dealt more adequately with the new challenges of the complex social world in which he lived.

I find reading Aquinas somewhat difficult. We have to do some translating to our own times to feel our way into the greatness of his work. Following is an example. I am commenting upon a piece of his *Summa Theologica* "On the Laws."

Is there an Eternal Law?

By "Eternal Law," Aquinas meant something very similar to what some of our contemporary evolution deniers call "Intelligent Design." But these contemporary science-deniers need to hear what Thomas says about "Eternal Law."

> *A law is nothing else than the dictate of practical reason in the sovereign who governs a perfect community. Now it is manifest, supposing that the world is ruled by a Divine Providence, that the whole community of the universe is governed by Divine Reason.*

By "sovereign" Aquinas means a king, the top leader of any society known at that time. By "perfect community" Aquinas means any grouping of humans in which all the aspects of society (political, economic, and cultural) are manifesting in a specific scope of geography. With this down-to-Earth picture in the readers' minds, Aquinas uses the word *"supposing"* when referring to a world *"ruled by a Divine Providence."* The word "supposing" indicates analogical thinking. Following is a restatement of the meaning of what Aquinas is saying: "Let us *suppose* that, just like we experience a king in our human societies, there is a KING that rules the whole universe. If so, then the Divine Reason of this Eternal KING is like unto a Law. Aquinas goes on to say what this "Eternal Law" is like.

> *And therefore the plan of government of things, as it is in God the Sovereign of the universe, bears the character of a law. And because the Divine Reason conceives nothing according to time, but has an eternal concept, therefore it is that this manner of law must be called eternal.*

Thomas Aquinas and Aristotelian Worldliness

For most 21st century persons, these sentences require much interpretation. Aquinas is still using his "supposing" or "analogical" thinking and he is also using the taken-for-granted, two-story metaphor known to everyone in his times. In terms of the meaning of the above sentences for Aquinas' existence and ours, we need to consider carefully this sentence: *"Divine Reason conceives nothing according to time, but has an eternal concept."* This "eternal concept" exists only in the "Mind of God." And that means that the "Eternal Law" is something that cannot be conceived from the point of view of our time-bound human minds. This "Divine Reason" which is the "Law" ruling the entire universe is, to us humans, Sheer Mystery. We may be experiencing this Sheer Mystery in our conscious guts, but we are not experiencing this Eternal Law with our minds. With our minds we are merely *supposing* Eternal Law as a thought project. What we are experiencing with our consciousness is Sheer Mystery.

In contrast to Aquinas, contemporary conservative Christians insist on using the term "Intelligent Design" for something that human beings can understand with their minds by reading their Bibles or listening to their Church teachings. In doing so, they are not on the same wavelength with Aquinas. If they were to notice that their so-called "Intelligent Design" is analogical thinking about the Sheer Mystery, then they would be able to see what Aquinas is saying to them about their lives. Aquinas is expressing his faith that the process of the whole universe is good – well ordered by a trustworthy "Orderer" whose order, design, rules, laws are incapable of being understood by human beings, but are nevertheless Good – that is Godly. Let us continue with Aquinas' remarkable logic.

> *Is there in us any natural law?*
> *Law being a rule and measure, may be in a thing in two ways: in one way as in one ruling and measuring, in another way as in one who is ruled and measured. Hence, since all things subject to Divine Providence are ruled and measured by the Eternal Law, it is manifest that they all*

participate to some extent in the Eternal Law, inasmuch by the stamp of that law upon them they have their inclinations to their several acts and ends. But among the rest the rational creature is subject to Divine Providence in a more excellent way, being itself a partaker in Providence, providing for itself and others. Hence there is in it a participation of the Eternal Law, whereby it has a natural inclination to a due act and end: such participation in Eternal Law in the rational creature is called natural law. Hence it is clear that the natural law is nothing else than a participation of the Eternal Law in the rational creature.

Putting this in our 21st Century words, Aquinas is saying that whatever we humans know about the Sheer Mystery of the universe is a participation of that Sheer Mystery in our finite human minds. Here are examples: If we know that mass and energy are two forms of the same reality, that is a participation of the Sheer Mystery in our human minds. If we know that gravity is not a force of attraction operating at a distance, but a bending in space caused by the presence of great mass, that is a participation of the Sheer Mystery in our human minds. If we know that the average Earth temperature is getting warmer as a result of our burning of fossil fuels, that is a participation of the Sheer Mystery in our human minds. Natural law, if that term can have meaning for us today, is simply what the human mind can currently know about the Sheer Mystery of the universe. Our contemplative inquiry into our own consciousness can also turn up "natural law" about the Sheer Mystery of what it means to be conscious beings. So with such careful translation, we can perhaps agree with Aquinas that there is such thing in our minds as natural law. But not Eternal Law. Natural law is what we know about the Eternal Law. About the Eternal Law itself we are still mystified. The Eternal Law in its wholeness and essence remains Sheer Mystery. Next we see the practical results of Aquinas' logic for human society:

Thomas Aquinas and Aristotelian Worldliness

Whether there is human law?
As we have stated above, a law is a dictate of the practice reason. Now it is to be observed that the same procedure takes place in the practical and in the speculative reason, for each proceeds from principles to conclusions. Accordingly, we conclude that, just as in speculative reason, from naturally known demonstrable principles we draw conclusions of the various sciences, the knowledge of which is not imparted to us by nature, but acquired by the efforts of reason, so too it is that from the precepts of the natural law, as from common and demonstrable principles, the human reason needs to proceed to the more particular determination of certain matters. These particular determinations, devised by human reason, are called human laws, provided that the other essential conditions of law be observed as was stated above.

So what does Aquinas mean by human law? He means whatever a human ruler, president, Congress, reform movements etc. finds it needful to add to natural law in order to make a society workable – for example: determining on which side of the road we are required to drive; what color of light means stop; or what corporations are allowed to do and what not to do. All such matters are not prescribed by our knowledge of natural law.

In a later part of his section on human law, Aquinas makes it clear that any human law that is not in accord with natural law does not have the standing of "law," and thus has no claim upon the conscience of the citizen to be obeyed. It can be disobeyed. It needs to be changed to be a true law. Here is a modern example: Any US law about energy that is not in accord with the natural law concerning global warming (climate crisis) does not have the standing of law. It does not have a claim upon conscience to be obeyed. So the current laws permitting the mining and transport or tar sands oil should not be counted as laws: they should not be obeyed or enforced by the police. Here are Aquinas' words on this point:

Every law framed by man bears the character of a law exactly to the extent to which it is derived from the law of nature. But if on any point it is in conflict with the law of nature, it at once ceases to be a law: it is a mere perversion of law.

Catholics who claim to revere Thomas Aquinas as their top theologian and yet deny climate science and evolutionary science need to notice that Aquinas does not support them in this attitude. And Protestants, who claim that the Right-wising of our lives begins and ends with faith alone, need to notice that Aquinas' statements about Eternal Law actually express his "faith" that all the processes of nature and history that are happening to us are trustworthy gifts of that Eternal Enigma, "whose" ways are mysterious and forever unknown to us. This means that Aquinas might be viewed as supportive of a radical Protestantism that claims that God is not "a person," that "person" is just a metaphor that expresses our devotion to this Ground of Being that is the source and the terminator of all things.

From this tiny piece of Thomas Aquinas' vast work, we can see that he is a practical ethicist (even a revolutionary one) as well as an ecclesiastical reformer. He is a mediating thinker between the rising Aristotelian science (objective thought) and the church's collective wisdom (authoritative thought about our primal existence). He is much concerned to give credence to the best science of his day as well as give credence to the Church's vast collection of deep wisdom. With regard to Church wisdom Aquinas is a type of mystic and a devoted person of deep trust. These qualities were not as prominent among many of the thinkers that came after him. Aquinas wanted to assure his generation that they could absorb Aristotelian science as far as it goes. He also wanted to convince his generation that such wisdom does not go the whole way to our "Final Blessedness." We still need to access the Grace of God ministered by the Church to open in us the "supernatural virtues" of Trust, Hope and Love. These gifts of God are essential to our true fulfillment, and they are missing from the greatness of Aristotelian wisdom and virtues.

Thomas Aquinas and Aristotelian Worldliness

Aquinas ends up with a two-story stack of wisdom – the natural and the supernatural. The separation between these two categories of meaning was increased. The more mystical thought of Augustine tended to interlace natural and supernatural. For Aquinas, the supernatural is separate and firmly on top, but this top layer is on top of something valid – the natural realm and wisdom, which is also a gift to us from the same Sheer Mystery that gives us the healing grace carried by the Church. It was Aquinas' affirmation of natural wisdom that the established Augustinian theologians found objectionable. Aristotle did not square with their more mystical views of nature. Also, the practical consequences involved in admitting this wisdom distressed them. Aquinas and his whole religious order were a revolutionary force within that time. They did not win the majority mind right away, but they did more or less win eventually. Had they not won what they won, we today might not be the science-loving Western world that we are. Or perhaps the science-loving Western world would have evolved, but the Church could not have been able to minister to it.

As the post-Aquinas flow of events unfolded, the unleashed natural sciences began to challenge the Church half of Aquinas' two-story stack of wisdom. Let the science of evolution be our example. The scientific understandings that went into the composition of the Genesis myths does indeed conflict with today's cosmology and biology. When conservative Christians insist on a literal rather than mythic view of Genesis, they are in serious tension with the evidence for species evolution and with the evidence for a 13-to-14-billion-year-old cosmos. In spite of the fact that the scientific community has already won this war with the intelligentsia, there is still a huge percentage of the U.S. population that reject evolution and contemporary cosmology. As Christian theologians, it remains for us to do for our time what Aquinas did for his time, namely to reconcile science and religion.

But before we return to questions of how the Christian religion needs to be recast in such a way that the ongoing work of science is an enrichment rather than a nemesis of our "faith," we need to explore another major turning point in Christian church history. This next turning point had much to do with that word "faith." When Martin Luther claims that our lives are "made righteous" by faith alone, only a small minority of contemporary people understand what he was taking about.

Chapter 10

Luther and the Reform of Authority

A great deal of new thought and a number of new experiments in Christian living arose between Thomas Aquinas (1225-1274) and Martin Luther (1483-1546). In Aquinas' own lifetime a very talented scholar, Duns Scotus (1266-1308), criticized Aquinas' too-easy synthesis between Aristotle's philosophy and Augustine's creative authoritarianism. The result of Scotus' thought was to render philosophy less "religious" and theology more thoroughly dependent on authoritarian doctrine. This direction was further developed by William of Ockham (1288-1347), leaving rational concepts as a mere naming of particular experiences emptying reason from what Paul Tillich called its "theonomous" potential, that is, its capacity to house symbolic meanings that reach into talk about Ultimate matters. Such "nominalism" left Christian theology even more dependent upon the sheer authority of the Church, rather than on an intuitive, scholarly reasoning for its verification.

In Luther's lifetime another great thinker, Desiderius Erasmus, created what Diarmaid MacCulloch suggests was a reasonable layman's Christianity somewhat in the vein of C. S. Lewis' *Mere Christianity*.[8] Erasmus was skeptical of rigid authoritarianism,

---

[8] MacCollouch, Diarmaid, *Christianity: The First Three Thousand Years* (Penguin Books: 2009) page 599

Luther and the Reform of Authority

irrational mysticism, Augustinian pessimism about the human fall, and Luther's radical Christian reforms. In spite of the fact that the Roman Inquisition tried to ban all Erasmus' writings, he skillfully made himself popular among the lay royalty and escaped persecution in spite of doing some controversial Biblical translation and promoting a thoroughgoing pacifism in that violent age.[9]

In another post-Aquinas thread, the German theologian, Meister Eckhart (1260-1328), developed a rather controversial and "too-wild-for-Erasmus" mysticism. Many other mystics preceded him and followed in his wake. During Luther's lifetime in the wildly violent and enthusiastically religious Spain, Teresa of Avila (1515-1582) and John of the Cross (1542-1591) also developed Christian mysticism as a powerful option that was supportive of the Roman Catholic Reformation and also manifested overlaps with Luther's Protestantism.

Luther was an original voice, even though he learned much from earlier challenges to the authority of the Roman Church. Here are two key precursors to Luther's reform: (1) A Britisher, John Wycliffe (1330-1384), was a thoroughgoing Augustinian but critical of Roman overreach and the oppression of lay thinking. He promoted the first translation of the Bible into English. With enthusiastic support from prominent laity he lived to a nonviolent death, but the Roman Church dug up his bones and burned them. His followers, the Lollards, had to live in hiding from a reactive scourge. (2) The Bohemian (Czechoslovakian) priest Jan Hus or John Huss (1374-1415) similarly supported lay Biblical literacy, translated the Bible, and most controversial of all distinguished himself by serving both the bread and the wine to the laity. He was burned at the stake mostly because of that liturgical change. But his followers kept an underground movement alive, and their influences were not ignored by Luther, Calvin, Zwingli, and others.

---

[9] op. cit: page 602

Luther and the Reform of Authority

Martin Luther

Martin Luther was the beginning of a new type of Christian Reform movement. He was advantaged by the reform movements and other ferment that happened before his time, and by an increasing restlessness in the German-speaking region with the Rome-based authorities. He was also helped by the invention of the printing press that enabled a widespread and quick distribution of his writings and his Bible translation. Nevertheless, it was the foundational level of his critique of Roman Christianity that made his Reformation a deep turning point, picked up by other competent reformers, and carried forward to this day. I will focus on this core level of his Reformation in Christian understanding and practice.

Let us begin with his redefinition of faith. Rather than meaning *belief* in a set of authoritarian dogmas, "faith" was recast, with help from Paul, as an act of the will, better called "trust" than "belief." Here are some words of Luther quoted by H. Richard Niebuhr in Niebuhr's essay "Faith in Gods and in God."

> *Trust and faith of the heart alone make both God and idol . . . For the two, faith and God, hold close together. Whatever then thy heart clings to . . . and relies upon, that is properly called thy God.*

This means that if your nation, right or wrong, is what your heart clings to, then that nation is your God. If the "racial superiority" of your race is what your heart clings to, then the "honor" of being that race is your God. If wealth and the privileges of wealth is what your heart clings to, then wealth is your God. If the authoritative teachings of your religious group are what your heart clings to, then those teachings or that group is your God.

So how does Luther spell out what it means to have faith in the "Reality" that Luther holds to be the God of Christian faith? Here is a quote from his essay "A Treatise on Christian Liberty."

Luther and the Reform of Authority

It is a further function of faith that it honors him whom it trusts with the most reverent and highest regard, since it considers him truthful and trustworthy. There is no other honor equal to the estimate of truthfulness and righteousness with which we honor him whom we trust. Could we ascribe to a man anything greater than truthfulness and righteousness and perfect goodness? On the other hand, there is no way in which we can show greater contempt for a man than to regard him as false and wicked, and to be suspicious of him, as we do when we do not trust him. So when the Soul firmly trusts God's promises, it regards him as truthful and righteous. Nothing more excellent than this can be ascribed to God. The very highest worship of God is this that we ascribe to him truthfulness, righteousness, and whatever else should be ascribed to one who is trusted. When this is done, the soul consents to his will. Then it hallows his name and allows itself to be treated according to God's good pleasure for, clinging to God's promises, it does not doubt that he who is true, just, and wise will do, dispose, and provide all things well.

This passage cannot come alive for us until we are clear what Luther means by the word "God" in addition to the devotional meaning he is giving this word. Luther assumes as his, and as the true Christian object of worship, the same Reality that we explored in the earlier chapters with the aid of Isaiah, Second Isaiah, Jesus, Paul, Augustine, and Thomas Aquinas. So what does Luther mean by this God who does all things well? We can assume without doubt that he means the same Sheer Mystery that we viewed in the writing of Aquinas, Augustine, Paul, Jesus, and both Isaiahs. That is, "God" points to: the metaphorical "King" of the universe, the Final Reality, the Reality that is present in every event. *So in each and every event of our lives we are facing a Mysterious Power that is true and just and wise and will do, dispose, and provide all things well.* Whether you are confronting the birth of your grandchild or the death of your daughter, you are confronting the God who does all things well. Whether you are confronting the success of your political revolution or the seeing your nation carried off into exile, you are confronting the God who does all things well. This is the trust that saves you from despair and transforms you into a blessed state of life. You allow yourself to be treated according to that Sheer Mystery's good pleasure – to be born in the century in which you are born, to live with the gifts and limitations that are being given to you, to face and deal with the challenges that you face, and to die on the day given to you to die. This trusting surrender does not mean fatalism toward some already determined destiny. Your choices matter. Your actions can change the course of history. You are a co-creator with God of outcomes over which you do not have full control, but for which you do bear responsibility. This "God-given" freedom, this responsibility is also part of the good pleasure given to you by the Sheer Mystery that is doing all things well. This radical trust is the "revolutionary thing" upon which Luther founded his Reformation of Christianity. Such trust is both humbling and strengthening – for no power is greater than the Power so trusted. This trust leads not only to freedom, but also to the universal love that the commandments can describe but cannot awaken. According to Luther, trust alone awakens both love and freedom.

Luther, in accord with Augustine and Paul, understands that faith is a gift, not an accomplishment. Such an understanding permits him to see faith as predestined from the foundations of creation. We have nothing whatsoever to do with the accomplishment of faith. By grace we are saved from our estrangement with the Realty in relation to which we are estranged. Reality must break through to our bound will and release it into its freedom to love Reality. But this grace is lived through faith, through the freedom that is part of this faith. So it remains for John Wesley to later insist that faith is 100% our action as well as 100% the gift of God. Wesley's insistence undermines the wooden sort of interpretation that later Calvinists gave to a belief about predestination. It is also true that in Luther's thought no support is given for living a passive Christian life. Faith for Luther meant action, such as: "Here I stand" in opposition to the entire Roman

Church. He experiences his conscience to be utterly captive to The Word of God: "I can *do* no other."

This clarified foundation for Christian understanding has far reaching consequences. First of all, it means that healing or salvation is a God-given opportunity offered directly to each individual person. The relation with God is personal, direct, and without need of an authorized priesthood that has been passed along since Peter. This did not square with the then current Roman Catholic belief that such "grace" comes only through the institutions of the Church and its sacraments. Further, grace, as seen by Luther, was no longer conceived as a fluid substance that flowed into the believer who is eating the Eucharist or attending a ritual, or hearing a sermon. Luther provided a new understanding of grace. Everything about salvation or the healing of the soul was seen as a personal relationship with the Almighty who meets each of us everywhere, in nature, in history, as well as in the Church's witnesses, teachings, and rituals in so far as those witnesses and rituals were properly embedded in the original breakthrough recorded in the Scriptures. This need not mean an idolization of the Bible into which so many later Protestants have fallen. Luther understood that the Word of God was in the Bible, not that the Word of God was the Bible. Luther did not have the benefit of modern historical criticism of the Scriptures, but he was critical of certain books of the Bible, especially those he found moralistic. He likened the book of James to straw.

So, the Word of God in the Bible was not the literal words of Latin or Greek or German, but a cosmic message of Good News that your life was being blessed with forgiveness from all your wayward thinking and living, that your past was being approved as your now unchangeable given, that a fresh start in living was being offered to you for your future, and that everything that is going on now or will go on in the future is being provided by THAT POWER that does all things well. You had only to accept this WORD, trust it, and keep on trusting it through thick and thin. This is a courageous life, but it was not a self-constructed life. It is

Luther and the Reform of Authority

the grace of God alone that is moving you to find and respond in this faith, and this grace sustains you in this faith. You did not create faith or invent it or anything of the sort. You were destined to it from the foundations of time. Or we might say that this faith is simply the REAL YOU coming into its AWESOME own.

With a great deal of consistency and careful thought, Luther re-established the practice of Christianity from this starting point. His "priesthood of all believers" was a rejection of the laity-clergy split, replacing it by defining laity and clergy as different but complementary functions. His service of both bread and wine undergirded this direction. He reduced the number of sacraments to Baptism and the Eucharist – that is, to (1) an affirmation of the basic nature of the entry into faith and (2) the nurture of faith through this deep ritual for the rest of our lives. Confirmation, Marriage, Ordination and Extreme Unction remained useful rituals for enriching these key life passages. Protestant practice would continue ministering to people during these turning points of their lives, but Luther felt that "sacrament" was too powerful a term to signify these practices. And he saw the established understanding of Penance to be so wrapped in clericalism that the role of confessing our sins needed a whole new understanding. Luther believed that sin was such a vast sea of estrangement that we never know everything for which we need forgiveness. Therefore confessing to a priest was too narrow to be an all-purpose ministry for our need to confess the fullness of our estrangement.

Also, Luther left the monastery and married a Lutheran convert among the many previous nuns – thereby again rejecting any clergy/laity split in levels of holiness. Luther also accepted from the wider critique of traditional practices – anything he felt did not fit into his profound rediscovery of the roots of faith. He also saved what he viewed as core heritage and practices. He gave preaching a more prominent place. And he was a joyous companion at table talk among feasting companions. He was far from alone in making the Reformation happen, but he deserves his central place of honor in this turning point in Christian history.

Reformation Implications

The Reformation was a glorious reinvigoration of Christian practice, but it also had tragic consequences: leading to both unnecessary, as well as necessary, trans-European warfare between Protestant and Catholic regions, costly civil wars in some places, and much rigidification on both sides of this divide. Also, the implications of Luther's radical faith and freedom were taken up by wave-after-wave of reform movements, which were then persecuted by earlier versions of Protestantism itself. Such fragmentation of Christian religious practice was not altogether new, but it was vastly increased by the Reformation, and this fragmentation had its downside. It set the stage for hearing in our times cries for unity and commonality among religious bodies who have so often emphasized one part of the vast truth of the Christian revelation and neglected parts that other groups preserved. Creative ecumenical dialogue is now needed to counteract the negative aspects of this dispersion.

Protestants and Catholics of all sorts have tended to preserve the image of authority, both the authority of Scripture and the authority of each institutional system. A deeper test of truth is now seen as needed – deeper than what "my group" says or what "my group" says about Scripture. Such a test has always been there, but hidden and secondary. Authenticity was always there competing with authority to be the final test of Christian truth. But seeing authority as valid only if it breathes authenticity was not yet established by the Protestant Reformation. Luther reformed authority, but he did not end it. Authenticity was not yet fully clarified and made the primary judge of Christian practice. This development did happened, however, in the work of my next selection of a major turning-point figure in my abbreviated history of Christianity: Søren Kierkegaard.

Chapter 11

Kierkegaard and the End of Authority

The fourth huge turning point in Church History began in an out-of-the-way place back in middle of the 19th Century. Søren Kierkegaard (1813-1856) lived in Denmark on the periphery of the great debates that went on in Germany, France, and Spain. Kierkegaard participated in that ferment, but history was slow to hear from him. Nevertheless, as we look back and calculate his influence on philosophy and Christian theology, few persons of his era stand out more than he. Hegel (1770-1831) was his chief foil. Schelling (1775-1854) was an encouraging teacher. And the Russian Dostoyevsky (1821-1881), whom he may never have read, was perhaps his closest companion in launching a revolution in Christian thought. Nietzsche (1844-1900), (whom Kierkegaard, as far as we know, never met or read) was destined to become his most important companion in a basic critique of Western philosophy.

Kierkegaard has been known by many as the dismal Dane because of his writing on dread and despair, but I have found his book on despair (*The Sickness Unto Death*) to be one of the most illuminating and hopeful books I have ever read. We might better characterize Kierkegaard as an anti-Hegelian comedian, as one of the most brilliant satirists who has ever lived. He pictured Hegel as a rational system builder of beautiful systems in which the actual

Hegel did not live. He satirized Hegel as one who built a huge and beautiful mansion, but lived alongside it in a doghouse.

Kierkegaard emphasized the individual existing person as the truth that was being omitted from the thinking of his time. H. Richard Niebuhr may have appropriately criticized his work as too focused on the solitary person and too little attentive to the communal nature of the Christian life. I believe that Niebuhr was right about this, but it is the role of a great prophet to overemphasize the missing pole in the great polarities of life. Today, we need to clarify that there is no authentic solitude without authentic community to occasion it, and there is no authentic community without authentic solitude to create it. I am glad that the Christian theologians, who have been living and writing in Kierkegaard's wake, have learned to emphasize the communal pole as a correction to Kierkegaard's emphasis on solitariness. The communal thinking of H. Richard Niebuhr or Dietrich Bonhoeffer was not a return to the collectivistic rationalism that suppresses and ignores individual human existence. Rather this fresh communal realization has been built in full honor of Kierkegaard's history-ripping breakthroughs. The views that a relevant Christianity needs to oppose are not those of solitude or communal life, but those of individualism and collectivism.

Beyond Plato and Aristotle

Kierkegaard not only gave new inner life to the interpretation of Christianity, he moved beyond the philosophical contexts in which Christianity had been articulated ever since the thought of Plato and Aristotle became known to the Christian movement. Kierkegaard ascribed to himself a type of humility that to him meant a surrender to Reality. In this context he felt humble about honoring in himself what he called "the cockiness of genius." Perhaps his most cocky statement had to do with Western philosophy. He suggested that prior to his emphasis the whole of Western philosophy was a footnote on Plato. This did not mean he saw no truth in this long heritage, but it did mean that he emphasized the experience of the existing person in a way that moved beyond Hegel and all the philosophical systems that had come before him. Kierkegaard also contrasted Socrates' emphasis on concrete lived experience to Plato's systematizing. This philosophical emphasis gave Kierkegaard an important context for his theological writings, the deliverance of religious truth from the rationalism and moralism of his times.

An Attack on Christendom

Kierkegaard's Christianity moved beyond Protestantism and Catholicism in a thoroughgoing manner. Though he was clearly a follower of Luther's understanding of faith, he saw the whole establishment of 19th Century Christianity as a betrayal of the Jesus Christ "revelation." He especially opposed any sort of authoritarianism that moved the discovery of truth beyond what can be verified in personal experience. Though it remains true that there was a type of existential orientation in the authority thinking of Augustine, Aquinas, and Luther, and many others, Kierkegaard helps us to abandon entirely the notion that Christianity has an authoritarian reference point. Neither the Bible nor the Church fathers (and mothers) have any authority over the depth existential experience of the individual Christian.

If we cannot find resonance in our own individual lives with a Christian doctrine, creed, writing, poem, story, etc., then that witness has to be either abandoned or it has to be interpreted in a way that is existentially persuasive. It may, of course, be the case that many sayings and teachings of this long-standing tradition are true to our personal existence, but we have yet to "grow up" in our consciousness in order to appropriate them. Indeed, most of Kierkegaard's theological writings are aimed at assisting us in that growing-up process. I will illustrate his theological gift with a quick survey of some core insights in his book, *The Sickness Unto Death*.

The Sickness of Despair and
How Despair is a Fresh Definition of Sin

Faith, according to Kierkegaard, is not the opposite of vice or disbelief: faith is the opposite of despair. This is a key contribution to Christian theology. Sin is not immorality. Sin is a sickness of the "soul" – a sickness in the most primary quality that makes us human, our consciousness of our consciousness. This sickness may lead to immoralities and also to sick moralities, but sin itself is not immorality. Sin means that our basic attentionality and intentionality are corrupted in a fundamental and horrifying way.

Kierkegaard tells us what that sickness is. He gives us a livid description of the sickness he calls "despair." All of us create despair in our lives when we flee from or fight with Reality. Why? Because Reality cannot be fled, and Reality cannot be defeated. We do not always experience the despair that we are in. We only experience our despair when we are courageous enough to experience it. Why is courage needed? Because if we experience our despair fully, it is the most horrible experience that a human being can have. Rather than endure their despair, human beings often commit suicide. Very few people commit suicide for any other reason than to escape their despair. When a returning war veteran kills himself, it is almost always because he is despairing over being a person who participated in an overwhelming amount of violence, or who in some other way is finding it difficult to handle his traumatic memories. When a mass murderer kills a bunch of adults, college students, or children and then kills himself, he is, in all likelihood, acting out some despair over himself or over how he is being perceived by others. We often see quite functional persons take their lives in the wake of being jilted by a lover or some other interruption of their self-created world. The event that sets suicide in motion may seem trivial to an outside observer, but to the despairing person some sort of upending of his or her world or vital self-image has in all likelihood occurred.

Kierkegaard and the End of Authority

Kierkegaard describes how these suicidal or potentially suicidal persons are bearing a pain of despair so intense that most of us cannot even imagine it. Most of us are not in touch with our despair. Most of us view any whiff of despair that comes up for us as if this were just a smoking fireplace in our house. We leave the house until the smoke clears away, and then we go back into our familiar living room and sit down again.

But there are also those who carry the harsh pain of despair as a deep secret while outwardly being a circumspect, ordinary, quite careful person. Such respectable appearing persons are the ones who may surprise us with their suicide.

But few despairers stay at this point of complete closed-in secretiveness. Rather, they plunge into debauchery or into noble work, whatever seems to dull the pain of their despair. This desperate plunge leaves a clear trace that their condition is despair.

And finally, Kierkegaard describes the defiant despairer who may be defiantly active in creating a false self to substitute for the real despairing self. This actively defiant despairer is a curious phenomenon, for this self-created self can with a single choice be returned to the nothingness that it is. A second type of defiant despairer uses his or her own despairing self as an excuse to protest against Reality. With his typical humor, Kierkegaard suggests this caricature of passive defiance: it is as if an author were to make a mistake on a printed page and then that this mistake becomes conscious of its self and uses itself to prove that this author was a very poor writer.

The defiant ones are the most conscious of all despairers, but consciousness alone does not heal the despair. The turn to "faith" means trusting that the realistic living of what is truly here and truly possible is the best-case scenario for living. From the perspective of such faith, despair is a doorway to health, for it reveals where realism is being avoided. Despair seems to be a horrific thing, but since it is only the result of lying to ourselves, it can disappear as our lying ceases. <u>Trusting Reality is the health that is built into Reality itself.</u> Trust of Reality is the Garden of

Eden from which we have been expelled through eating from the "lie" tree. This psychological analysis of sin and faith is one of the key contributions of Kierkegaard to the theology of a vital Next Christianity. This vision of sin and faith illuminates the long history of Christian witnessing and shapes the witnessing of a meaningful Next Christian practice.

The Authority of Authenticity

As previously noted, both Roman Catholic and Protestant expressions of Christianity have given strong emphasis to authority as a primary test for "Christian" truth. The authority of Scripture, the authority of tradition, the authority of ecclesiastical personages have been assumed to be an ultimate test of Christian truth. Personal experience has always played a role as well – at times it competed strongly with the authority principle. But today, as we seek to dwell, think, and work toward a vital Next Christianity, authenticity becomes the sole test of Christian truth. A theological statement has "authority" only if it has existential resonance. This is a primary characteristic of what I am calling "a post-Kierkegaardian era of vital Christian formation."

Authority of a secondary sort will still play a role (*We will still treasure the Bible and the great souls of our heritage.*), but the role of authority is now quite secondary to the role of authenticity. We might say that the authority of authenticity is now more primary than the authority of authority. From now on the Christian truth about life can only be validated by authenticity, not authority. This is a radical change. It places us on a narrow path with huge ditches on both sides. On the right side of the road is the ditch of authoritarian dogmatism. On the left side of the road is the ditch of absolute relativism that denies any certainty whatsoever, including authenticity. The absolute relativist tends to view authenticity as one more form of authoritarian dogmatism; hence the absolute relativist rejects authenticity as a reliable test of truth.

Kierkegaard and the End of Authority
Existential Truth

In order to be truthful, we must give relativist thinking its due. Any truth that a human being has created is uncertain. My latest and best theology, my philosophy, my view of being a husband or a parent, my healthcare plan, my worldview, my social ideology – all these things have at best only approximate certainty. All these human creations have room for improvement. All these human creations may be wrong in major ways. I don't know how wrong they are. I don't know how right they are.

Anything that human beings have created is uncertain. Einstein's theory of gravity, Darwin's theory of evolution, the Pope's latest proclamation, my favorite commentator's latest rant – none of these creations by human beings are certain. All these views are without certainty. They are no more than approximate, and they are all open to improvement. Science, which in an earlier century spoke of discovering the laws of nature, has now become more modest. A law of nature is now seen as the most recent, best-case bit of order, created by humans to approximately match the empirical data so far gathered by the experts on the topic to which this "law" applies. In other words, a law of nature is merely a guess that has not yet been refuted. We have no absolute certainty arriving to us from the work of scientists. This does not mean that all guesses about nature are equally worthy, for the facts have refuted many guesses, and the guesses left standing are those in terms of which we can most successfully conduct our living. And even more humbling is the realization that the mystery of life is not being reduced by our scientific advances. Rather, the mystery grows stronger in the light of our new discoveries. The more we know about nature the more we know we don't know.

Absolute certainty is not a characteristic of anything created by the human species. Furthermore, absolute certainty does not drop into the human mind from heaven or from some other realm. Anything that the human mind can possess is uncertain. We hear it said that nothing is certain except death and taxes. Even that is an exaggeration. Death is certain, but taxes are not. Death is not created by a human being, but taxes are.

Your and my ideas about death are not certain, but death is certain. What does it mean to say that death is certain? In answering this question we discover a fundamental clue to the nature of existential truth, the sort of truth that Kierkegaard promoted. Doing theology in the wake of the Kierkegaardian breakthrough means embracing the existential type of truth we have to experience in order to understand fully any verse of Christian scripture or any valid witness to the Christian revelation.

Death, whatever else it may be, is not a human creation. We humans did not create death. It would have been the last thing our hyper magical minds and egos would ever have been concerned to create. We have created our ideas about death, but not death itself. In this sense death is certain, a certain truth. What else is certain? Life is certain. As the poet Rumi noticed, "Life and death are two wings on the same bird." Every experience as experience is certain – as certain as death. Our descriptions of an experience are approximate and capable of improvement. Thus our descriptions of experience are not certain. Nevertheless, the experience itself is certain.

Let's say that a truck runs over my toe. I am going to experience something, something more than the sight of the blood oozing from my shoe, something more than the pain in my foot, something more than all the ideas flowing through my mind. What sort of truck was it? Who was driving it? All these considerations have uncertainty built into them. Do I need to go to the hospital? Which one? How do I get there? All these sort of considerations have uncertainty built into them. But one thing is certain. I have had an encounter with Reality in the vicinity of my toe. This is certain with the same certainty that death is certain. This is *truth* of an existential sort.

Therefore, let us be clear that the increasingly popular human view that there is no certainty is not certain. In fact, that view is not true. There is certainty. When people say, "The only certainty is uncertainty," that is not true. Any experience that comes to me from Reality is certain. I will inevitably have my thoughts and opinions about that experience, and all those thoughts and opinions are uncertain. *But, let us notice that the experience that all my thoughts and opinions are uncertain is certain! Why? Because that experience of uncertainty is an experience.*

If we say that we cannot sort out the certainty of experience from our thinking about experience, we are not telling the truth. We can. It is true that thinking is constantly going on and that thinking is producing "screens" through which we are viewing our experiences. This *truth of experience* may seem to imply that we never have an experience that is certain, because experience is always being limited by those relative screens of thought through which we are looking at our experiences. But we can experience those screens and notice that they are not the experience we are seeing through them. From time to time we can notice ourselves testing different screens through which to view the same experience. We can also notice ourselves allowing our experience to tell us which of several screens is best for describing our experience. So who is doing this noticing and this choosing of screens? It is "I" – the contemplative inquirer into my own "I"-experiences. It is "I" who can see the difference between thinking and experience.

If we say that what we are experiencing is not certain, we are talking about our self-created ideas about our experience, not about our experiences themselves. By experience we mean whatever is certain within that maze of thinking and responding that is being humanly created in response to that experience. Such certainty is what we are pointed to with the word "authenticity." Such certainty is what we are pointing to with the term "existential truth." Such certainty is what Kierkegaard uses to criticize Hegel and the rest of Western philosophy. Such certainty is what Kierkegaard expects Christian theologians to use to test, understand, or proclaim anything that has to do with Christian faith – trust of Reality, love, freedom, hope, peace, or any other such word. All these words are meaningless unless they are used to point to something real, authentic, convicting, challenging, healing, redemptive, etc.

Everyone has denied, is still denying, or can in the future deny these existential certainties. This capacity for denial is also an experience about which we have certainty. The widespread dynamic of denial is as certain as death and more certain than taxes. The widespread dynamic of denial is a part of our experience. But let us not view this widespread denial of certainty as necessary. There is no excuse for it. It is not necessary. This, too, can be our experience. We can experience the experiencing of our experience as an absolute certainty, and we can experience that the denial of that experience as unnecessary.

The writings of Søren Kierkegaard transport us to this kind of certainty, to this authority of authenticity. His philosophical description of human experience puts us in position to better understand the Christian heritage. For example, if you are experiencing in this moment your experience of the Awesome and are thus filled with Awe, let me welcome you to the Kingdom of God, to the Reign of Reality, to the Eternal Tao, to the Enlightenment of profound humanness, to the Truth, the Life, and the Way of Jesus. Those who created so much of our religious vocabulary join together in welcoming you and me home to the absolute certainty of our Real experience. Also, you and I are being welcomed to the historical wake of Søren Kierkegaard and thereby called to a fresh future of Christian witnessing and theologizing. This awakening means a new era in the history of Christianity. Luther conducted a reform of Christendom. Kierkegaard has led us beyond Christendom, beyond all authority to an Awe-sustained authenticity.

Chapter 12

Kierkegaard's Descendants and the Social Gospel

What does it mean to claim that the obscure Dane, Søren Kierkegaard, was the beginning of a whole new era in Christian history – a turning point as deep or deeper than the turning points represented by Paul, the Gospel of John, Augustine, Thomas Aquinas, and Luther. Here are four mid-twentieth century theologians whom I believe to have most fully embodied the wake created by Kierkegaard – Rudolph Bultmann (1884-1976), Paul Tillich (1886-1965), H. Richard Niebuhr (1894-1962), and Dietrich Bonhoeffer (1906-1945). Two other prominent mid-twentieth century Protestant theologians were also deeply influenced by Kierkegaard – Reinhold Niebuhr (1892-1971) and Karl Barth (1886-1968). In this same period two existential theologians within the Roman Catholic community also stand out: Karl Rahner (1904-1984) and Jacques Maritain (1882-1976). There were renowned mid-twentieth century women who also breathed the air of this new flow of Christian resurgence – Simone Weil (1909-1943) a French woman of Jewish origins who became captivated by the best of Roman Catholic existentialism, but refused to be baptized because of her critique of Roman Catholic authoritarianism; and Suzanne de Dietrich (1891-1981) another French woman who was deeply impacted by Protestant neo-orthodoxy, an organizer of the Student Christian Movement, a social activist, a feminist, and a renowned teacher of Biblical writings. And somewhat later, Mary Daly (1928-2010) added to the Kierkegaardian attack on Christendom an equally skillful attack on the patriarchal qualities of Christendom. Obviously, there are many other prominent persons within this Kierkegaardian wake – including the teachers, colleagues, and students of the luminaries mentioned.

All of these mid-twentieth century theologians moved beyond Kierkegaard in their emphasis on social justice. Kierkegaard lived in a quiet place in a quiet century. He did not live to see the communist critique of capitalism, two world wars, deep economic crisis, horrific poverty issues, global uprisings, feminist critiques, racial protests, ecological crisis and much more. Theologically, Kierkegaard did not live to be impacted by the work of Walter Rauschenbusch (1861-1918), initiator of the Social Gospel Movement in which sin was effectively restated as a social matter and redemption enmeshed with the fight for justice for the poor. This social gospel theme was powerfully carried forward by Reinhold Niebuhr, who might be characterized as a Rauschenbusch-Kierkegaardian existentialist. H. Richard Niebuhr, Dietrich Bonhoeffer, Paul Tillich, Rudolf Bultmann, and Karl Barth also support this emphasis on social justice and a disciplined communal life that fights for justice as well as nurtures individual Christians.

Later in the 20th century, further work was done within this stream of communal life and social justice. Much Christian renewal has taken place in the areas of feminism, racism, economic equity, and ecological responsibility. Mary Daly gave a colorful and powerful impetus to the importance of women's experience and equality as a necessary correction in Christian practice. Martin Luther King Jr. (1929-1968) was a student of Reinhold Niebuhr. He applied Reinhold Niebuhr's social passion as well as Gandhi's to U.S. racial justice. Pierre Teilhard de Chardin (1881-1955) and Thomas Berry (1914-2009) are prominent Christian ecologists. And there are still others that could be mentioned, including the Peruvian priest Gustavo Gutiérrez (1928-), the initiator of

Kierkegaard's Descendants and the Social Gospel

Liberation Theology, who, among others, further developed the Christian response to hierarchical rule and grueling poverty. Liberation theology thinking has now been applied to racism, the oppression of women, the oppression of gay and lesbian persons, and so on. All these names and thousands of others can be said to have moved beyond Kierkegaard's more personal focus toward the communal life and social justice aspects of a fully developed Next Christian practice. Nevertheless, these twentieth and twenty-first century developments are not a rejection of Kierkegaard; they indeed owe a debt of gratitude for their lucidity to this not-so-dismal Dane. Also, we might say that Søren Kierkegaard was himself a social revolutionary in his headlong attack on the basic philosophical and intellectual structures of Western society.

The Church as Social Pioneer

Operating in the wake of the Kierkegaardian breakthroughs, H. Richard Niebuhr focused on the community of faith and on the ethical thought and action of this faith community. One of his most startling contributions was his redefinition of the true church and how it includes being pioneers in social history. By "pioneer" he meant moving first into a new arena, similar to a scientist leading a new frontier of rational understanding or an artist pushing into a new edge in beauty or realism. The true church is a pioneer in social wisdom and justice. Niebuhr writes:

> It (the true Church) is the sensitive and responsive part in every society and mankind as a whole. It is that group which hears the Word of God, which sees His judgments, which has the vision of the resurrection. In its relations with God it is the pioneer part of society that responds to God on behalf of the whole society.[10]

---

[10] "The Responsibility of the Church for Society" Chapter 5 *The Gospel, The World and the Church* ed. Kenneth Scott Latourette (Harper Bros. 1949)

Kierkegaard's Descendants and the Social Gospel

If some part of the Roman Catholic organization is sensitive and responsive, that part, not the whole of it, is the Church. If some part of the Southern Baptist Convention is sensitive and responsive, that part, not the whole of it, is the Church. If some part of the United States of America is sensitive and responsive, that part, not the whole of it, is the Church. Clearly Niebuhr is developing a view of being the Church that is at variance with the popular view. According to Niebuhr's view, the true Church is not a specific set of religious organizations; it is a dynamic in human history. Sometimes we use the term "invisible Church" to point to what Niebuhr is indicating, but Niebuhr is pushing beyond the way that most of us use the term "invisible Church." The Church is a direction of response – toward God, the Final Reality. The Church is the sensitive and responsive portion of the entire human species, those who are sensitive and responsive to the Final Reality faced by us all. Notice that this means that the true Church is a dynamic in history in which people who are not practicing Christians may also participate. This dynamic of the sensitive and responsive portion of humanity defines the term "Church." The People of God are those who serve God. This means that engaged Buddhists may be the people of God, and that Jews and Christians who hang back from such sensitivity and responsiveness are not the People of God. The following diagram has been helpful.

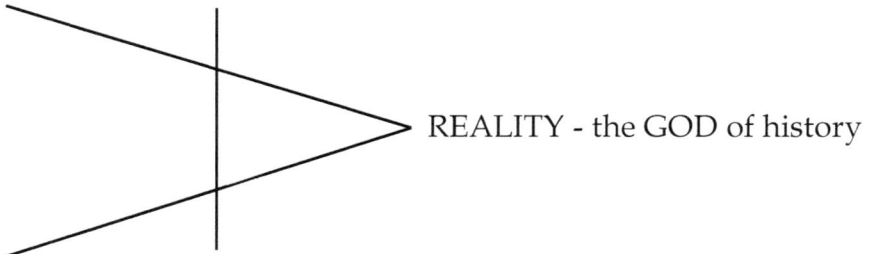

The vertical line divides any group of humans or humankind as a whole into two parts. The part on the right side of the vertical line is moving toward God on behalf of the whole society. The part on the left side of the vertical line is not moving toward God. The front portion of this "wedge" of humanity is sensitive and responsive in Trust of the REAL – sensitive and responsive in Love toward the REAL, toward all humankind, toward the whole Earth – sensitive and responsive in the boldness of the Freedom found in such Trust and Love toward the REAL.

All this language needs to be made concrete in terms of the historical issues that confront us. In the essay quoted above Niebuhr spells that out:

> *In ethics it (the Church) is the first to repent for the sins of a society and it repents on behalf of all. When it becomes apparent that slavery is a transgression of the divine commandment, then the Church repents of it, turns its back upon it, abolishes it within itself. It does this, not as the holy community separate from the world, but as the pioneer and representative. It repents for the sin of the whole society and leads in the social act of repentance. When the property institutions of society are subject to question because innocent suffering illuminates their antagonism to the will of God, then the Church undertakes to change its own use of these institutions and to lead society in their reformation. So also the Church becomes a pioneer and representative of society in the practice of equality before God, in the reformation of institutions of rulership, in the acceptance of mutual responsibility of individuals for one another.*

Women, the Earth, and the East

H. Richard Niebuhr spoke passionately about racism, nationalism, and economic imperialism, but he said virtually nothing about the oppression of women or ecological ruin. He lived slightly before the full flowering of these two challenges. The first issue of Gloria Steinem's radical-feminist MS. Magazine appeared in 1971. A radical feminist movement was already underway at that time, but the startling effects of that movement were still in the future when Niebuhr was alive. The effects of that movement have now become huge: every woman, man, and child in North America and Europe have been deeply affected. Even the reactionary minority that still opposes this trend have been affected: they use the gifts that this movement has brought them to oppose its further expression. And the liberation of women is spreading to every patriarchal village in the furthest corners of the planet. The women who launched and sustain this movement were and are pioneers. Some of them were practicing Christians, and some of those Christians brought with them the pioneering spirit articulated by H. Richard Niebuhr. And the pioneering on this topic is far from over. Honored standing and civil rights for gay and lesbian citizens is a companion movement along with the honoring of women's experience, its contributions, and its role within human society.

A similar story can be told about ecology. Ecological sanity has now become a critical topic among the challenges, the vision, and the action of every progressive person and the clearest articulators of Christian ethics. Those of us who are fighting the deniers of climate crisis or the foot-draggers on reducing untenable pollution are the pioneers on these topics. The many ecological movements are another expression of the true Church within which many practicing Christians are participating as part of their pioneering Christian practice. Furthermore, the lead edge in the climate crisis portion of this ecological pioneering has moved into a new intensity. Completely shutting down the tar sands industry is being actively pursued. A movement has been built that proposes a moratorium on coal mining and burning. Investment in oil and gas industries is being successfully discouraged within public institutions as well as within "green" organizations. However strong the difficulties and the opposition to change in this area may be, and however insidious the lying on the part of fossil fuel companies and their supporters will continue to be, moderating global warming has become an edge issue that the People of God are raising to the level of slavery abolition. Indeed, a type of civil war will surely be fought on ending the fossil fuel addiction and building an alternative energy infrastructure.

Kierkegaard's Descendants and the Social Gospel

A third movement of crucial importance is the impact of the Eastern religions upon the consciousness of the Western world. Hinduism, Buddhism, Taoism, etc. have helped us redefine religion as a practice that assists us to access our true human essence. Christianity, at its best, is also such a practice. And the human essence, that any effective religious practice assists us to access, is the same human essence accessed through an effective Christianity. Whether we call this essence "true humanness," "Holy Spirit," "enlightenment," or some other positive name may not matter, for what matters most is our participation in this profound humanness, not the name we call it. Such an understanding provides a fresh foundation for meaningful interreligious dialogue. All the religions of the world are learning from each other in a truly amazing way and extent. Religions have always learned from one other, but for many centuries there was considerable isolation of the Western religious heritages from those of the East. Today, however, every large world city houses almost every religious practice on the planet. Among the early-to-mid-20th-century Christian theologians, very few dealt with this interreligious development. Paul Tillich wrote his last essay on Buddhism. Most of the other mid-twentieth century theologians gave even less attention to this development. But in the 21st Century, the dialogue between Christian practitioners and Buddhist practitioners (as well as other religious heritages) is a virtual necessity for being a pioneer in religious formation.

The Meaning of Revelation

In a book entitled *"The Meaning of Revelation"* H. Richard Niebuhr provides much clarity about how we need to think about "revelation" in the context of our future Christian thought. Other religious communities may use the term "revelation" differently, but within the Christian community, we need to distinguish this important term from a number of other usages. We do not mean hearing a piece of news as in "What Alfred said was a revelation to me." Also, we need to give up the idea that Christian revelation means a magical implant of Hebrew or Greek words into the minds of our primal authorities. Also, inadequate is the notion that Christian revelation is an unusual psychological experience of strong emotional or visionary content. And we need to clarify that Christian revelation is not an arms-length experience, such as a new discovery in the empirical sciences. Christian revelation happens to persons, to our stories about what it means to be human, and to what it means to be humanly related to other humans, and to history as a whole.

Christian revelation is about historical events that happen to communities of people. The individual persons of those communities are involved of course, but the revelation is a public rather than a private happening. Also, the revelation is about an event that reveals Reality (God) to that community in such a way that it entails an understanding that can be applied to every event. Such a revelation challenges our current mental pictures of Reality, so it would be wrong to say that we arrive at a revelation through the exercise of our reason. Yet it would also be wrong to say that a revelation opposes reason or that revelation is of such a nature that no thought can be given to it. Rather, a revelation is meaningful in such a way that it can become the basis for much thoughtful application to all the events of our lives.

For example, the Exodus from Egypt was a revelatory event. In saying this we are not talking about an arms-length scientific-history approach to what factually happened in (according to one plausible guess) 1290 BCE. We are talking about what happened to a group of people in their understanding of Reality as a whole. Our scientific knowledge of this ancient event is very scant and quite approximate. Indeed, the historical scholars disagree about almost every aspect of answering the question, "What actually happened?" But let us suppose that we have this much common agreement about what factually happened: A group of slaves made it out of Egypt, ineffectively pursued by the Egyptian military, into the eastern wilderness where they wandered southward toward mountain foothills where they stopped to reflect on this matter. In this bare-bones scientific depiction, the event is entirely meaningless.

To see the revelation that these people saw entails joining with these people in their interior experience – joining with them in the dawning that dawned on them about the way that Reality works in all the events of their lives and ours. So what dawned? What dawning can be gleaned from this many-layered, told and retold story?

First of all, an experience of history-making freedom had dawned on them. They saw that Reality is not some sort of recorded drama just playing out its grooves, that humans can make choices that thoroughly change the conditions under which they are living. They further saw that they could choose to trust this freedom-supplying Reality to be their Benefactor in the future. They saw themselves as chosen for freedom by Reality and they choose to choose Reality back. As they prepared to live out this fresh understanding, they realized that their lives did not have to be organized in the same way that their lives were organized back in Egypt. Their new basic rules opened with the deeply interior "commandment" to trust this freedom-providing God over all the other loyalties that Egyptian society had offered them. Further, they saw that their freedom enabled them to give first-rate standing to every member of their group. They did not need one set of rules for the all-powerful and another set of rules for the un-powerful. One set of rules will do. We don't know what those very first set of rules were. The rule-delivering story was elaborated over many centuries. But let us guess that those first rules (or very old ones) included: Don't kill one another; Don't steal from one another, Don't mess with another's spouse; Don't lie before a settlement judge. Added to this quite basic stuff were some recommended inward attitudes that also took the place of their Egyptian training. Perhaps we can claim that they discovered that anarchy would not do, that their new won freedom did not mean living with no rules at all, just as it did not mean returning to hierarchical civilization's style of rule-making. It meant a fundamentally fresh approach to rule-making – one that was rooted in the WAY IT IS, as far as they could see into that Mystery in their specific times.

As the history of this people unfolds some of their attempts to make rules that are based on loyalty to Reality seem pretty weird to us today, even gross. They were creating social order for another time and place. The core Exodus revelation is not about the legal details – each century brought its own struggle with fresh challenges and the invention of additional legal details. The major prophets, like Amos, Hosea, and Isaiah, were working with problems that come up when you have a royalty and an aristocracy. Jeremiah handled this interesting topic: What does our Exodus blessing mean when our nation is being carried away into exile? Jeremiah announced the "Word of God" that a religious community loyal to Reality can exist without a nation, living in the midst of a foreign land. God, he preached, is going to establish a new covenant, one written on our hearts rather than rooted in a nation.

I can resonate with all of this. I grasp myself as a member of this community. These are my ancestors in religious practice. It does not matter that I was born in Oklahoma of ex-Europeans, or if my parents had come from Africa. Moses and Deborah and Amos and so on are my people. This is my religious group. This revelation of Reality has happened to me. And this revelation applies to all the events in my life. Reality for me is still a freedom-giving Power that respects me and expects me to use that freedom to establish a workable social order.

Similarly, Jesus, seen as the Christ, is another revelatory event. It is my revelatory event because I have chosen to make those who have experienced this event my people. I find this revelatory event shows me something true about every event that is happening to me, and that is happening to my species of life. While the depth of meaning in this event is still unfurling with ever-new implications, here are some things that have already clarified for me. It is possible for me and for humanity to experience a more inward exodus from a still deeper slavery – the exit from our estrangement from Reality and the despair that estrangement occasions. The healing of my estrangement is not complete, nor is it complete for humanity as a whole, but being among those to whom the Jesus Christ event has happened, we are in some measure dead to estrangement and raised-up to newness of life. This sort of healing is what is taking place in every event. Nothing can separate us from the "Love" of this healing process that characterizes every event in the ongoing flow of real time happenings. I, or anyone else, who can see our estrangements and their tragic consequence, can also see that we are all welcomed home to Reality. We can see that you or I do not have to become a new species or a different sex or anything like that. As we are, we are welcome home to Reality, and we can welcome this Welcome as the context for all our living.

A Redefinition of Christian Theology

In the wake of the post-Kierkegaardian turning point in Christian history, the meaning of "theology" has come into question. Etiologically, the word "theology" means the study of God. But if by the word "God" we mean Reality in its most inclusive, awesome, totally mysterious quality, then "theology" is simply "the study of Reality" with a capital "R." Theology is *Real-ology*. Christian theology is the study of Reality as each and every event of Reality as *revealed* through the revelatory event symbolized by the words "Jesus Christ."

This Real-ology includes the insight that a valid Christian theology is not an abstract philosophical pursuit by a systematic thinker who wishes to complete his or her rational worldview. Christian theology is not about a worldview, it is about witnessing to an event of revelation that happened to a community of people. Further, Christian theology is not an individual pursuit, even though theologians are individuals and every individual can be challenged to construct his or her theology. Nevertheless, the task of each individual Christian theologian is a communal task – the inclusive understanding of what has happened to a community of people who are witnessing to a particular historical event that is a revelation of Reality as Reality encounters us in every event. Such theology is an ongoing task. It is never finished, because life moves on. Each new learning in each new moment of history must be integrated within this revealed perspective that governs the life of this specific communal body within which theologizing functions as an aid to total living.

Let us examine in more detail what these statements in the above paragraph mean. Not all, but many religious heritages have revelatory events that call its members into being. This is certainly true of Judaism and its view of the Exodus. Islam sees the teachings of Mohammed as such an event. Buddhism refers to the Bodhi tree moment in the life of Siddhartha as the dawn of the Awake One or Buddha. Buddhists may not see themselves as doing theology, but they practice a form of theoretics or Dharma teaching that accomplishes the function that theology accomplishes in Christian communities. Each of these revelations of Reality can be meaningful and useful to each of us, but the practice of a Christian practice with other Christian practitioners requires a Christian theology that prioritizes the Jesus Christ event as a window into the nature of Reality as Reality confronts us in every event.

Is the word "theology" appropriate for the religious theoretics of Buddhism, Hinduism, Taoism, and other religious traditions that do not use the word "God" to mean a devotional relation to Reality with a capital "R"? My answer is, "No." "Theology" is a good word for the theoretics, past and future, of Judaism, Christianity, and Islam? My answer is, "Yes." All three of these traditions are rooted in the ancient Arabic/Hebraic heritage that discussed Final Reality as the "object" of their use of the devotional word "God." In all three of these vast heritages, there is a type of atheism at work. Here is a way of dramatizing the core teaching of the Islamic heritage: "There are *no gods*,   (long pause)   save the Final Reality."

Kierkegaard's Descendants and the Social Gospel

Christian Theology and Philosophy

The Jewish theological heritage exists prior and independent from the Greek heritage usage of gods, goddesses, and God. Eventually, Judaism, Christianity, and Islam mingled their God-theoretics with the philosophical works of Plato, Aristotle, and their philosophical descendants. This has created the term "philosophical theology." Philosophy and theology have a close relation because they both seek to clarify basic life truths and seek to do so in an all-encompassing way. Nevertheless, the term "philosophical theology" spawns misunderstandings with regard to the quality of Christian theology needed for a viable Next Christianity. In the definition of "Christian theology" that I am recommending for a vital Next Christianity, it is important, I am convinced, to strictly distinguish philosophy from theology. So what is philosophy?

Philosophy is the attempt to build an overview of thought for a specific culture at a specific time in history. We can describe three branches or modes of philosophical thought that have distinguished themselves in recent centuries: (1) **analytical philosophy** which focuses on the meaning of words in the culture as well as a clarification of logic and the quest for objective factual grounding, (2) **existential philosophy** which focuses on the description of the inner experience of the person in his/her intimacy with other persons and his/her personal relations with the world, nature, the cosmos (i.e. Reality as a whole), and (3) **metabilt philosophy** (also called systematic philosophy or metaphysics) which focuses on pulling together in some sort of cultural overview the analytical and existential approaches to truth. In this paragraph I am doing some metabilt philosophy by attempting to sketch an overview of philosophy itself. However interesting it might be to dwell more thoroughly on such philosophizing, my aim here is simply to say that **theology is not** any one of these three modes of philosophical theoretics.

Kierkegaard's Descendants and the Social Gospel

Let me put this point as emphatically as I can. To speak of a philosophical theology is as inappropriate and confusing as to speak of a feline dog or a canine cat. We can authentically speak of a philosophy of religion (or even of a philosophy of religious theoretics), for philosophy has the job of reflecting upon anything and everything in order to put together illuminating overviews of thought. But a philosophy of religion is not a theology. A philosophy of religion holds religion at arm's length, even though some participation in the topic of religion is needed to philosophize about it. But theology does not hold its religious insights at arm's length. Theology is about the truth of personal commitment, a truth to live by, a truth to be devoted to, to die for, to give meaning to my life, my work, my birth, my being, my death, and to the entire life of my theological community as well as my planet and humanity as a whole.

Perhaps there have been and are philosophers who have made philosophy their religion, their primary life passion, but such a "religion" is, from the perspective of a fully clear Christian theology, an idolatrous religion. Philosophy is a creation of the human mind, and any human creation is an idol when it takes the place of devotion to that Power that creates the human and all the potentials for human creation. This demotion of philosophy from the role of ultimate concern does not mean a contempt for philosophy. Indeed, once demoted, philosophy becomes a critical part of living along with music, politics, and sewage disposal.

Like philosophy, Christian theology is also a work of the human mind. So theology itself cannot be our Christian God. Theology points to God, and begins its reasoning from its core revelation of God. Theological reason, as H. Richard Niebuhr so aptly put it, is a reason of the heart: it begins with a heart-felt response to the truth about Reality revealed in the Jesus Christ address. "Christian theology," as that term is used in the Kierkegaardian wake, begins with a heartfelt commitment, and then uses the skills of the human mind for thinking through what that commitment means with respect to every aspect of everyday, down-to-Earth living. Such theology does not become our ultimate concern, it is a work of obedience to our Ultimate Concern and like all finite things it is ongoing and changing. Indeed, there is no Christian theology; there is just Christian theologizing.

So why do theologians get mixed up with philosophers and philosophy? Theologians speak to themselves and others as cultural beings, so they are impelled to theologize about everything: a society's philosophies, sociologies, psychologies, economics, politics, everything. Paul Tillich wrote a book entitled *Theology of Culture*. This book was not a philosophy of culture; it was a theology of culture, including the philosophizing that was going on in Tillich's culture. Tillich, Bultmann and other theologians have been very clear about the fact that theology has two poles: (1) the revelatory event in which their theology is rooted and their devotion grounded and (2) the cultural scope of meanings held by the people that they intend to address with their "Word of God." They do not want to reduce the Word of God to the insights of their culture. And they do not want to speak the Word of God in a language or style that addressed some other culture of humans, but cannot address the current culture to whom they are speaking.

For example, Bultmann has been accused by some of his critics of reducing the New Testament message to a 20th Century existential philosophy. But this is not at all true. In fact, Bultmann has also been criticized by some existentialist thinkers for being too preoccupied with the New Testament proclamation. Bultmann is, above all else, an exegete of New Testament texts. His *Theology of the New Testament* is his classic work. He is being a theologian, not a philosopher, in his work of rendering those New Testament texts meaningful for 20th and 21st Century persons.

Here is another way that Christian theology is different from philosophy. Theology is rooted in a specific **community of commitment**. We can speak of Jewish theology, Christian theology, and Muslim Theology. We can break this communal nature of theology down further to Roman Catholic theology, Protestant theology, Lutheran theology, Methodist theology, and so on. In each of these cases the theologian, though an individual, speaks on behalf of a community, to that community, and for that community to the world. We can also speak of an Old Testament theology, a New Testament theology, a Second Isaiahian theology, a Pauline Theology, a Markian theology, a Johannine theology, an Augustinian theology, a Tillichian theology, a Bultmannian theology, and so on. Such theologies, named for an individual person are also communal in nature; these theologians drew from and spoke to a community of people. And these theologians speak on behalf of that community of faith to the wider world. I myself in this book am doing theological writing on behalf of a community that I am calling "a Next Christianity." I am using what I have learned from the many theologians mentioned above, plus adding and subtracting what I believe I have experienced with regard to these common topics.

It is important to say once more that Christian theology is an **unending task**. It should perhaps be called "theologizing." Bultmann died in 1976 at the ripe old age of 92. My key mentor Joseph Wesley Mathews died a year later at the age of 66. I am writing theology more than three decades beyond the ministry of these mid-twentieth century theologians that I count as great warriors of God within the Søren Kierkegaard wake. But in this wake, theologizing continues. Even though I have learned from these giants at least 90% of what I say in my Christian theologizing, I speak to a later historical community of Christians and others living within 21st Century encounters. And I speak on behalf of my community of Christians as it journeys into a future beyond me.

Finally, though Christian theology is communal in nature, it is also **universal** in its emphasis. The job of Christian theology is to articulate what it means to be loyal to a Jesus Christ understanding of the Final Reality that is operative in *every* event. So Christian theology can and is called to speak about everything: every theologian, every religion, every philosophy, every culture, every science, every humanity, every political and economic issue, everything. But the Christian theologian speaks about everything from a point of view that is rooted in a specific revelatory event in history – namely, Jesus understood as the Christ, spelled out in the New Testament, carried through many centuries, and powerfully revived through the interpretations of that revelation as updated by the post-Kierkegaardian theologians I have cited.

* * * * * * * *

In summary, Christian theology is a work of thought, a rational theoretics about everything from the viewpoint of a revelatory event in relation to which a community of people are witnessing to what is Real for everyone. Christian Theology is a "Real-ology" that uses hot symbols like God, Messiah, Jesus Christ, cross, resurrection, sin, grace, and others. This theology must interpret those hot symbols for 21st century people and their approaches to truth. We are required to think of these theological interpretations not as dogmas or literal history, but as witnessing to our personal experience in a manner that awakens the personal experience of others and allows us to understand the healing power of the original interpretations of Jesus as the Christ as a "Word of Reality" to us today. Theology is ongoing and changing because everything is changing.

I have already mentioned how important for recent theologizing have been: (1) the changes in perception about women's experience and women's equality, (2) the ecological crises, and (3) the impact of Eastern religions. We could also mention increased awareness about the scandal of needless poverty, inept money systems, and the challenge to develop a polity and an economy that is thoroughly post-hierarchical. The theology of a Next Christianity will be our reasoned witness in relation to how this Reality-inspired pouring-out-of-life can be appropriately lived in the 21st Century. As the Gospel of John put it: the Jesus Christ revelation shows us "The Truth, the Way, and the Life." We theologians are called to creatively think through what that primal essence of living means for each new decade. This "thinking through" defines the meaning of the term "Christian theology."

Kierkegaard's Descendants and the Social Gospel

Theology's role within a vital Next Christianity will be to see our pressing challenges through the lens of this basic Christ-Jesus breakthrough and then creatively interpret and live our current challenges from that point of view. Such theology will be in dialogue with every historical event, every other religious community, and every insight that crops up from any source. I repeat, in the post-Kierkegaardian era, *Christian theology is not a fixed set of doctrines. It is an ongoing invention of fresh understanding of this religious community's grand heritage and of the fresh communication of this Christ-Jesus Way of living within our era and our everyday moments of living.*

Part Three:

A Reconstruction of Christian Practice

"a next Christianity"

The transition to Part Three is the most important transition in this proposed manifesto. It is a transition from interpreting the past for the sake of the future to the task of envisioning a specific sociological future with the help of the past and in terms of our current challenges in the present.

I have been describing a particular past, not the whole past of Christian forms in all places. Diarmaid MacCulloch does that more inclusive job quite well in his 1184-page book *Christianity for the First Three Thousand Years*. But my visit to the past has been more specialized and in many respects quite different from MacCulloch's. I am thinking on behalf of a particular thread of memory and my hope of extending that thread into the future.

I am looking through the eyes of my mentor Joe Mathews and his mentors and mine: H. Richard Niebuhr, Paul Tillich, Dietrich Bonhoeffer, and Rudolf Bultmann. I have examined the importance to me and these mentors the work of Søren Kierkegaard, John Wesley, Martin Luther, Thomas Aquinas, Benedict, Augustine, John, Luke, Matthew, Mark, Paul, Jesus, the Old Testament Prophets, the Genesis Texts, and Moses. That list leaves out a number of people in this thread of history that have also influenced me significantly, such as John Calvin and Jonathan Edwards. I have also treasured to a considerable degree, Teresa of Avila and John of the Cross, but the whole history of Spain and its horrific Moorish and Jewish conflicts I have omitted from my story. I have also omitted the whole Eastern Church. My story has been a Western story. I have also omitted within this Western story the Post-Lutheran Counterreformation, Pope John's Second Vatican Council, and much else which I have noticed and learned from, but do not count central to my story.

My projection of a Next Christianity is deeply Protestant, exclusively Western, and selectively Western with great emphasis on Paul, the Gospels, and the Prophets. This is why I am naming the future that I am going to envision "a" not "the" reconstruction of Christian practice. Also, the word "reconstruction" needs a bit of definition. I do not mean a return to some previously constructed Christianity. The Next Christianity that I will describe is post-Christendom, post-Roman-Catholic, and post-Protestant. I am also envisioning this Next Christianity to be in service of building and sustaining a social world that I call "post-civilization" – that is, a post-imperial era that I have described, with help from my friends, in a book we named: *The Road from Empire to Eco-Democracy*.

I am envisioning an almost entirely new sociological reconstruction of Christian religious practice. I see this sociological reconstruction illuminated by a Christian theology that is in a number of ways post-Joe-Mathews and post mid-twentieth century. Much change has happened to my world and to me over that last 37 years. I have seen the need for greater justice for women, gay and lesbian persons, and racial groups. I have benefited from reading and knowing some great religious women – Simone Weil, Mary Daly, Charlene Spretnak, and others. Promoting ecological sanity has been a deep influence. Much new depth has entered my life through interreligious dialogue – the ministries of reformed Buddhist teachings and the psychological/spirit illuminations of A. H. Almaas. Nevertheless, I firmly remain a practitioner of a Christian theology and religious practice. I am committed to an experience-based conviction that this heritage has contributions to make that only this heritage is likely to make to both interreligious dialogue and to the inner qualities of the emerging secular world.

Therefore, I ask you to read the following chapters in the understanding that a Christian practice need not be seen as your or my or anyone's only religious option. Furthermore, the mode of Christianity I will suggest need not be seen as anyone's only Christian option. And it will surely be true that even those of us who choose to create a Next Christianity within the above-described stream of influences will disagree about many matters, and I believe new and better directions will emerge from these disagreements. Nevertheless, I am projecting my best vision. I want to envision a Next Christianity that is appropriate for me, and many others with similar experience-based convictions about the need for a Next Christianity.

Chapter 13

An Existential Trinitarianism

As we turn our attention to the future of Christianity, we need a fresh view of the Trinity. We can no longer talk about three Persons in a metaphorical heaven and convince ourselves that this has something to do with our lives or with a meaningful Christian practice. We cannot say to ourselves too many times that *another world* beyond the stars, whether real or metaphorical, is no longer meaningful talk. Angels and devils, God and Satan, gremlins and fairies are all as questionable to us as the tooth fairy. We have to begin a vital Christian resurgence with at least this much honesty.

For those of us who have moved into this "post-two-story" universe of theological thought, one difficult challenge is understanding how that old mythical thinking was meaningful to our Christian ancestors. Early Christians were talking about their Spirit lives. In that sense they were existentialists, just as much as we super-scientific and post-Kierkegaardian contemporaries. So let us inquire into how we can talk about our experience of the Trinity in our own lives, and do so in such a way that it enables us to see what our ancestors were talking about in their own lives. To create a viable Next Christian practices, we need to be able to share with our world the same experience earlier Christians were sharing with their world, even though our talk and their talk will be very different.

An Existential Trinitarianism

The Three Faces of God

Here is my one sentence 21st Century summary of an existential understanding of the Triune heritage:

The Experience of God has three faces:
The Awesome, The Awed Ones, and the Awe itself.

In this simplified statement we can see how these three "Faces" belong together as parts of one experience. How can there be Awe without the Awesome that is Awe-ing us? How can there be either the Awesome or the Awe without the human beings who are the Awed Ones?

The **Awesome** is the first face, the Almighty mystery of it all, the Parent of all things, the primal Source, the Void of origin and the Void of ending, the Fullness of overall connectedness, the Power that powers the coming into being of all things and the going out of being of all things.

The **Awed Ones** are those human beings who are participants in the community of the Awed. Christianly speaking, they are the Body of the risen Christ. Jesus, understood as the Christ, is the first comer, the ultimate exemplar, an elder brother of the sons and daughters who comprise the Awed Ones. Each Awed One is entirely human and entirely "reborn" – "virgin born" by the Awesome Almightyness of it all. As we join Jesus in devotion to the Awesome, we become the Awed Ones along with Abraham, Moses, Isaiah, and other Awed Ones who preceded Jesus as well as those who follow Jesus in the Christian story of the People of God. And there are members of the Awed Ones who are not members of the Christian fold. As the Gospel of John's Jesus was given to say, "I have sheep who are not of this fold." Jesus Christ is symbolism for a cosmic, planet-wide, communion of the Awed Ones. The membership boundaries of this communion are unknown to any human being.

An Existential Trinitarianism

The **Awe** itself is the depth of the whole experience of the Triune God. Without the Awe there is no experience of the Awesome and there are no Awed Ones. Awe is the inner Spirit Reality of the whole Triune Happening in our lives. In our 21st Century understanding of the Trinity, we need to understand first of all what we mean by "Awe." This, and this alone, tells us what we mean by "Holy Spirit." Holy Spirit is not an enigmatic spook from some other realm. Holy Spirit is that down-to-Earth profound humanness that occurs in real human beings when the Awesome occasions Awe in the Awed Ones. Awe is not a psychological or sociological creation of humanity, but the advent of the Eternal in the temporal human.

Awe is dread of the Awesome Almightyness, and Awe is fascination with our powerful relationship with the Awesome Almightyness. Thirdly, Awe includes accessing our courage to be this intensity of dread and fascination. In Awe we dread the Almighty; we are fascinated with the Spirit power of this relatedness, and we access our courage to be the Awed human in our specific history.

There is a reductionistic form of mysticism that views the experience of Awe as entirely passive. It is true that dread and fascination happen to us and are not caused by us, but without the courage of living that dread and fascination, it is as if these intensities never happened. This is why we can say, and must say, that Christian trust is a deed, an act of courage, a risk of a person's whole life, freely taken by the person involved. Without that courageous, freely-taken deed of trust in Awesome Reality – no Awe happens. The possibility of Awe may have happened, but the possibility was not embraced.

Further, to see the tie of this existential Trinitarianism with the traditional second-story mythic Trinitarianism, we need to clarify that the Awe experience needs to be viewed as more than a finite psychological process. "Awe," as I am using that term, means the Presence of the Eternal in our finite psychological apparatus – in our bodies, our emotions, our minds, our consciousness. In our

An Existential Trinitarianism

finite psyche we feel the dread and the fascination, but the gift of courage to embrace and live these extreme intensifications is an operation of the Eternal in our own finite body, emotions, mind, and consciousness. By our own power, we do not achieve Awe or cause Awe. Awe is something that strikes us, upsetting our familiar finite relations of living with something "miraculous" – if that word can be used to mean the Presence of the Eternal within the flow of time.

Awe is the Presence of the Awesome Almightyness. We do not produce Awe; Awe attacks us or occupies us like a visitor from outer space. In Christian vocabulary we can say that Awe is a gift of grace, where grace is an action of the Eternal upon our lives in ongoing history. Awe can also be called our authenticity, our essence, our true Being, but when we say this, we mean something more than our finitude. We must insist that our true Being is an Eternal Presence. Kierkegaard described Spirit (which I equate with Awe) as a relation between the finite and the Eternal. Kierkegaard says that Spirit is not the finite and it is not the Eternal but a third term, the relation between the two. And this relation is not set in motion by us, but by the Eternal that posits the whole relation. And that relation includes the Freedom to courageously enter into a relation of creative dialogue with the Eternal. Such a life means becoming our "essence" as Christ like beings. That commonly neglected essence can also be called "sonship or daughtership sired by the living God." In order for "the Awed Ones" to speak of both Jesus and we are "in Christ," we must hold not only for Jesus but for ourselves both the finite and Eternal poles of the relation of which Kierkegaard speaks.

Such poetry is intended to call our attention to how the absolutely distant Wholly Other is One-with the absolutely near Awe that blows through the absolutely finite human Awed Ones. There is no experience of the Awesome Wholly Other without an experience of Awe within some historically temporal Awed One. So the experience of Reality ("God" in Christian faith) has three faces; Reality has these same three faces for anyone who

experiences Awe, whatever religion or quasi-religion thos
are practicing in order to beckon the Awe. If slaying a pig and
drinking its blood is a ritual that occasions Awe in the members of
some ancient tribe, those Awed Ones are experiencing all three
faces of the Christian Trinity: the Awesome, being an Awed One,
and the Awe itself. The transformed disciples of Jesus, in their
reflection upon what had so deeply Awed them, created the
theorizing that came to be called "the Trinity." But the experience,
so theorized, is a universal experience – an experience potentially
accessible by humans in any time or space or culture. In that sense,
"Awe" can be another word for human essence, human
authenticity, or simply the true Being of being human.

The Otherness, the Nearness of the Otherness in the Awed
Ones, and the Awe itself are three faces of one experience that
carries each Awed One beyond the estranged human "will" that is
clinging to finite passing things into a Will that is not our own
invented "will," but an un-will-Will that is also called "Freedom."
Obedience to being this Freedom is obedience to a new Will created
in us by God. But enough on this Triune poetry; we need more
description of Awe itself.

AWE
as Trust, Love, and Freedom

Awe is not one state of being, but a whole ocean of states of being: Awe includes TRUST in WHAT IS happening to us. Awe also includes LOVE of self, others, and the Ground of our Being. And Awe includes FREEDOM from egoic compulsions, superegoic restraints, and fatalistic cop-outs. Embracing Awe means living a healed, liberated, bold, history-bending life.

Trust

Awe includes Trust in the Awesome encounters of our lives, a Trust that is given to us by the Awesome Source of our Being. This Trust is our entry into the community of the Awed Ones. This

An Existential Trinitarianism

Trust begins with some consciously experienced despair that turns out to be the doorway that leads from some devotional falseness toward a dedication to that All powerful Void that is the source of all things and the Tomb of all things. This Trust is the dawning of the good news (perhaps proclaimed to us by an Awed One) that we are forgiven, welcome home to Reality – Reality as our home, our gift, and our demand for realistic living. We are welcome home in spite of our prodigal escapades into the swamps of debauchery, arrogance, addiction, foolishness, malice, emotional hardness, terror, despair, hopelessness, and other wording that points to illusory living. This Trust completes its manifestation in our lives with our courageous willingness to be forgiven, our true deed of welcoming our welcome home to Reality.

This waking up to reality of our unreality, experiencing our welcome home to Reality, and welcoming this Welcome is a drama that manifests in simple everyday experiences. Following is a story, taken from many years ago in my life – a story that illustrates the above dynamics of Trust.

I was a young Chaplain in the U.S. Army stationed in Bad Hersfeld, Germany guarding the East German border with an Armored Cavalry Battalion. It was a small base with one chapel. I and my one assistant and jeep driver were responsible for this building and all the activities that were to go on in it. The core of this story developed on the occasion of a Three-Star General's inspecting our base, including my chapel. He came to my chapel trailed by three others, including my base colonel. My assistant and I, each being an over-mental type, had made too many halfway preparations for this inspection. There was a pile of songbooks on a back bench that should have been in their racks. There was a pile of materials in the back hall with an Army blanket thrown over them. The General made notes about this and gave them to my colonel. The next day I was called into my colonel's office. I don't remember all that he said to me, but I remember this one line, "Captain Marshall you are probably the most well-educated man on this base, but sometimes you remind me of an immature little boy." I may have gotten out of that office without breaking into tears, but that holding-it-together condition did not last. I tried to dismiss what he said by angrily noting that this colonel never attended chapel, but that did not work to get rid of the truth of what he said. I was experiencing the opening of a "despair doorway" in my life, having to do with my not paying attention to all the details of my life. This external set of happenings was occasioning an internal crisis in my life, raising the deep question "Who am I?" I was clearly in denial about having a good bit of growing-up to do. At such a moment we can try patching up the shattered world, getting drunk to forget all about it, and so on. Suicide seemed a bit extreme to me for this particular jolt.

Fortunately, I recalled from my Christian heritage that my life is forgiven. I, the immature little boy, was welcome home to Reality. The whole world had not come to an end. I was just facing some growing-up I needed to do. Life is still livable. I can open to an unfamiliar future, one in which I become better at paying attention rather than sweeping the details under some blanket. When such real happenings confront you or me, they need not wipe us out. Reality remains trustworthy.

Such a mundane story illustrates the cosmic (or Holy) yet down-to-Earth dynamics of Trust – that ever-deepening Trust that can for every anticipated future carry us through even the most horrendous doorways of despair into a thoroughgoing "welcome home" "uttered" to each of us by the WAY LIFE IS.

Love

Awe (Holy Spirit) also manifests as Love. This Spirit Love is a love of my own self in my deepest self-reality and it is a love that loves the neighbor with the same love that the self is loved. This Love is also a love of the Ground of our Being that supports all things in being as well as yawns before us as the Grave on all beings. This Love is an enchantment with Being as a Whole, a curiosity to know the Truth, an openness to live Real Life, and a

An Existential Trinitarianism

willingness to walk the Way of Spirit Love. Like Trust, this Love is a gift. It cannot be achieved. It happens to us as we are rocked by the hot intensity of life into an existential crisis that raises this core existential question: How be I? What style, what presence, is possible for me as I walk through all the moments of my life. And like the life of Trust, the life of Love must be chosen by me. It is a gift, but this gift must be assertively accepted.

Sometimes fiction describes the hot moments of Spirit Love better than our biographical memories. In *The Lord of the Rings*, J.R.R. Tolkien tells about how an experience of "Spirit Love" appears in the life of the hero of his story, Frodo.

The scene is a council meeting in which the topic is: who will carry the dangerous ring to the mountain of doom and cast it in? The young hobbit Frodo is among those at this meeting. He has been bearing the ring, and the more powerful figures at the council are not good candidates to do so, for the ring bestows such power that it tends to turn these rather superlative persons into evil forces. So, during the pause after this question was asked, Tolkien tells us about Frodo's inner workings:

All the council sat with downcast eyes, as if in deep thought. A great dread fell on him (Frodo), as if he was awaiting the pronouncement of some doom that he had long foreseen and vainly hoped might after all never be spoken.
An overwhelming longing to rest and remain at peace by Bilbo's side in Rivendell filled all his heart. At last with an effort he spoke, and wondered to hear his own words, as if some other will was using his small voice. "I will take the ring," he said, "though I do not know the way."

This is a fine expression of how our true nature of universal Love can break through our ordinary states of consciousness and becomes the orientation of our lives. "It is like some other will," Tolkien says. Yes, our comfort-oriented will resists such callings to the tasks of Love. But our deep Self, our Awe Self, our Spirit blown "no-self" can appear, can arise from the deepest realms of our being. Such Love is not unnatural or otherworldly. Such Love is simply our True Being. Yet to receive this Love as the active force in our living, our familiar self-constructed self must be set aside. As Frodo does his task of love, he has to fight with his own inner feelings and mental stories. And he has to fight the same temptations in the lives of his companions. Love is an action, a task, a living that contradicts the greed and ambition, moralism and sloth, power craze and sentimentality that can and does so often rule our living.

Freedom

Freedom is the raw, overall answer to the question, "What do I?" "What do I with this one life?" Freedom, like Trust and Love, is a gift of our true nature not an accomplishment. As we first awaken, we find that our wills are bound to some narrow purposes or addictions. The challenges of Reality viewed through the Message of a forgiven past and an open future provide us with the possibility to step forth into our essential Freedom. This essential Freedom is a liberation from the passions of the ego-self, the qualms and habits of the superego, and the pessimism of our excuse-making fatalism. This liberation opens us to the incredible power and emphatic persistence that characterizes essential Freedom. Freedom appears as responsible actions constructed and carried out by our own selves, without dependence on the advice or approval of others, or on the seeming dictates of our circumstances, or on whatever principles that constrain our minds. Freedom is an act that is self-created out of nothing, except the raw depth of Freedom itself. And each Free act is performed within the ambiguity that every real situation spreads over our longed-for but never present moral certainty. And finally, we can notice that though Freedom is a gift from Reality, it must be freely chosen in order for it to be the character of our living. Freedom is a gift, but it does not manifest as something passive. It feels like a possibility that has to be risked – perhaps with an agony of struggle over against my still tempting forces of bondage.

An Existential Trinitarianism

I will illustrate the feel of this Freedom with my experience of choosing to end my first marriage and begin marriage with my current wife. My first wife and I were members of a religious order of families. We had four children and were prominent members who had been with this order from its beginning. This marriage had not been a horrible arrangement; there had been love and common purpose. But for the previous eight years I had been holding together a marriage with which I did not feel comfortable. The two of us were not on the same page in our sensitivities and responsiveness with regard to what we were "called" to do with the rest our lives. Also, I had fallen in love with a woman whom I felt was an ideal partner for my anticipated "rest of my life." My religious order was not opposed to all divorces, but they did not favor breaking up marriages in which both members were committed to staying in the order, especially marriages of our "antiquity" (23 years). To make a long story short, I was constrained by the order to maintain my current marriage or leave the order. The order had been the first truly satisfying vocation of my life. Leaving this work and this beloved group of friends was almost unthinkable. I had some criticisms of the order concerning its polity, its moralism, and some of its policies, but I could have remained in the order as a reformer of all these matters. Perhaps that is enough detail to illuminate the ambiguities in relation to these two options: reconstruct my married life at the expense of leaving the order or stay in the order and maintaining a marriage with which I was not happy.

I was alone with this decision. Who could I ask? Neither my parents nor my children could understand. Only a very few members of the order understood my situation and supported my perspective on remarriage, but they could not make this decision for me. Furthermore, both options were plausible in their own way. The remarriage had great promise in terms of a new intensity of nurture and growth, but it entailed a reconstructing of my vocation from scratch. I had only a vague idea about how that would work out. Staying in the order would preserve a meaningful vocation that might be further improved, but this direction entailed in a number of subtle and grievous psychological downsides. There was no right answer, or perhaps there were two right answers. So I had to leap into the unknown, for there was no final rationalization that could with absolute certainty support the leap. I knew by that stage in my life that such Freedom was a characteristic of the Holy life, but that did not lessen the Awe of this deep transitional challenge.

Freedom like Trust and Love is an Awe experience, a bubbling up from the depths of life that is infinitely mysterious, dreadful, fascinating, and requiring a maximum expression of courage.

The AWESOME
as Void, Demand, and Fullness

In one of his books (I can't remember which one), Søren Kierkegaard defined Spirit (and therefore Awe) as this happening:

When an external situation occasions an internal crisis, raising an existential question, from which we want only to flee, we are having a Spirit experience.

On the next page I have drawn a chart that spells out what this Kierkegaardian sentence means to me after so many years of thinking about it. This chart is content for a thousand sermons, but I will only comment briefly on how the Awesome operates in history to occasion our opportunities for Awe filled living.

An Existential Trinitarianism

HOW THE AWESOME OCCASIONS AWE

Awe — The Awesome Dynamics	No-Thing-Ness VOID	Eternal Presence DEMAND	Every-Thing-Ness FULLNESS
Awe happens when the **External Situation**	**Endings** Insecurity Loss Solitude Mystery Frustration Guilt	**Intensity** Aliveness Glory Engulfed Inspired Called Anointed	**Beginnings** Possibility Giftedness Camaraderie Clarification Victories Significance
occasions an **Internal Crisis**	Emptiness Too little hope	Scalded Too intense aliveness	Overwhelmed Too much possibility
calling forth an **Existential Question**	Who am I?	How be I?	What do I?
from which we wish only to **Escape.**	Hanging onto the past Hiding from awareness	Fogging over the Now Defense of old habits	Waiting for the future Floating above engagement
The JC Event			
The opportunity and willingness to **open to Spirit** rather than escape from Spirit means:	Oblivion is my name. **Trust** is my Being. Lucidity Forgiveness Letting Be	Equanimity is my style. **Love** is my Being. Strength Enchantment Compassion	Resurgence is my vocation. **Freedom** is my Being. Liberation Boldness Attuned

An Existential Trinitarianism

No-Thing-Ness – Complete VOID

These words point to a mysterious Power operating within every event in the cosmos, the fragileness of every being, the vulnerability of every being. We are seared with the inescapable consciousness that endings, endings of all sorts, take place in our lives. It is as if Death walks with us in every event. And this is not just our own death. It is the End of the cosmos. Every moment is an apocalypse. The end of the world is happening now. Every finite thing is coming to naught, is being naughted, is returning to the Abyss out of which it arose. As the various forms of endings assault our lives, we keep asking afresh, "Who am I now?" My parents die: Who am I now? I lose my job: Who am I now? My view of my essential self comes undone: Who am I now? This is our first core existential question from which we tend to flee.

We hang on to the past or hide our heads from these naughting experiences. But if we accept the Jesus-Christ Word of forgiveness, restoring us to a fresh-start in Reality, we discover that the oblivion experiencer is just who I am. Trust in the Almighty Void is my true Being. And, I can continue in an unending journey into lucidity, forgiveness, and letting-be WHAT-IS.

Eternal Presence – Scalding DEMAND

These words point to the Mysterious Presence of an intensity of aliveness that can feel scalding to our aloofness or ontic sloth. Such intensity is the appearance of a "How to Be" that answers the question of "How Be I?" for all time. But we flee from this Infinite Demand into our favorite forms of fogging out. But if I open to this Demand, then equanimity is my style. Love is my being. I am enchanted with this too intense aliveness with which Reality is loving me. I am strong with an unheralded strength we might describe as a "courageous heart." I love myself and all other selves and wish for them to enjoy this same state of strength and enchantment that has captivated and is captivating me. Compassion for the sin-sick humanity from whom I am emerging

An Existential Trinitarianism

(and among whom I dwell) fills the "heart" of my devotion to Reality.

Every-thing-Ness – Overwhelming FULLNESS

These words point to the Mysterious appearing of possibilities so overwhelming that I flee into all sorts of postponements and floating above the fray of real engagement. I hear the dreadful question, "What do I?", but I do not answer with doing the Freedom that I am being set free to be. I hear Jesus challenging me about moving mountains with a grain of Trust, but I do not want to embrace such visions. I hear Jesus saying to Peter, "Feed my sheep," but I prefer to feed my ego. When loving Reality is our passion, we can see that every new possibility is a great gift. We can see that "Resurgence in my vocation." "Freedom is my being." I am on a journey into still further liberation, boldness, and attuned working within the actual course of history that is taking place.

The AWED ONES
as Hospital, Communion, & Vanguard

As a community of people, the Awed Ones are like a **hospital** for the despair-sick, malice-sick, bondage-sick persons who contact this community of Awe Ones. We are all sick in these ways, so this hospital function never goes away. It is primary. It is both the introduction of people into the community of the Awed Ones, and it is an ongoing nurture of their Awe-health over the long haul of their lives. Forgiveness and a fresh start is the never-ending message of this hospital ministry.

The Awed Ones are also a **communion** of saints. We usually think of "sainthood" as the state of the very few who meet certain outstanding criteria, but the communion of saints, as first introduced by Paul, was actually composed of ordinary, quite humble people, very few of whom were outstanding in a public way. Anyone who has received the gift of being in Awe is an Awed One. The Awed Ones are the Body of Jesus Christ in its full

An Existential Trinitarianism

glory. We cannot take credit for being an Awed One. It is a gift. It happens to us and what has happened is nothing more or less than the appearance of our profound humanness. We have to receive profound humanness consciously and live it intentionally. But even the capacity to opt for this profound humanness is a gift of the profound humanness for which the opting is being made. In other words, the main quality of the communion of saints is noticing and accepting our forgiveness for all the estrangement that has and may still characterize much of our living. The saints are those who have joined in living contact with the Awed Ones of history and thus experience this "righteousness" that was imparted at our creation and is being re-imparted as we accept our forgiveness for all our tragic departures. As saints we are still sinners, but as Paul put it we "Awed Ones "press on toward the full stature of Christ Jesus." This "pressing on" does not mean "accomplishing," for this "righteousness" remains a gift. "Pressing on" means further openness to receiving this gift of "righteousness," – this gift of the essential profound humanness of Awe-filled living.

Thirdly, the Awed Ones are a **vanguard** force in the course of history. Through their dedication to realistic living they become part of a key minority within humankind – a minority that leads in the progressive movement toward greater realism, sanity, and justice. I will say more on this topic in the next chapter. But for now let us notice that this vanguard of Awed Ones are not all Christians, in the sense of practicing a Christian religion. Any person, practicing any religion or no religion, who is Awed by the Awesome and consents to be Awed is a member of the Awed Ones. And these Awed Ones are the key vanguard in the positive bending of history. In Christian language the Awed Ones are *the resurrected body of Christ Jesus.*

Such religious language is the talk of Christians, but this Christian talk is about a dynamic that is cosmic and historical – the Awed Ones includes millions who do not talk Christian talk. *Those of us who do choose to talk the Christian talk and theologize relevantly*

An Existential Trinitarianism

will find much help in this Existential Trinitarianism of the Awesome, the Awed Ones, and the Awe itself.

Chapter 14

History and the Age of Spirit

Joachim of Flore (1135-1202) suggested that there were three overlapping ages, the Age of the Father, the Age of the Son, and the Age of the Spirit. His work is valuable as a counter to the notion that history is going around and around in static circles. Joachim saw that history is going somewhere and that new periods of history begin long before old periods end. His Age of the Father ran from Adam to Jesus. His age of the Son begins with Isaiah. His Age of the Spirit begins with Benedict. I find his periods rather artificial, but his underlying notion of history is intriguing.

In my discussion of the Trinity in Chapter 13, I emphasized personal authenticity and the experience of Awe, spelled out as Trust, Love, and Freedom. This is an emphasis on the Holy Spirit third of the Triune experience. Beginning with Søren Kierkegaard, Christian theology has emphasized authenticity over authority. Authenticity is an emphasis on Holy Spirit. The authority emphasis of Christendom was rooted in the concern to preserve the centrality of the Jesus Christ revelation. It was an age of emphasis on human "Sonship," The Awed Ones.

Since the work of Søren Kierkegaard we have been opening an Age of Spirit in Christian theology and practice. And this development is replacing an Age of Second-Face emphasis. The theology of Moses and the Prophets emphasized becoming ever

History and the Age of Spirit

more clear about the life of devotion to Almighty Reality, the First Face of the Triune experience.

In suggesting this fresh Joachim-like model of the history of triune awareness, we need to underline that all three faces of the Triune experience of God appear in all three eras of theological emphasis. In the Old Testament we find all three: The Almighty Lord of history, the People of God, and the Spirit of God.

The theology that characterized the early centuries of Christian theology emphasized the Second Face, but this did not mean that the First Face was abandoned. The Almighty God of history was heatedly protected against a Gnosticism that denied the importance of the First Face. Also, the Holy Spirit was given reflection in the Bible as well as in second and third century theology. But attention to the Holy Spirit did not have the emphasis and heat that was poured out with regard to the basic nature of the Jesus Christ breakthrough.

As we participate in a post-Kierkegaardian era in Christian theology, Holy Spirit has become front and center. This does not mean, however, that we are going to neglect the Awesome and the Awed Ones and focus only upon the Awe. We are going to find ourselves approaching a further clarification of all three Faces of the God experience. Through our skill in clarifying Awe, we will be enabled to further clarify the Awesome and the Awed Ones.

We need to guard against overemphasis in our Holy Spirit emphasis. For example, it is misleading to proclaim that God the Almighty is dead, that Christ is dead, and that only Holy Spirit is important to us from now on. There is no Awe without the Awesome Otherness that Awes us. And there is no Awe without the Awed Ones who are being Awed. One of the ways we can see an overemphasis upon the Third Face of the Trinity is in a neglect of the God of history, of historical issues, and of our historical responsibilities. My name for this neglect is "the estrangement of aloofness." History has been a core theme of the Bible and in most eras of Church history. History is certainly a core theme in this manifesto for a Next Christianity. If we do not retain our love of

History and the Age of Spirit

history, we lose our love of God in the Christian sense. We drift off into experiences of timeless states of being and ignore the ongoing flow of time within which these deep experiences are happening. The unstoppable flow of time is an encounter with the Awesome Almightyness.

Following is a diagram that helps us picture the relations of Spirit and history, as well as a view of the Trinity from a historical outlook:

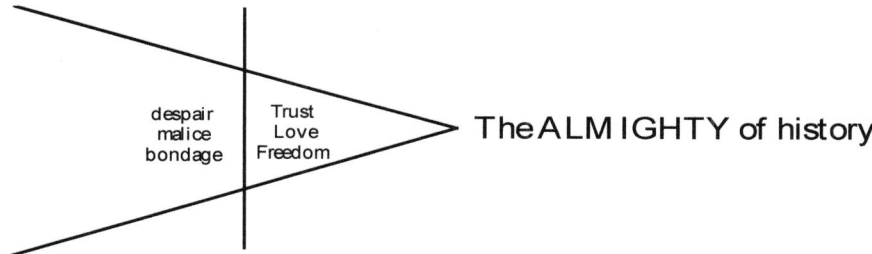

In this diagram God the Almighty is confronting the wedge of humanity entering the future. Humanity can be pictured as a wedge because the wider scope of humanity is the least sensitive and responsive to the Awesomeness of history that is Awe-ing us. The most sensitive and most responsive portion of humanity narrows to a point occupied by the most prophetic members of our species in this particular moment in history. The line that seems to separate the sensitive-and-responsive from the insensitive-and-irresponsive is a poem about the decision to accept the Call to be the Awed Ones in history. This dividing line is not a clear line among a literal population. No person is completely insensitive to Reality or completely irresponsive to Reality. Nevertheless, we can define the Awed Ones (or the People of God) as those for whom being sensitive and responsive to Reality has become the main course of their lives. In spite of imperfections in this regard, our lives can be directed by the Call to embody Trust, Love, and Freedom as described in the last chapter.

The above diagram also holds the insight that the states of Trust, Love, and Freedom are not a form of aloofness from time, but a sensitivity and responsiveness taking place in time – within the history in which we confront the Almighty Reality toward which this sensitivity and responsiveness is directed.

We could also misunderstand this picture in a moralistic fashion – thinking that we must get busy trying to be sensitive and responsive. Such moralism is countered if we remain aware that our states of Awe (i.e. Trust, Love, and Freedom) are gifts of Reality not accomplishments by humans. Humans embody and enact those gifts, but they get no credit for creating them. The Awed Ones are servants of the Almighty. Such servants humbly be what they are being be-ed by Reality to be.

Finally, the above diagram may also seem to damn most of humanity to despair, malice, and bondage. Again, that is a bit misleading, for the gifts of Trust, Love, and Freedom can appear in any life from time to time. But it is also true that the ruling characteristic of humanity as a whole is fallenness. However many trips we have made to the "mountaintop" of Enchantment with Being, we still participate in the swamp of estrangement from Being. To whatever extent we share life with the majority, we share in their despair, malice, and bondage. And to whatever extent we share life with the Awed Ones, we share in the cruciform principle shown to us by Jesus – the truth that the majority hates this challenging minority of Awed Ones. We are continually choosing between: (1) the glory of being hated as an Awed One and (2) the temporary comfort of being accepted by the majority on its way to the doom of despair. Herein is the truth of history revealed by Moses, the prophets, Jesus, and all the other enlightened followers of this heritage.

The Mission of the Awed Ones

The sensitive and responsive minority of Awed Ones play a healing role in history. They are the saviors of humankind. They are the reconcilers of humanity to Reality. They are the deliverers from the karma of despair to the liberation of the Awed life of

Trust, Love, and Freedom. This healing task is never finished. Not only are humans stubbornly addicted to their current estrangements, they keep inventing new estrangements and new versions of the old estrangements.

The temptation to estrangement from Reality is part of every human being's constitution. In the story of his forty-day fast before beginning his ministry, Jesus, our symbol of profound humanness, faced the tempter. All of us who have been restored to our Freedom face the temptation present because of that very Freedom to freely decide to no longer be free. In order for Freedom to remain in our lives, Freedom must be lived through the ongoing exercise of that Freedom. Most of us have already experienced Freedom at some point in our lives, and perhaps we can also recall our retreats into new forms of bondage.

Furthermore, there is a widespread unconsciousness about the already established estrangements of the general society. This unconsciousness is tragic, for it means an unrealism heading toward despair. It also means an acting-out of that despair as malice toward truth, motivated by a reactivity in defense of illusions. Consider the illusions of civilization in both its capitalist and communist forms; both tend to deny or minimize the impending climate catastrophe. Both manifest various levels of inattention to waning fresh water sources, to soil loss, to starvation and social chaos. Our estrangement from facing these challenges and dealing with them has grim consequences. It is an understatement to say that there is no end in sight for the work of bringing humanity's estrangements into awareness, articulating humanity's forgiveness, and beckoning humanity to fresh starts in realism.

Witnessing Love

The "work" indicated in the last sentence of the previous section has the classical name "Witnessing Love." We, the Awed Ones, bear witness by both living a realistic life and telling others about its possibility and the path that must be taken from despair to Trust, from malice to Love, and from bondage to Freedom. One of the great discoveries of our era is that the experience of despair is both the hell we want to avoid and the doorway to the glory of authenticity. We must pass through the hell of a self-aware experience of our despair in order to see our desire and longing for authenticity. We do not cry out for forgiveness of our estrangement until the hell of it begins to be intolerable. This fact presents us with the most disagreeable part of the task of Witnessing Love – assisting people to consciously experience their despair – the very last thing on earth any of us want to experience is our despair. Fortunately for the witnesser, most people have already been brought to self-aware despair by the everyday actions of the Almighty in their lives. So the witness can often move immediately toward sharing the good news that there is a way out of despair – that despair is a doorway to the forgiveness of estranged living and a fresh start in the realism that knows no despair. Realistic living knows no despair, because Reality supports realism rather than judges it. Our despair always means that we are not fully engaged in realistic living.

The Awed Ones' task of Witnessing Love has three aspects that correspond with the following three aspects of Paul Tillich's description of the grace happening: (1) the awakenment to despair, (2) the dawning of acceptance, and (3) the acceptance of acceptance.

Here are the parallels in the work of Witnessing Love with Tillich's aspects of grace: (1) The witness stands firm in support of the harsh truth that estrangement exists and is headed to or is already arriving at the doom of despair. (2) The witness meets the despairer with the healing message that each specific life is received just as it is, that the past is approved as the unalterable origin of this particular life's goodness, that the future is open to a mode of realism that is now possible, and that the whole cosmic drama of things is the wholesome world of my one and only livable life. (3) When this good news is heard, the witnessing person has only one aspect of Witnessing Love left to do – beckoning the forgiven one to step forth in an acceptance of the forgiveness – a step that is challenging because it means the surrender to the judging action of the Almighty upon our estrangements and embracing an undeserved "WELCOME HOME" by Reality in spite of our unworthiness for any fresh start.

The term "beckoning" I have taken from the story of Jesus walking on the water and responding to Peter's request to join Jesus in such walking. Peter says, "If it is really you, call me to walk to you on the water. Jesus responds, "Come on then." These three words summarize well the beckoning dynamic of Witnessing Love.

Peter does step down from his safe boat and walk on the water making for Jesus. Then out on the water of his stormy life, he notices the strength of the winds and waves and begins to sink. The temptation to estrangement is always present! Peter calls out to Jesus, who holds out his hand and pulls Peter back to his feet on the wild waves of Reality and then asks Peter this challenging question: "What made you lose your Trust like that? It is Trust in the goodness of Reality that keeps Jesus, Peter, you, or me on top of the waters of realism and out of the depths of despair.

On almost every page of all four Gospels, Jesus is presented as an example of what Witnessing Love looks like.

Justing Love

In addition to Witnessing Love, Justing Love is a companion aspect of the work of Love carried out by the Awed Ones. The meaning of this made-up term is that our Witnessing Love is carried out alongside our caring for the human body, the mind, the emotions, and the whole social life of humanity. In the New Testament stories about Jesus, we see Justing Love as the call to give water to the thirsty, feed the hungry, visit the prisoners, heal the sick, care for the poor, render justice to everyone, and prepare the society for the challenge of facing up to the entire drama of historical unfolding.

History and the Age of Spirit

In our recent centuries, Protestant theologians like Walter Rauschenbusch and Reinhold Niebuhr challenged the more Evangelical types of Christianity for their overemphasis on Witnessing Love. Rauschenbusch established a tradition called "the social gospel." The liberation theology of Gustavo Gutiérrez also opened minds to the social justice component of the work of the Awed Ones.

Social structures need to be seen as coagulations of human choices that typically fail to care for people fully enough. Therefore, the Love of people includes changing those structures toward forms that are more just, sane, workable, and worthy of being the ways we live together in a realistic manner – in a manner that gives everyone an opportunity for survival, social liberty, and the pursuit of happiness. In a fully elaborated Christian theology and ethics, we presuppose that "happiness" means Trust, Love, and Freedom. Yet, the focus of Justing Love is upon something else than opening these Holy Spirit depths of personal living. Justing Love focuses upon the opportunities to enjoy the material, mental, emotional, and social conditions that provide possibilities for all human life, both for profound living and for the ordinary supports for all human living.

Loving God in the Christian sense, means loving what we are truly encountering in world history and in our actual everyday lives. It can seem at first that the calling to "Love What Is" might result in a passive or ultraconservative sort of ethics, but that would be to ignore the truth that the given or actual Reality always includes possibility. There is no *actual* that does not include the *possible*, and there is no *possible* that is not rooted in some *actual*. If loving the actual excludes loving the possible, then we need to rip the word "actual" out of the English language. And if loving the possible excludes loving the actual, then we need to rip the word "possible" out of the English language. Actual and possible are two wings on the same bird – Reality. However paradoxical that statement may sound to our philosophical minds, it is simply the truth: Realty includes both the actual and the possible. Here is an illustration of what this insight means in social practice:

Thinking Outside the Fossil Fuel Box

As long as we insist on thinking inside the Fossil Fuel Box (the actual), there is no way to envision a genuine alternative to fossil fuel use, and there is no way to chart a path from our hopeless *here* of impending climate catastrophe to a hopeful *there* of a viable alternative energy system.

I was rocked into seeing afresh the importance of seeing the energy *possibility* beyond the norm of current thinking by an article by Gail Tverberg entitled "Renewables; Good for Some Things; Not so Good for Others." This article, though written by a progressive person of good intentions, is an example of thinking inside the Fossil Fuel Box. She begins with this assertion: "Renewables that we have available today won't replace all of today's fossil fuels in any reasonable time line." The phrase "reasonable time line" excludes a full grasp of the *possible* that is present in our *actual* situation. To be realistic, to "Love What Is," we must think of an *unreasonable time line* if we are going to avoid the worst-case scenario of the climate-crisis catastrophe – "unreasonable," that is, in terms of the thinking that goes on inside the Fossil Fuel Box.

The Tverberg article is a good analysis of how difficult the transition from fossil fuels to a wind-and-solar-based system will be. And clearly there will have to be a period of transition, for this is an enormous leap, and we will need to use the energy of fossil fuels to make this leap. But overall the Tverberg article amounts to a huge victim image about making this needed energy transition under any circumstances. And the article leaves out of consideration some very important facts, without which the *technological possibilities* are invisible. So let me sketch some of those facts:

(1) It is now technologically possible to fuel jet planes with liquefied hydrogen cheaper and safer than with jet fuel. This also

has implications for trains, trucks and other transport means and major equipment.

(2) Hydrogen can be produced from any energy source – fossil, solar, wind, etc. Hydrogen is not an energy source; it is an energy currency like electricity. Electricity and hydrogen, operating together, can connect any energy use to any energy source. The economics and efficiency of energy conversion to hydrogen is rapidly improving. For storing energy hydrogen can replace batteries in many important applications. Storing energy is a key innovation for replacing the easily stored fossil fuels. Hydrogen is a lightweight and efficient energy-storage medium compared with batteries.

(3) Unlimited growth in the overall use of energy is not a necessary prediction. We are currently so wasteful in energy-use practices that we may be able to cut the overall use of energy in half without lessening what we need energy to do. This is not a welcome truth to energy sellers, but to government policy makers it is a primary opening to useful progressive action.

(4) The building of an infrastructure to distribute energy through electricity and hydrogen may be far cheaper over the long haul than maintaining the current energy infrastructure, especially if we figure in the damage done by harsher and more frequent tornadoes, hurricanes, desertification, flooding, and the social chaos that will attend a continuation of the current energy system.

So what are the blocks for using the power of fossil fuels to arrive at a post-fossil fuel energy system? The main block is populations and their politicians who are continuing to live inside the Fossil Fuel Box of understandings. Plus it is energy companies that have already located fossil fuel sources and built long-range business plans based on selling those "goods." Such companies will have to be severely regulated, perhaps nationalized, perhaps outlawed if we are going to leave some of that fossil fuel product in the ground. This requires a political shift from big money control of our governments to popular control by an enlightened population. That may seem like an impossible challenge. But it is *the* challenge. It is *the* possibility within our actual situation. We have the basic technology for making a transition from the fossil-fuel system to a solar-and-wind energy system. The technological challenges are a real limit on the speed with which the transition can be made, but not the main limit. It is the political limits that fundamentally control the speed of the transition.

We have not yet begun the energy transition in earnest. With a full political dedication to the transition, it might shock us how quickly this enormous shift could be conducted. Just suppose that all subsides to fossil fuel companies were removed. Just suppose that 90% of the profits of fossil fuel companies were used to subsidize the transition. Just suppose that government support for thoroughgoing energy conservation got fully serious. When we look at history carefully we see that change can happen rapidly when the economic and mental factors line up together. Consider the story of the automobile or the computer chip. Technology when well financed and widely purchased is an almost irresistible force for change. And investors don't care what they invest in; they will go with whatever is going. Our core block is politicians who are bought by and defended by the current economic establishment.

In conclusion, there are reasonable grounds for being unreasonable with respect to the "reasonable" thinking that goes on within the Fossil Fuel Box. Reality is always unreasonable with respect to the inherited form of reasoning. Reality is always alive with possibilities that shock to the roots the reasonableness of inherited reasoning.

For a reference on these possibilities of hydrogen, see **David Sanborn Scott**, Ph.D., Vice-President (for Americas) International Hydrogen Association, Founding Director, Institute for Integrated Energy Systems, University of Victoria, Canada, author of *Smelling Land: The Hydrogen Defense Against Climate Catastrophe*.

Also see a fuller analysis of the energy crisis in chapter three of the book *From Empire to Eco-Democracy* authored by myself, Ben

Ball, Marsha Buck, Ken Kreutziger, and Alan Richard. Climate responsibility is a primary social justice issue of our times.

Here is a second illustration of Justing Love, loving the REAL as both *actual* and *possible*. It may seem impossible at first for gay and lesbian individuals and those of us who respect and love the gay and lesbian individuals in our lives to Love the actual world in which gay and lesbian individuals are misunderstood, considered abnormal, despised, and oppressed. But this actual world is the only world we have. We have to live in it, and to live in it wholeheartedly, we cannot love only the possibility of correcting that world but not the actual world in which that possibility exists. That would be a split love, seeing life as two great powers – one evil, one good. Such a view is the Manichean heresy in relation to the one good Reality of classical Christian theology.

At the other extreme, it would be a lack of Love for Reality to exclude the possibility of correcting the illusory living within this actual world. Gay and lesbian oppression is based on a set of illusions. And all illusions are vulnerable to the judgment of Reality. In other words, Reality is on the side of respect for gay and lesbian individuals. Reality is defending them from oppression, opposing their enemies, holding before us all the possibility of revealing the illusory nature of all grandiose thinking about the glory of being heterosexual. But this possibility of ending these gender illusions as well as this established malice toward some of our citizens can only be healed by some of us paying the cost of standing for the truth. Standing for the truth of possibility in this actual world of illusory living results in some sacrifice on the part of the first defenders of that truth. This is called in Christian theology, "the cruciform principle."

In the cruciform principle we face yet another crisis of faith with regard to affirming Reality as good. How can Reality be good if the cruciform principle is part of Reality? Christian theology has grappled with that issue in this way: Reality loves (forgives) sinners (the illusion dwellers) by sacrificing Reality's truest sons and daughters for the healing of these sinners. For we who are the

Reality lovers, this means that we become the servants of the despairing rather than their self-righteous rulers and despisers. With our own bodies and blood, we enact Reality's forgiveness for the illusion dwellers. And we do not forget that it has been the bodies and blood of other servants of Reality who brought to us our awakenment and our awareness of the healing forgiveness for our own illusion dwelling.

Yes, loving Reality is a humbling life. It humbles our prideful illusion dwelling. It humbles our reluctance to live in the actual world of illusion-dwelling people. It humbles our lethargy and fear to embrace the possibility of being a healing force in this Spirit-sick, illusion-dwelling, despairing *actual* world.

Presencing Love

A third task of Love carried out by the Awed Ones is simply being there in history as a resource for and a continuity of profound human living and Loving. Sometimes Witnessing Love and Justing Love are secondary to simply preserving within a group of humans the grand secrets of true authenticity – plus the methods of preserving these treasures and living them.

Love is a quality that manifests in Witnessing Love and Justing Love, and yet the Love that we are discussing is not absent when no actions are being done. The Love of Reality, self, and neighbor can be present in a state of complete stillness, in a moment of contemplation, in a practice of prayer, in a Presence of sitting or standing in a room of people or no people. Love is manifest in action, but it is not produced by action or accomplished by action. Love is a transformation of the action that is continually taking place in human life, a transformation from malice to Loving.

After we are dead our Loving presence continues. It continues because Love is the essence of humanity, so any human who Loves is touching into something Eternal – something that is simply there for every living human being, and generation of human beings to come. We are not talking here about having a legacy. The legacy of our specific Loving presence may be forgotten by humankind, but the ramifications of that Loving presence live on. It cannot be killed. Killing the biological organisms of those who Love does not kill the manifestation of Love. All deeds, including the deeds of Love, are finite expressions that wear out, become obsolete, and are perhaps forgotten. But the Presence of Love lives on.

That living on of Loving Presence is our immortality, our resurrection, our reincarnation. Love is joined with Freedom and Trust in Reality as the Holy Spirit that does not die. Our biology and our deeds do not live on, but The Spirit of Love blows on. To whatever extent we have shared in manifesting this Love, it blows on from our days on Earth, our grave, our pyre of fire, our rot of bone.

The communal life of both Christian congregations and monastic orders has, at their best, carried out the Presencing-Love task. In some circumstances the most appropriate response is just being there in Presencing Love. Even when Witnessing and Justing Love are functioning as our foremost focus, we have to create the Presence of those groups of people who do the witnessing and put their bodies and minds into the tasks of justice.

Therefore, community building among the Awed Ones is an outcome of Presencing Love. Among those Awed Ones who are committed to a Christian practice as their means of staying alive, Presencing Love promotes the recreation of the next institutional forms of the Christian religion. Upon that controversial issue, I will reflect in the next chapter.

Chapter 15

Post-Christendom Institutionalization

Religious institutions, especially Christian religious institutions, have earned a bad reputation. Many of these institutions have become turned-in upon themselves, corrupted by their need for money, overly accommodated to the shallowness, sentimentality, and bigotries of their communities, and often so authoritarian in style that honest thought is almost entirely excluded.

Also, many liberal Christians and Christian alumni have become so individualistic in their sensibilities that every sort of disciplined community or institutional form has become suspect (i.e. oppressive until proven otherwise). Some Christian--identified persons who have embraced a relatively sound 21st century theology have resisted membership in any Christian religious institution or group. Therefore, a proposal to envision a next institutionalization of the Christian religion may seem questionable, old fashioned, Medieval, just plain futile, or wrong.

No Next Christian Institution can be Authoritative

As pointed out in Chapter 11, the deep currents of 20th Century Christian theology have become lucidly aware that no Christian institutions can be authoritative for all Christians. Both Roman Catholic and Protestant Conservatives who still hold the notion that their institution of religion is the one and only Christianity are being dismissed as bigots by most thoughtful people. Furthermore, in this era of planet-wide interreligious dialogue, it is becoming preposterous to claim that a Christian practice of any sort is the one and only valid religion. The more clear we become about what "valid religion" means, the more clear we become that every long-standing religious tradition has become "long-standing" through centuries of cultural change precisely because of its many elements of "validity." I have recently written a whole book (*The Enigma of Consciousness*) aimed at defining "religious validity" as any finite, humanly-invented symbolic practice that enables us to become more "accident prone" to the experience of the accident of recovering aspects of our profound humanness. In other words, religious formation has been a continually emerging part of human societies because there is an enduring need for some sort of restoration from our illusions to our authenticity. We need that dynamic for our survival, thriving, realism, justice, courage, and other elemental aspects of being true to the depths of our humanity.

We now have abundant Christian theological writing that has clarified how the deepest dynamics of Christianity are revelations of how human life is for all humans in their essential state. Therefore, it is not surprising that these same dynamics show up in other religions. H. Richard Niebuhr defined the true Church as that part of any society that is sensitive and responsive to the depths of what is going on in history. This means that "the true church" is a term that points to a dynamic of history, not a religious institution. Nor is the true church confined to a specific set of religious institutions; it is a cosmic dynamic of sensitivity and responsiveness to WHAT IS HAPPENING. This means that Christians must become clear that the "true church" or "communion of saints" is not the same as membership in a particular religious group. A Christian religious group can be defined sociologically, but no sociologically defined group can be the boundary within which "true church" exists.

Post-Christendom Institutionalization

So how does this vision of the "invisible true church" relate to the task of building a Next visible institutional form of the Christian religion? Clearly, the builders of a Next Christianity will need to seek to give institutional form to this universal dynamic of "true church," and at the same time be an embodiment of Christianity's core revelatory event – that is, clear about what the Jesus as Messiah witness means with regard to being fully human in relation to the Fully Real. Clearly, this is a challenging calling, but a doable one.

We who take on this task will also need to remain clear that a sociological reconstruction of the historical tradition of Christianity is no more important than a sociological reconstruction of Buddhism or any other religious tradition. Nevertheless, a reconstruction of Christianity can be viewed as important for millions of people. It can even be viewed as important for enriching the ongoing interreligious dialogue. Indeed, let us approach the task of Christian reconstruction with the understanding that the Christian pool of Holy journeying has something to contribute to the overall discussion that is needed by humanity as a whole.

As soon as we begin to see what fresh Christian institutions are needed, we confront a barrier within ourselves and within our general culture. Many of us, perhaps most of us, have come to distrust institutions of any sort.

What is an Institution?

The need for institutions in human life needs some undergirding for many people. The very word "institution" makes us think of organizations we could do without. But let us look at the concept "institution" more carefully. The English language is a social institution. If English is our only language, we could hardly recommend doing without it. Indeed, we require some language institution in order to pursue any life that we have in mind. Art is likewise a set of social institutions. Education is a set of institutions. We are not usually opposed to having such institutions. Typically, we are more friendly toward cultural institutions like language, art, and education than we are toward economic and political institutions. Religious institutions are also cultural institutions, but we often distrust them the most.

Every essential social process of human socialization needs to be institutionalized in order to become a real life functioning. For example, the economic aspect of every human society can be described as three sets of essential processes: resource processes, production processes, and distribution processes. Each society institutionalizes these essential processes differently, but no society can escape organizing all three in some manner in order to: (1) access from the Earth needed riches, (2) produce those riches into products and services people need and want, and (3) invent effective ways of distributing those products and services to those who use or consume them. Similarly, the term "Religious formation" can be the name for an essential social process that every fully functional society needs to institutionalize for the benefit of that society.

In other words, our sensibility to our profound humanness and the sharing of those sensibilities with others needs to be institutionalized in order for this essential social dynamics to become fully manifest. Satisfying this need does not mean settling for the failed institutions of religion that still hang around. And correcting this state of religious decay can mean more than reforming the old institutions. It may mean creating whole new styles of religious institutions – institutions that fit our experience of how profound humanness is experienced today and how people access that humanness. Accessing our profound humanness has many names: enlightenment, salvation, blessedness, holiness, the quest for our essential wonder, and more. For such terms to be filled with meaning and rescued from misunderstandings, we need institutions in which we house effective practices, relevant ethics, workable communal associations, and the supportive theoretics

So What is Religion?

Religion is a social institution that gives form to the essential religious formation process of accessing our profound humanness. Every long-standing religious tradition has had its force in human life because it was a creation of social institutions that assisted people toward their need for a profound embodiment of their humanness. It has happened in 20th century Western culture that our institutions of research physics assisted some people to access aspects of their essential awe and wonder. To the extent that this was so, those research physics institutions were also religious institutions. But research physics does not usually define its essential function as awe accessing. Other institutions do define accessing the profound awe of being human as their essential function. Such institutions can be properly called "religion." Of course many religious institutions fail to perform the above stated essential function and even mis-define themselves as having some other function. They may even lie about the function they are performing, which is all too often creating an escape from the sobering awe of human authenticity and focusing instead on some sort of superficial, socially un-disturbing, tensionless irrelevance.

As an example of religious organizations that are fulfilling the religious function, many creative institutions of Buddhist practice are now taking root in Western societies. The practice of meditation is being taught with the expectation of enabling some sort of profound accessing of our true humanity. A student asked his Buddhist teacher if practicing meditation would cause enlightenment. "No," said the teacher, "enlightenment is an accident, but meditation will make you more accident prone." I view this statement as helpful in forming a general definition of religion. Religion is a humanly invented practice that makes you more accident prone to your essential awe, wonder, true being, profound humanness, enlightenment, depth healing, salvation – choose your term and define it with your honest experience.

The word "religion" has often been abandoned in favor of the word "spirituality." People say that they hate practicing a religion, but they claim to have a spirituality. If, however, "spirituality" means a practice that enables one to access profound humanness, then "spirituality" and "religion" have the same meaning. I prefer the word "religion" to "spirituality" because "religion" has a more down-to-Earth quality. "Spirituality" can too easily drift off into intellectualism, individualism, and sentimentality. The word "Religion" has a chance of meaning a crass down-to-Earth social process, a regular group practice and a regular solitary practice that we do daily, weekly, monthly, and yearly for a lifetime. So defined, religion is one more social practice along with education or sewage disposal: religion is something we do, join, enact, in a word *practice*. "Religion," so defined, is not merely a set of beliefs or a worldview, although it is true that a religious practice typically includes thinking and systems of thinking about the practices in which such thinking plays a part. Further, "religion" is not merely a set of moralities, although it is true that the profound humanness that a religion assists us to access does become manifest in moral patterns. Religion is a finite social process with the purpose of assisting us to access the Infinite.

What is a Christian Religion?

A Christian religion is a religious practice that has roots in the Christian heritage. Christianity is a long history of effective practices (as well as perverted practices). And like meditation these practices can make one more accident prone to the accident of our essential profound humanness. Christianity at its best has been clear about the importance of the communal life of a religious practice. This includes an understanding of the difference between Christianity as a "communion of saints" and Christianity as a religious institution. While the older theologies sometimes claimed

Post-Christendom Institutionalization

that the communion of saints only existed inside a Christian Institution, we now know that this is not true. As John's Jesus says, "I have sheep who are not of this fold." That sentence can be allowed to mean that whatever Christian institution we come up with, the communion of saints (i.e. the Body of Christ) will include people who are outside that finite grouping. "The Body of Christ" can be allowed to mean "the Awed Ones," wherever these dedicated-to-profound-humanness people appear through that enigmatic accident of "second birth" occasioned by the Awesome Almightyness that is operative in the whole of human history.

The rebuilding of a Next Christian religion must surely be done by Awed Ones who treasure the core of Christian heritage. But let us not forget that we who are these Awed Christianity rebuilders must not claim that Awed Ones appear only in the institutions we are building. We need to retain the principle that "God only knows" who are the members of the communion of the Awed Ones – thus its invisibility to the eyes of humans. That is, we are experiencing a fresh definition of "the communion of saints" as all those of whatever religious practice or lack of religious practice who are indeed Awe-sensitive and Awe-responsive to the Awesome and thereby being the Awed Ones in history leading all humans toward an Awe-filled Commonwealth of realistic living. If we use the New Testament term, the Awed Ones are the "Kingdom of God."

As we proceed with building Next institutions of Christian practice, we must also maintain our awareness of yet another deep mystery – namely, that all the people within whatever institutions we build will be sinners, that is persons deeply or somewhat estranged from their membership in the communion of saints. The religious institutions we build will be hospitals for the *sin-sick* as well as places for communion among those who are *being healed* of their sin-sickness – their despair over Reality, their malice toward all, and their bondage to the compulsions of misdirected willfulness.

Post-Christendom Institutionalization

Church as a Communion of Saints

The *communion-of-saints* vision of the Christian Church remains primary in our understanding of the past, present, and future of Christianity. Jesus did not see his task as founding a new religion. He was calling his followers to be a communion of saints, a new Israel, a true Israel. His call was to become members of an Eternity-based Kingdom being established right now on Earth by the God of History. Paul likewise saw his task as creating communities of saints that included both circumcised Judeans and uncircumcised Gentiles. Both groups of people were manifesting the same communion of Holy Spirit. Paul initiated other novel religious practices, but all this was taking place within a Hellenistic/Hebraic subculture that was not yet calling itself "Judaism." In fact, in Paul's lifetime neither Judaism nor Christianity had emerged as separate religions. Paul was initiating first steps beyond the Hebraic subculture, but first steps that did not mean "new religion" to Paul.

Church as Religious Institutions

Chapters 6 through 11 contain illustrations of how the original communion-of-Christian saints, as it moved through history, built religious institutions. So when we use the word "Church" today (as in "What Church do you attend?"), we typically mean a religious institution. As already indicated, religious institutions are needed in order to sustain over time the teachings and practices that are useful for accessing our own communion-of-saints qualities and for awakening others to this possibility being offered to humanity from the Sovereign Power confronted in the flow of history. So here is the key point: *Within our current era of Christian history, a new style of religious institution is needed. We need Christian institutions in which **authenticity** rather than **authority** is the ruling emphasis.*

Many people who are clear about the inadequacies of our inherited Christian institutions have stopped participating in those

Post-Christendom Institutionalization

institutions and become what is often called "Christian alumni." These alumni plus many Christian reformers and revolutionaries who retain active roles in the inherited institutions have become averse to religious institutions. Their jaws tighten up when someone even suggests building new and better Christian institutions. These antiauthoritarian, freedom-loving, spirited, independent revolutionary souls are the hope for a Next Christianity, but like the proverbial "cats," they will not be easily herded. And *herding* is not what we want to do. We want a community of free, creative, independent thinking Christians. Yet, what we find to be our first obstacle toward establishing a Next Christianity is that the very people who can build a Next Christianity see religious institutionalization as a form of "herding" people. One key to countering this "fear of herding" is to make sure that our next institutional forms have a thoroughly open-ended quality, and that the members have genuine responsibility for the unending emergence of the needed institutional changes.

And here is a second hitch to successful Christian institution building: our over-commitment to rigid views of democratic process. The quality of these new Christian institutions needs to be derived, maintained, and improved from the living experience of being a communion of saints – people who are experiencing their profound humanness and creatively leading from the perspective of that profound humanness. Not everyone experiences this communion of saints with the same intensity. Many members of any group will be strongly resistant to precisely those religious methods, communal forms, disciplines, and social missions that are most needed. Therefore, well-enforced religious patterns are needed to create healing communities and radical missional impacts upon the general society. So how do we handle that resistance to effective forms and methods?

Here is part of the answer to that question: The deep seriousness that arises from our profound humanness needs to be balanced with a form of consensus building that replaces all the top-down church politics of the Medieval and Modern centuries.

Post-Christendom Institutionalization

So what does this new polity look like? Consensus need not mean total agreement by everyone involved. It can mean statements of direction that a group can go along with for now without flying apart. A disagreeing person can *stand aside* from supporting a decision without leaving the group. If a disagreeing person feels that a given direction is some sort of life-or-death violation of what it means to be part of the Christianity rebuilding effort, then that person can vigorously ask the group to reconsider the controversial direction. And if the group cannot be convinced to do so, then that disagreeing person can simply leave that group and create something else. Consensus building must be understood to be that serious and that honest. Such consensus building is not a top-down oppression and must not be accused of being so. If everyone is given their opportunity to be heard and every issue is approached within the notion that truth is something being discovered in our own experience of living, then overt oppression need not be the outcome.

Also such consensus building will include rejecting rigid beliefs as the unifying structure. It also means abandoning huge buildings or regional temples that form an economic anchor around our revolutionary necks. It means maintaining the Spirit or Awe-level inspiration for a disciplined cooperativeness that is purely voluntary, but open to useful order. It means a deep humility about honoring the authenticity and skills in one another without falling into the illusion that all saints are equally saintly or equally skilled. To start with, it means opening our minds to the need for these new institutions and opening our creative imaginations toward the unprecedented social forms that will be needed.

Leadership within this new direction becomes *the* (I repeat *the*) most challenging topic. First of all, it means abandoning the old model of an ordained clergy; the old clergy/laity split cries out to be abandoned. Full responsibility falls on all members of the here envisioned Next Christian practice. There must not be two levels of commitment. This means taking with new seriousness the well-worn Lutheran slogan of "the priesthood of all believers." That phrase traditionally meant a rejection of the Roman Catholic version of clericalism. It was an argument for release from subservient dependence upon "Church" authority for interpreting the tradition, and thus an opening for each lay Christian to read the Bible in his or her native language and think through for himself or herself the implications for Christian living. But a majority of Protestants have not yet fully challenged Protestant clericalism. Some Protestant laity have retained a subjugation to their clergy that is even more oppressive than the Roman Catholic version.

Other laity and clergy have misinterpreted "the priesthood of all believers" to mean that each person, clergy or laity, can simply think and act however they like with no truth-demanding obedience to a core Revelation. That would be a departure from a key aspect of Christian wisdom. The Medieval authoritarian pattern did have the virtue of maintaining the understanding that a revealed Truth for our living had entered history through the Jesus-Christ event. Our understanding of "the priesthood of all believers" does not mean some anarchy of individualistic overemphasis.

Rather, we will need to emphasize the "priesthood" word in that phrase. "Priesthood" implies a Spirit maturity and a set of theological and interpersonal skills. Priesthood implies that we hear the Word of God and know how to address the Word of God to other human beings. To embrace "the priesthood" of all members of a Next Christian community of persons means that every member has the responsibility of thoroughness in their own Spirit journey and in their own skills of witnessing and living from that ruling Word of God that undergirds this entire effort. Also, it means facing up to the inevitable fact that some members will be more skilled and more mature in Spirit and in an appropriate sociological journey than others. So while all members are leaders, all members are also followers of the leadership of others. While it is true that a recent member to the Christian journey may address the Word of God to the most mature member, it also remains true

Post-Christendom Institutionalization

that the most mature member has more leadership calling than those who have just begun to put their Christian living together.

Also, the entire structure of a Next Christian institution depends upon favoring strongly the most mature members in the ongoing task of creating the new designs and maintaining their effective application and improvements. And all this means a new intensity of awareness on the part of everyone about who is providing Spirit quality leadership and who is relatively naive or confused about the difference between ego-based and Spirit-based behavior. Being obedient to the Spirit of Christ is a possibility that a group of people can obey, but this direction will challenge us and ask us for a humility and a wisdom that is very far from customary.

Therefore, What Next?

So what do these intuitions of fresh sociological directions tell us about the social forms for a Next Christianity? The following three chapters provide some responses to that question: (1) We need to see that the commonality of the Next Christianity is in large measure composed of effective **religious methods** well learned and applied by trained leadership, (2) We need to view at least the following four forms of gathering as primary structures: **Circles, Assemblies, Guilds, and Retreats**. And (3) we need to remain clear that our new communal forms and religious methods are not means of being aloof from world history, but forms of nurture, training, and planning for responses to world history – that is, for "**The Eternal Mission to Planet Earth.**"

Chapter 16

Christianity as Healing Methods

One of the most important breakthroughs in the redefinition of religion and thus in our development of a Next Christianity is the understanding that religion is not fundamentally about thinking, dogma, or a worldview: it is about practice. Religion is something you do – daily, weekly, yearly, for the rest of your life. Thinking is part of what you do, but it is a supporting part of this core thing: PRACTICE. "Practice" means doing group rituals, viewing core icons, telling core stories, doing solitary exercises, building group consensus, conducting cooperative actions of truthful witness and social justice, carrying out group disciplines, and more. Thinking is part of each of these things but not the core definition. Various sorts of intellectual work are included in an inclusive religious practice, such as doing the sort of theologizing illustrated in these chapters. But, we should never again speak of having a theology. We should only speak of doing theology or theologizing – that is, of pushing our theological edge still further into the abyss of the unknown.

And by "practice" I mean practicing a Next Christian religion. There are many religions and many Christian religions, each of which may define religion somewhat differently. Understanding religion as practice opens another deep discovery: our methods of practice are as important as our theological understandings. Religious methods are important content to be learned by the practitioners of a Next Christianity. In this chapter, I will describe some specific healing practices, which I will also call "methods."

Healing Methods

If we were practicing Buddhism, we would begin by learning the practice of meditation and experiencing for ourselves how that practice works for us in making us more accident prone to the accident of enlightenment. A next Christian practice can include meditation practices that we learn from Buddhism or elsewhere. Similarly, we can adopt dancing, chanting, toning, feasting, fasting, or whatever from wherever. Some of these religious methods are optional, rather than essential to a Christian practice. Other methods are basic to a Christian practice. Some of the methods Christians need to practice can be used anywhere – such as consensus methods, workshop methods, and leadership methods. I will not describe these important but generally-used methods in this chapter. I will focus on five key methods that are uniquely needed for a Next Christian practice.

Method One: Conducting Profound Dialogue

I will describe first a religious method I call "profound dialogue." We all tend to have an interior council of "great people" with whom we dialogue: a parent, a teacher, an author, an artist, an activist, a personal friend, a person in the distant past, a contemporary, and many others. As a religious practice, "profound dialogue" means bringing these "great people" into our consciousness, through remembering or reading their words – hearing their voices, their music, their poetry – seeing their paintings, their sculpture, their architecture. These people are "great" because we have found them inspiring, evoking Awe within us, assisting us to access our own profound greatness of awe-filled, Reality-breathing living.

The various voices that have spoken to us have taken up a place in our memory and tend to talk to us more or less all the time. Our practice of profound dialogue begins when we take charge of this interior council of "great voices." We can seat these speakers as we want them seated. Some of them are on the front row of our circle of interior council members. We consult them first or most often. Others we have seated further back. We consult them with reservations or infrequently. We can order our interior council in accord with various subjects or topics or ways of aiding us. This is our council, our creation, our interpretation of our personal history of being inspired. It is also our future resources for further inspiration. We have the power to listen or not, accept what they say or not, correct them, enrich them, or shut them up. This religious practice is a dialogue, not a monologue. We are not only listening. We are not only speaking. In a dialogue we listen for truth and we speak back: we do both as a way of appropriating more realism in our living.

Since this is our very own council meeting, we do not need to play defensive games with it. We are not passive pawns of our inspiring voices, nor are we closed to what these voices have to share with us. In the practice of dialogue, we go to these "great people" willingly and actively for the enrichment of our lives. We may disagree with them, fight with them, and even unseat them from our interior council, but we maintain a continuing humility of being open, curious, aggressive learners.[11]

In order to see how this universal dynamic of interior dialogue can be uniquely Christian, let us apply this general human dynamic to the topic of a Next Christian practice of dialogue with the writers of the Bible. Using the marvelous work of the historical scholars of our Christian origins, we have a relatively clear picture of the historical Jesus, distinguished from the Jesus of Paul, the Jesus of Mark, the Jesus of Matthew, the Jesus of Luke, and the Jesus of

---

[11] For more in the interior council, see Joe Mathews talk "Meditation" in *Bending History*, John Epps Ed. (Resurugence Publishing: 2005)

Christianity as Healing Methods

John. We can now dialogue with the historical Jesus. Rudolf Bultmann was among the first to scientifically separate out the earliest historical layer of the Mark, Matthew, and Luke texts. This work is summarized for the public in his classic book *Jesus and the Word*. A more recent work, *Jesus, a Revolutionary Biography* by John Dominic Crossan adds interesting details to a plausible view of the historical Jesus. And I have recently read and been impressed by *Jesus Before Christianity* by Albert Nolan, who created another plausible picture of this historical figure's address to our lives today. Nolan has assisted me to better understand Jesus' identification with the destitute and with his attack on the moralistic piety of the prosperous. He has better illuminated my own struggles with hierarchical society and its injustices and hypocrisies.

Having clarified what I mean by the historical Jesus, I can view the word "Jesus" or "Jesus Christ" in the writings of Paul as a dialogue with Paul rather than a dialogue with Jesus of Nazareth. I might say that I am in dialogue with Paul as a resurrected embodiment of Jesus – that is, with Paul as an ongoing member of the Jesus Christ breakthrough in history. If next I read the Gospel of Mark, I am in dialogue with Mark, not Jesus. When I see Jesus as a character in Mark's fictional drama, I can dialogue with this Markian Jesus as a fictitious character much in the same way as I can dialogue with Harry Potter as a fictitious character in the writings of J. K. Rowling. In a much deeper sense I can also dialogue with Rowling and her insights into profound humanness that she is embodying in her fiction. My wife Joyce and I have recently read aloud *David Copperfield* by Charles Dickens. I find myself now in dialogue with many of the vivid characters of that Dickens novel. But on an even deeper level I am in dialogue with Dickens and his profound insight into people that he was able to share with me through the creation of his characters.

Similarly, in the fiction of Matthew and the fiction of Luke and the fiction of John, I need to be clear that I am in profound dialogue with Matthew, Luke, and John (or whoever these writers actually were). These dialogues are as significant as the dialogues I have with the characters in their fiction, including Jesus as a character in their story. These Gospel writers, like Paul, can be viewed as the resurrected profound humanness of Jesus. The Jesus figure in Mark, Matthew, or Luke is what we might call historical fiction – that is, some memories of the historical figure of Jesus still influence their fiction. But in the gospel of John, the tradition of fictionalizing Jesus has leaped all previous bounds and gone into wholesale development of sermons by whoever it was who wrote this Fourth Gospel. In my most profound dialogue with "John's" piece of fiction, I have had to remain clear that I am in dialogue with a most amazing theologian who has made Jesus into a spokesperson for his (or her) edge theologizing.

The considerations just summarized illustrate the sort of religious methods needed for Scripture study/dialogue within a vital and responsible Next Christianity. There is no authority of the Bible involved here. There is a great love of history. And this love of history is part of the religious methodology needed for a Next Christianity. In the context of loving our own history, we Next Christian practitioners can be enriched by learning the history in which the Christian writers of the past lived and witnessed and loved.

Also, these methods of Scripture study/dialogue include a great love of the actual text and a great love of the profound humanness that the text writers are describing. And we can dialogue with each fictional Jesus as we can also dialogue with the fictional Harry Potter or David Copperfield. But we do not view these fictional characters with a literalistic or an authoritarian attitude. We look to them for clues to our own profound humanness in our own historical moments. And to do this dialogue well, we will need to be aware of the historical circumstances of Mark, Matthew, Luke, John, Dickens, and Rowling. We need our love of history to read our Bibles.

Ignatius of Loyola emphasized dialogue with Scripture. But he, like Luther, viewed Scripture authoritatively, and he, like Luther, knew that the authority of Scripture had to be appropriated personally. So he created a method for doing that. He asked his retreat participants to take characters from the biblical story and have a conversation with them. He asked them to imagine a mini-drama: me, Peter, me, Peter, me, Peter, me, Peter, me. As Ignatius knew, it requires profound imagination to invent such dialogue between these ancient characters and the emerging "me" in my historical times. I believe that Ignatius' religious method can be updated for a Next Christianity. But today it is important to move away from Ignatius' authoritarianism into a Next Christianity's authenticity emphasis. Let us insist that our religious methods fit the times in which we live. Our dialogue with Scripture or with Augustine, Ignatius, or Luther needs to be based on authenticity, not authority. What did these ancient witnesses see about profound humanness that can inform me in my own experience of and quest for profound humanness – a humanness that I am proposing to live within the historical flow of my historical times and as an outflow of my love of the historical challenges I face and the responses I am going to make?

In summary, Method One helps us address both the solitary and communal aspects of our profound humanness. It is a needed method for rooting our authentic life in history, in time, in the past as well as the future, and for living within the now of decision.

Method Two: Metaphorical Translation

Following is a description of a method that is closely related to the method just described. In order to carry out dialogue with Biblical writers or other Church fathers and mothers, here is a method for translating insight from the older two-story mythic language into a language or poetry that resonates with the full round of thinking and living that we must do in the 21st Century. As lovers of history we can learn to take seriously the imagery of these former times in which our Christian heritage was composed, and yet re-say the core meaning of this old language in imagery taken from our times. Only if we learn to practice an effective method of metaphorical translation from **then** to **now** will our dialogue with Christian Scriptures and other ancient witnesses come alive for us and for those to whom we witness concerning our Christian-based discoveries of profound humanness.

Kierkegaard likened reading the Scriptures to receiving a love letter. Our purpose is hearing what our lover is saying to us. Whatever trouble we have to go through to open the envelope and translate the letter is preliminary. We do that only in order to get to the message that the letter has for us. When we are reading love letters from Reality written 2000 years ago in some no-longer-spoken language, we have some work to do to be sure we are hearing appropriately. Fortunately, the language scholars have done some of the work for us. We can read the love letter in our own contemporary language, but the metaphors in which we think and the meanings we assign to specific words are still there to deal with. So we must learn a deeper kind of translation, namely translating meanings from a two-story mythical storytelling era to our one-story ways of speaking about profound experiences. We cannot honestly believe in a supreme being in some next-door world. And if we are honest, we need to admit that we have had a hard time understanding that Jesus and others used that old poetry meaningfully to talk about their real lives. We are tempted to dismiss these old Scriptures (or large portions of them) as irrelevant to us. Or we are tempted to read into these supposedly authoritarian documents whatever we want them to say. To find an appropriate way to read a two thousand-year-old love letter from Reality is a challenge. Using the word Reality instead of God is a start, but even here we will find it necessary to ask ourselves what we mean by "Reality," and if what we mean by "Reality" corresponds with what earlier Christian witnesses meant by "God." Also let us explore how using the devotional word "God" adds something to using the more neutral word "Reality."

Here is an example of doing metaphorical translation with one familiar verse: *Blessed are you poor, for yours is the Kingdom of God.*

(Luke 6:20 RSV) The authors of *The Five Gospels* favor this textual translation: *Congratulations, you poor, God's domain belongs to you.* I suggest that the word "destitute" is a better textual translation than "poor," because poor in our world today can mean a state much more well off than the state of those to whom Jesus was referring. And I suggest that "Fortunate" rather than "Congratulations" would also be a better textual translation. So now we have for a text: *Fortunate are you destitute, God's domain belongs to you.*

With this text, we still have some puzzling features. Whether we use "God's Domain" or "The Kingdom of God," we still have to ask what was being pointed to by Jesus. As we have already developed in previous chapters, Jesus clearly understood the word "God" in the Old Testament manner – a devotional word for WHAT IS – that is, for the Almighty Reality that confronts us in every happening. "Reality's Domain," as Jesus used that term, points to the arrival in history of a way of being for human beings that is serving God rather than serving the opposite of God, which Jesus calls "Satan's Domain." Before our literalistic minds conjure up an otherworldly figure with horns and tail, let us insist that Jesus was pointing to something going on in his experience, namely the fact that humans were fleeing from and fighting with God's Domain. The fallen state of humans was being symbolized by a powerful "kingdom" symbolized by its own supermundane king. Serving this evil king clearly meant not serving the Truth, the Real, the WHAT IS. So serving the evil king meant serving an illusion – some sociologically empowered lie about WHAT IS. The pronouncement that God's Domain was coming in Jesus' lifetime meant that people were being healed from their illusions and restored to their REAL lives. Satan was being defeated, tied down by a stronger force, and humans were being released from Satan's prison to live their REAL lives in glorious freedom, love, and trust in Reality's love for them.

We can now suggest the following metaphorical translation of the above verse for our lives in the 21st Century: Fortunate are those who are devoid of the benefits of our evil age, for they are ripe to participate in the realistic living of their lives. Now we have a translation of that particular love letter from Reality (that particular Word of God) that this verse holds for us. We may not be happy with it, for we may not find ourselves among the destitute, and thus we may seem to be left out of the "good news." Apparently, someone in the early church had this same feeling, for they "improved" Jesus saying to mean "destitute in spirit" (Matthew 5:3) rather than the simply "destitute" in the more literal economic sense. We can assume that they meant that the Domain of God was also happening in the lives of people who were not literally destitute, but was occurring among those who were joining the destitute in being "not of this evil world." So the point of the verse is not that having no worldly goods is itself a blessing. No, the blessing is having weak ties to the Satanic kingdom and thus an openness to living a realistic life.

With that polemical and cryptic "yell out" on some Galilean hillside, Jesus clearly got the attention of the destitute and the rich by reversing a taken for granted view that it was the rich who were being blessed by God and that it was the destitute who were in a state of lesser honor or no honor at all.

We certainly must not take from this verse the notion that poverty is a good thing. Jesus clearly saw that it was good for the rich to provide for the poor, and that it was good for everyone to help everyone with their fundamental needs. Nevertheless, we can share in Jesus' distrust of riches, for riches commonly serve as a bond with Satan's kingdom that needs to be given up. It is as true now as it ever was that "Where your treasure is, there will your heart be also." Augustine, as we have seen, taught that if a wealthy Christian's heart was at rest in the Domain of God, that person would generously provide for the poor and generously provide for the work of the Church throughout the Empire. He fought for this view against both the views of the arrogant rich and the views of perfectionistic Christians who were making wealth itself an evil thing. Augustine's view enabled the cultural conquest of the

Roman Empire. If the perfectionistic view had prevailed, we might never have heard of Christianity in the Western part of the world.

So what is the Word of God in this verse to each of us today? Let each of us answer that question for ourselves because the Word of God comes to each person personally and directly from Reality as each person is encountering Reality. For me the verse means that I am called to be detached from whatever wealth and benefits this world is providing me and to fully devote those gifts toward the liberation of both those who seek their significance in amassing wealth and those who are destitute and who are also dishonored for being needy. I also face the Demand of Reality to greatly lessen the vast inequality between rich and poor.

What I have attempted to illustrate with this rather elaborate metaphorical translation of a single verse is that we can approach each verse of the Bible with these four basic steps:

1. What does the text say in the language in which it was written as translated into the language we are using?
2. What did the text mean in the understanding of those who first said it, heard it, wrote it, and preserved it?
3. What is being said to me today from the Mouth of Reality as I am confronting Reality in my own life?
4. What does this Word of God ask me to do in my own living?

Each of the chapters of Part One and Two are further illustrations of the method of metaphorical translation. In Chapter One I did some metaphorical translation of the texts written by Isaiah and Second Isaiah. In Chapter Three I did some more metaphorical translation of Jesus' sayings and of the Church's use of the title "Christ." In Chapter four I did some metaphorical translation on Paul's use of the words "God" and "sin." Similarly, metaphorical translation was done with texts from John, Augustine, Thomas Aquinas, and Martin Luther. In every historical era before our own, we encounter in Christian witnessing a use of the two-story metaphorical language. That language has to be translated for our era, or else we fall into one of two serious Christian "heresies": (1) Supposing that all these early witnesses were insensitive and superstitious fools, or (2) Reading into their words our own superstitious misreading of their message to us.

Can Ordinary Christians Read the Bible and Study the Saints?

Yes, is my answer to this question. But it is a serious question, because metaphorical translation is not easy for most members of our culture. Therefore, the metaphorical translation method cries out to be carefully taught to the well-educated, the poorly educated, and the mis-educated of our emerging communities of Christian religious practice. We will need to view this skill as basic, like breathing, like sharing our lives, like gathering together weekly in committed circles for religious practice. There is no reason for avoiding metaphorical translation or skirting it with any member of our Next Christian practice. It is part of the methodological catechism that every teenager and elder can be taught to learn as fully as driving a car safely or working a computer skillfully. There will, however, be various levels of competence in understanding the history of ancient times and therefore understanding how a specific text can address us in our times. Those in our groups who are the most skilled with metaphorical translation will need to view themselves as servants of the rest, and the rest will need to welcome that service. Any excuse for avoiding this core method is bogus.

With such reservations in mind, we can still do Bible reading and discussion as an essential part of a weekly meeting of Next Christians. In my own meetings with other people most of whom are not Biblical scholars, we have found that these four questions can yield very meaningful conversations with almost any passage of Scripture:

1. What words or phrases did you hear?

2. How would you put the message of this text in your own words?
3. How does this message address you personally?
4. What does this message challenge you to do?

The Method of Metaphorical Translation is necessary for accurately accessing the Bible and other ancient texts as guides to the Christian revelation as a discovery of our own profound humanness in its contemporary setting.

Method Three: An Existential Study Method

The Western religions of Judaism, Christianity and Islam all emphasize the extensive study of their heritage. The practitioners of Eastern religions also study their heritage, but their emphasis tends to be upon the nonintellectual methods such as meditation, chanting, dancing, and other bodily movements and non-movements. These methods also appear in the West. Sufi Muslims place great emphasis on the nonintellectual methods. So do Jewish and Christian mystics, although it is interesting to note that the most famous Christian mystics almost always insisted on writing a book (or many books). Whatever be the trends in these different religious expressions, a Next Christianity cannot be true to the core of the Jesus Christ revelation without a vibrant study of its heritage and the basic love of history that I have been at pains to illustrate in every chapter of this call to create a viable Next Christian practice.

Many people, most of the time, simply skim written material, looking for highlights they agree with or already understand. That is not a good way to learn something. And it is a flaw in the general culture – a flaw that Christian practitioners can join others in correcting. My view is: if someone does not want to learn to study and study well, they are not yet ready for membership in a vital Next Christianity.

If in the communal life of my envisioned Next Christianity we are going to do serious study of the Scriptures, of the church fathers and mothers, and of contemporary theologians and ethicists, we will need to learn a competent existential study method. By this I mean a method that allows us to hear what an author is actually saying, and then hear what if anything he or she is saying that resonates with our own lives, that calls us into question, that challenges us, or that informs us at the level of our basic existence.

Charting is such a study method. This method can be spelled out in great detail, but here are its basic principles: (1) View the structure of the author's thought by constructing a visual picture of the text, its subparts, its relations, giving this chart your own titles, but your own titles for what the author is actually talking about. This picture is your gestalt, not of what you want to believe, but of what the author apparently believes and wants to say to you the reader. (2) The second step is grounding the key points of this chart in your own life experiences, working toward those "Ah Hah" moments where realistic insight emerges where it may never have existed before. (3) The third step is talking back to the author. Obviously, no author is perfect about everything, or says everything you would like to hear on the topic. So you will always have something to say in addition to thank you for the gift the author has given you. Trust your own intuitions and past awakenings to qualify you to have something to say to any author, however accomplished that author may be. With these three steps you are doing study, not skimming.

The same three steps apply to the teacher who is leading a group in a study process. He or she needs to do that same kind of study before leading the class through these similar steps: (1) The teacher needs to come prepared to make the structure and meaning of an author's text as clear as possible to everyone. (2) Then the teacher can assist the class to discover this clarity in their own lives. In a good teaching method, the teacher comes prepared to ask good grounding questions about all the key points in the text – questions that assist the class to recall and get out their own experience of and their own challenges by the key points of the study material. The teacher needs to avoid doing all the clarifying or all the grounding, but instead sees the teaching role as a sort of midwife role, enabling the class to conduct its own creative dialogue with the text. Such a teacher can include himself or herself as a member of the class in this clarity and grounding process. (3) The teacher can leave time at the end of the study for some general discussion of appreciation for and critique of the author studied. Time management is one of the key skills needed for leading an effective class process. Before teaching the teacher needs to plan the amount of time to be allotted to each part of the text, leaving adequate time for the most key issues and having a planned intent for how to end on time. Of course, a good study session will always be a surprise, so all these plans will need to be flexibly applied, as the occasion warrants.

Method Three makes possible the sort of serious study-life that is needed in a local, yet planet-responsible Circle of Next Christian practice.

Method Four: An Art-Form Conversation Method

Our methodological catechism needs to reach beyond language and poetry into all the arts, paintings, sculptures, architecture, music, dancing, drama, movies, novels, stories, singing, chanting, and whatever else we consider to be an artistic formation. Art assists us to experience our own experience by creating for us a virtual reality that can awaken us to our actual reality of feelings, sensibilities, realizations, repentances, forgivenesses, intentions, callings, whatever.

We tend to short-circuit our experience of art by jumping to rational interpretations or statements of pro and con before we have taken time to consciously appropriate the actual content of the art and the personal feelings and awarenesses that the experience of this art form awakens in us. So a method needs to be employed that allows us to have group conversations about art that take us through three important steps of understanding what art can do for us as an aid to our living. We can then take a fourth conversation step that specifically assists us with our Christian understanding.

Christianity as Healing Methods

Imagine that we are viewing a painting: here are the first three conversation steps:

Step one: **Objective impressions**: What shapes do you see? What colors? Where? what designs? What objects?

Step two: **Reflective feelings**: What objects seem pleasant to you? What objects seem unpleasant? What color would you like to subtract? What color would you like to add? Where to do see strong feelings expressed? What are these feelings? How do you feel right now? Where would you like to hang this picture in your house?

Step three: **Interpretive considerations**: What might you title this picture? What is its mood? What story could you tell that would lead to such a mood? So what is the picture about? What is this picture saying to you? What would you like to say back? Complete this sentence: It seems to me that this painting is about_____.

Then for Christian clarity, a fourth type of question can be asked such as: How does this painting tell us something about our experience of sin, our experience of God the Almighty, our experience of Holy Spirit, the transformative event of grace, etc.? Movies are especially good for assisting us to understand the nature of a Jesus-Christ-type event of death/resurrection as such transformational moments happen to ordinary human beings in their ordinary everyday lives.

Method Four is needed to help us be clear that profound humanness is itself more like an art form than a prose paragraph. And profound humanness can be accessed through art, perhaps more easily than through prose.[12]

---

[12] For more about this method see Brian Stanfield's book, *The Art of Focused Conversation* (New Society Publishers: 2000)

Method Five: Prayer as Persistent Intentions

"Prayer" is a much-misunderstood method in Christian practice because "God" has been a much misunderstood word. We need to focus first of all on clarifying that prayer is the exercise of our own *freedom* to which we are being liberated. In prayer we are taking the *initiative* to speak to Reality about our truth, concerns, hopes, confessions, gratitudes, or the simple joy of being in conscious dialogue with the Final Reality that we face. We have permission from our own Love of Reality to address Final Reality with personal terms like: Dear God, Blessed Mother, whatever. We do not need to take literally any of our personal sounding addresses, for we know that we are addressing an absolute Mystery about which we know nothing in a literal sense. We cannot presuppose to describe the Infinite with our finite minds. To insist upon a male designation, for example, says something about ourselves but nothing about God, unless "male" means power. But today "female" also means power. Clearly, the Infinite is neither male nor female. Anything said about the Infinite is actually said about our relationship with the Infinite, rather than about the Infinite Herself, Himself, Itself – surely this is clear.

So what sorts of things do Christians benefit from praying about? Here is an interesting gestalt of the types of topics that Christian heritage has emphasized for a practice of prayer: confession, gratitude, petition, and intercession. The benefit of doing any of these types of prayer is that we are programing our psyche to operate differently in the ongoing round of our living. We are rehearsing intentions that we will intend in the entire round of our living. Prayer is a responsiveness to the living challenges that we are actually facing. So with that in mind, here is a simplified summary of these four categories of prayer:

Confession means owning up to some reality in our behavior, our attitude toward life, our feelings, our thoughts, whatever. It means admitting the ways these bits of our living are escapes from the Whole of Reality or from our true self. Our confession may also own up to our fractured or troubled relations with other selves. Confession is an important initiative on the part of our consciousness because it is a beginning toward being where we are in our living, rather than pretending to be where we are not.

Gratitude means choosing the reality we are being given, instead of the unreality we might desire to substitute for the given Reality. In so far as the given Reality always includes forgiveness and the option of a fresh start in our living, we may experience grateful feelings for this welcome release from self-incrimination, self-underestimation, or self-victimization. But whether we have grateful feelings or not, the practice of gratitude is restorative to our solid here-and-now openness toward life. Life, openly lived, does provide its joys and exuberance, but the practice of gratitude does not mean forcing ourselves to have pleasant states of feeling. Gratitude is an intention that allows our real lives to produce whatever feelings and potentials life naturally produces. Gratitude can move into the very deep passion required to give thanks for enemies, tragedies, and challenges we wish in the first instance to avoid entirely.

Petition means choosing what to intend relative to augmentations for our own existence. Where do we want to go in our life journey? What do we want to have as states of being or worldly opportunities? Petitionary prayer is a courageous thing because we do not always receive exactly what we ask for, or what we thought we were asking for, or what we thought having our request would actually mean. A petition puts our life out there to be disappointed or surprised or amazed beyond all expectations. Petition is a powerful practice; it readies us to receive a future which contains that for which we are asking. Petitionary prayer programs our psyche to pursue opportunities as they present themselves. Petition is a powerful thing: it changes history. But petitionary prayer is not a magical means of controlling the future. Our petitions seldom work out exactly as we expect. History is in some way or another always a surprise, a surprise that can be intensely disappointing as well as overwhelmingly joyous.

Intercession means choosing what to intend with regard to other people, social systems, ecosystems, and the planet as whole. To intercede means to stand between a value and the threat to that value. To intercede means to put our body, our wealth, our reputation, our very being in the breach of creating solutions that handle the threats to what we value. Intercessory prayer means intending our being. Intercession is not asking some divine being to do something for someone. Intercession means requesting with our whole body that Reality change on behalf of some specific value or person that concerns us. In making an intercession we do not need to have a clear plan about how the requested change in history can happen or what our role needs to be in making this change. We can intercede for something that may seem or be impossible. An intercessory prayer is simply the programming of our psyche in a specific direction. We set up our own being to be on the lookout for insights and opportunities that pertain to the value that is the topic of our intercession. Both intercession and petition are an expression of our Trust in the possibility aspects of Mysterious Reality, an attitude that reaches beyond the limits of our familiar norms.

Method Five is a core method for accessing and living out a "personal" relationship with the always surprising, Final, Awesome Mysteriousness that is our God.

Conclusions on the Healing Methods for Christian Practice

There are many other methods that are important for the optimal practice of a Next Christianity, and much more could be said about each of the five methods summarized above. An exhaustive exploration of this topic would require many books. I have limited myself to illustrating this key point: *Good Christian-oriented religious methods are key to the creation of a vital functioning Next Christianity.* Each of the Methods summarized above are applicable to both solitary and group practice. There is no need to wait until we have a group who are willing to practice with us; each of us can begin now with 20 minutes to an hour set aside each day to practice some or all five of the above methods. We do this to beckon Spirit/Awe to appear and give foundation to our day.

As soon as we have one or two other people willing to practice a Next Christianity with us, we can meet weekly (perhaps more often) for a regular group beckoning of Spirit/Awe flowing from these Awe Ones among who we commune and from the Awesome Almightiness that is giving each of us our lives and life challenges.

Chapter 17

Circles, Assemblies, Guilds, and Retreats

The methods described in the preceding chapter and the theology described throughout all the previous chapters do not fit well into the inherited structures of Christendom. Never has the old dictum about new Spirit-wine requiring new wineskins been more appropriate than right now in this turning point of Christian history. Protestant, Roman Catholic, Eastern Orthodox, and all the other long-established expressions of the Christian religion are now in decline. Even though there are strong flare-ups of conservative backlash, the trajectory of Christendom is steadily down. In many once-Christian nations, the Christian alumni are greater in number than the active church members. And the most sensitive descendants of this complex set of religious heritages are the ones who are the most uncomfortable with attending the old institutions. Nevertheless, we can see within these obsolete containers occasional upwellings of valid insight and enthusiasm. We also see the supporters of these obsolete containers fighting against these positive trends in passionate defense of the indefensible.

In spite of these strong signs of decay, the old forms are going to last a while longer. Perhaps they need to last until the more adequate forms have come into being to replace them. Many pastors and other church leaders are already living a schizophrenic

Circles, Assemblies, Guilds and Retreats

life: (1) on the one hand, being administrators of what they know is a dying institution, and (2) on the other hand, building new social forms alongside the old for those who are ready for them.

My task in this chapter is to describe my intuitions about those new social forms. I do not intend this to be a rejection of the good work that many church leaders are doing within their dying institutions. I strongly support the work of assisting those institutions to die gracefully and helpfully in any way that they can. But for an increasing number of aware Christians, the imagining and building of new organizational forms has become first priority.

A New Birth of Intimacy

Archeological evidence seems to support the fact that pre-civilization peoples lived in tight-knit groups of about 150 adult members. Extrapolating from the size of the neocortex of various primates including humans, the British anthropologist Robin Dunbar concluded that the "mean group size" for humans was 150 members, with an "intimate circle size" of 12. However valid such research may be, it is remarkably suggestive of something being discovered by current religious experimenters. In our general society we are missing effective social forms of those two "intimate" sizes. We have circles of friends and various volunteer organizations in those size ranges, but the seriousness of purpose typical of groups of these sizes do not compare with the seriousness being attached to nations and states. Great pressure is being applied upon singular individuals to succeed within the fabrics of these huge social structures. We seldom sense a comparable urgency for our more intimate associations to succeed. Many people have very little life within intimate groups. They are basically alone within huge social collectives. Modern society in general can be said to suffer from both immense collectivism and lonely individualism. And when wealthy individuals game the collective society in their individual favor, human life becomes especially mean.

I am suggesting very strongly that the Next Christianity needs to "pioneer" strong social forms in the size ranges of 12 and 150, and do so on behalf of humanity at large. I am giving these new social forms of Christian practice names: The **Christian Resurgence Circle** and the **Regional Assembly**. The Christian Resurgence Circle, as I envision it, is a committed and disciplined group that meets for meaningful ritual, serious study, and intimate care for one another. The Regional Assembly is (ideally) about 12 of those Circles meeting together quarterly for a whole day or weekend. When 12 Circles of 12 people meet together, that is 144 people. That is my optimal picture of the next sociological design of the "local church" in my vision of a Next Christianity.

So let us explore in our imaginations this quite practical dream of 12 or more Circles of 3 to 12 adults meeting weekly in twelve places within driving distance, and meeting quarterly all together for Spirit refreshment, theological clarity and discussion, a Eucharist meal, plus planning and common work toward the expansion of a CRC Network and its mission to its region of Earth and humanity. This model for the next local church requires no church buildings, no janitor, no secretary, and no pastor. Living rooms and rented space suffice. And every member is pastor, janitor, and secretary in whatever proportion results from the skills and choices by the persons involved.

(1) The Magic of Circles

There have been various house church experiments going on in both conservative and liberal venues. Most of them strike me as theologically, methodologically, and missionally inadequate. They tend to carry forward the same dogmatic attitudes, moralism, and sentimentality that characterizes so many congregations. More interesting to me are the "base communities" launched within Latin American Catholicism by Liberation Theology priests and lay persons. These small groups of mostly working people push for new social justice for the poor, a theology of liberation, and an alternative to the overreaching hierarchical church structuring. Also instructive are the Sanghas of renewed Buddhism. Here also are disciplined small groups who are serious about accessing our common profound humanness. Whatever be their gifts or weaknesses, these groups are witnessing to a felt need for intense small group religious practice.

The Next Christianity being recommended in this book, envisions a type of small-group Circle in which the methods and theology described in this manifesto are operating. The name "Circle" is recommended because it emphasizes seating equidistant from a center, symbolizing a full manifestation of the "priesthood of all believers." This circle pattern has been pioneered by radical feminist movements, and it does provide fresh air for women. Such circling does not mean watering down the members to a common mediocrity, but rather the upgrading of all members to a fully competent leadership status. These envisioned circles are leader-full, rather than leaderless. There will be differences in leadership capacities, but even the most skilled and dedicated do not sit on raised platforms or take on special seating.

The specific experiment in small group practice in which I have been participating for over two decades has used the longer name "Christian Resurgence Circle," or CRC for short. Every new invention of religious practice needs to describe its practice and make clear what that practice is and what it is not. Here is a summation of what my group's 20-year exploration has envisioned a CRC to be and not to be:

A CRC Is Not:

A Church School Class
A Study Group
An Open-Discussion Group
A Circle of Friends

Circles, Assemblies, Guilds and Retreats

A Meditation Circle
A Spirit Group with Spirit leader
An Interreligious Dialogue
A Men's or Women's Support Group
A Peer-Counseling Circle
A Social Action Task Force

All these activities are good and may be led or participated in by CRC members, but they do not describe a CRC.

A CRC Is:

A CRC is a disciplined group who practice together (mind, Spirit, & body) with being a base community for a Next Christianity. This religious practice is designed for 3-12 persons meeting weekly for at least two hours. While the particular meeting times and disciplines are designed by each Circle, we have found that meeting face-to-face weekly for two hours is a baseline necessity. It is a viable continuation of the Sabbath heritage.

A CRC is rooted in Christian practice. By "Christian" we mean a basic loyalty to the history-changing and continuously transformative event of dying to our illusions and rising to authentic life – an event indicated by Jesus-as-Messiah, retold by word of mouth, and restated in Christian Scriptures and traditions. Such an understanding is outlined in this manifesto.

A CRC is rooted in the radical Christian theological awakening dating back to at least the innovations of Søren Kierkegaard. Such theology affirms radical social responsibility and continues to take in further respect for women's experience, equity topics of all types, ecological responsibility, interreligious respect & dialogue, and other edge topics of intense relevance to a Christian practice.

The CRC group practice uses a nurture design constructed upon the frame of Confession, Celebration, and Dedication.

A CRC is an ongoing experiment in religious innovation made by a whole network of CRCs acting together. As a whole group of CRCs we strive to evolve for ourselves and our descendants a structure of living practice that can become or influence significantly the base communities of a widespread Next Christianity. This networking is a key part of the whole pattern, for it can hold the balance between a commonality of religious practice and ongoing local experimentation. Each CRC needs to remain open to its own best intuitions without being so alone that it easily disintegrates into its own narrow egoisms. Being a vital Next Christianity requires both a planetary commonality and a local autonomy. How to balance those seemingly conflicting values is part of the sociological challenge we face.

(2) Quarterly Assemblies

An Assembly is conceived as a quarterly gathering of CRC members. These gatherings might be a 10 am to 4 pm Saturday event that includes an inspirational talk, breakout groups, a communion luncheon, and an afternoon of planning the common mission as well as the nurture and expansion of that regional group of CRCs. Such meetings would be carefully planned and carried out by leadership taken from all or most of the CRCs involved. Perhaps once a year they come together for an entire weekend. In my own experience, I have not yet experienced a sufficient number of CRCs in close enough proximity to experiment with these Assembly dynamics. Nevertheless, the eventual appearance of such a common structure seems to me absolutely necessary.

(3) Guilds

"Guild" is a generic name for any group that CRC members participate in or organize to do a specific service or to make a revolutionary input into their region. A Guild may be composed of members from some or all of the Circles as well as persons who are not members of a Christian Circle. And these region-wide tasks of social contribution are not carried out in the name of the Circles or the Assemblies, but are the contributions of bodies having secular names and organized in terms of making specific contributions that many different backgrounds of people may share in making. Calling this a "Guild" assumes that this organization would have only the amount of continuity needed for a particular social contribution, and that it might go out of being when its task is completed. Some Guilds might be ongoing or a significant period – such as an ecological organization, a theater troupe, a small business-help center, a coffee house & educational center, a cooperative-organic-food network, a protest organization, etc. Each of these organizations and/or operations would be composed of whoever is committed to that task and has the competence for it.

For example, if something does not already exist, a group concerned with **Climate-Crisis** would surely be needed. The common citizenry of every region needs to be mobilized for this cause. Also, every local region needs to find organized ways to promote "good" law making and its enforcement. It is not adequate to turn law making over to local old-boys clubs or to groups of political pros and their big business lobbyists. Local people need to design the spirit-of-the-law, if not all its details, and insist on the selection of representatives that carry out that spirit. People in every local region of the United States (or any other nation) need to work on the economic, political, and cultural aspects of every urgent topic.

One of the activities that might take place at a Quarterly Assembly of CRC members would be some discussion and planning concerning what service organizations (Guilds) are needed in this region, and which ones that already exist are in need of improvements that could be promoted by the members of this Assembly of Christians.

(4) Retreats

"Retreats" is another generic category for a wide variety of organizations – organization that might be viewed as the opposite of "Guilds," (Guilds might be called "Advances" rather than "Retreats.") By "Retreat" is not meant a withdrawal from mission

Circles, Assemblies, Guilds and Retreats

but a withdrawal in preparation for mission. "Retreats" are programs that have to do with awakening individual persons, training leadership, doing Spirit research, resolving polity questions or economic issues of the CRC Network, and more. Retreats can be constructed for CRC members and for the general public.

For example, one sort of Retreat would be an odyssey practicing a set of Spirit methods like those mentioned in Chapter 16. Another Retreat would be a theological and methodological Leadership Training School. Another would be a Research Symposium, working out new theological edges, methods of nurture, and needed missional thrusts. Another might be a conference of local CRC leaders for working out decisions that affect the whole CRC network or some part of it.

Enablement Offices

Each of the above organizations may require a volunteer or staffed enablement office to support their various functions. Some of these offices will be ongoing, staffed, and financially supported by Circle members and other interested persons. The nonprofit organization called "Realistic Living" in Bonham, Texas, is such an office. It is reasonable to hope that three more such offices might be opened in the next decade: one in Canada and on both East and West coasts of the U.S.

These ongoing enablement offices need to be composed of skilled people who are also CRC members, who are committed to the whole CRC Network, and who are willing to be thoroughly trained in the theology and methods of this specific venture in a Next Christianity experimentation. The polity of this arrangement needs to affirm both the participation of local circle members in the policy making as well as the independent creativity of these staffed offices. The Circles need to advise and financially support these offices, and these offices need to focus on serving the Circles that support them. These offices need to take care not to be behooved to monetary sources beyond the constituency of the CRC network.

Obviously, this is only a sketch of the organizational direction that a Next Christianity needs to take. Even though this pattern has overlaps with older patterns, the style and focus is very different. This is not a new denomination. It is not a monastic order. Overall, it is something significantly different from what Christian imagination has come up with in previous centuries. And this model is already something more than an off-the-cuff set of ideas; it is a consensus in the making among an expanding segment of Christian practitioners. And it is a consensus still in progress. This chapter is part of a manifesto with both a serious past and some yet to be written future.

A Leadership League

Without reinventing the clergy, we need to take seriously the need for trained leadership. We need to maintain the principle that every CRC member is a leader, and at the same time make provision for the preparation of self-selected leadership cores who have the devotion, commitment, theological training, and methodological skill needed to organize this novel and radical CRC Network and maintain its quality. A first experiment in launching such a Leadership League is outlined in the Appendix.

Chapter 18

The Eternal Mission to Planet Earth

A summary image is required for all the foregoing considerations about being the visible Church in history and choosing appropriate methods, theologies and institutional forms for that Next expression of Christianity. Many decades ago I saw the following image used to promote creative thinking about local church mission.

> *Suppose that you and I and others are on a space ship arriving to Earth from planet Wywang. On the side of our space ship is printed these words "Mission Earth."*

This picture can help us understand the radicality of being an expression of the true Church – of seeing in broad relief the task of creating that Next Christianity being described in this book. Indeed, being the true Church is even more challenging than being such an interplanetary mission: we are The Eternal Mission to Planet Earth. The word "Eternal" in this instance does not refer to some location beyond the stars, but to a trip we have taken without ever physically leaving planet Earth. We have died to our bodies, our emotions, our mind, our ego, and our personality as well as to our continent, our planet, our cosmos, and visited Eternity. No, we have not visited Eternity, we have come home to the profound humanness that is rooted in Eternity, a humanness that is just as mysterious as the entire cosmos is mysterious. We are breathing the final dread, fascination and courage of a state of Awe that is just as Awesome as the Void out of which all things come and into which all things return. We are still Earthlings, but Earthlings who have died and come back as resurrected Earthlings. By "resurrected" we mean having an Earthly embodiment that does not differ from every other humans' Earthly embodiment with this one exception: we are coming to every temporal experience from an experience of Eternity. We see every experience as an encounter with an Eternity experience that is our home, our true residence, our deep rest, our deep bliss, our deep roots of unconditional love for all beings among whom we dwell.

Here is another helpful story about this strange Eternal mission to planet Earth. I attended a musical many years ago entitled "Stop the World, I Want to Get Off." The gist of the story was about a man who in his ordinary life encountered a series of overwhelming challenges. When the going got roughest, he would cry out, "Stop the World, I Want to Get Off." The stage curtain would then close on his ordinary life and the man would reappear in a podium in front of the closed curtain. He would address the audience about his life, his feelings, his thoughts about it, and his considerations about what to do next. We, the audience, were aware that the real world never stops, yet I could identify with this man's desire to Stop the World, and more profoundly I could identify with his need to return to his ordinary life with a "having-stopped-the-world" perspective. Implied in this play is a radical perspective, a perspective derived from having the entire cosmos stop and then re-begin. This is another clue to the meaning of the "death-and-resurrection" symbol.

Jesus did not use the metaphor of stopping the world, and he certainly would not have recognized the metaphor of a spaceship arriving from outer space. But Jesus did use a metaphorical language that is just as strange to us contemporary Earth-walkers.

The Eternal Mission to Planet Earth

In order that you won't think that I am making this up, here is a quote from the premier New Testament scholar, Rudolf Bultmann:

> *The dominant concept of Jesus' message is the Reign of God. Jesus proclaims its immediately impending irruption, now already making itself felt. Reign of God is an eschatological concept. It means the regime of God which will destroy the present course of the world, wipe out all the contra-divine, Satanic power under which the present world groans – ... With such a message Jesus stands in the historical context of Jewish expectations about the end of the world and God's new future.*[13]

Bultmann shows how every teaching of Jesus implies this context of understanding. Furthermore, Bultmann insists that the earliest Christian community saw itself as an eschatological community, the community of the end time. He insists that every word of Paul implies an eschatological context. Paul saw himself calling his followers out of the old eon of Satanic living and finding standing in the new eon of the humanity of Jesus that had already come and was yet to come in its fullness. Indeed, every major Christian concept in Bultmann's 20th Century theology is an eschatological concept. "Faith" is an eschatological state of being. "Love" is an eschatological state of being. "Freedom" is an eschatological state of being. What does eschatological mean?

Bultmann interprets the eschatological metaphor existentially. He claims that we can translate the interior truth of the "eschatological" metaphor into something that we can experience. It can mean dying to the world with all its evil trends. It can mean dying to death itself, and being raised up to newness of life as a gift from the very same power that created us and that is killing our clinging attachments to this world. The meaning of the healing event we call "Jesus Christ" can include: leaving this world, joining Eternity, and returning to our ordinary lives in this world as new born beings.

---

[13] Bultmann, Rudolf; *Theology of the New Testament* (Charles Scribner's Sons, New York: 1951) page 4

The Eternal Mission to Planet Earth

It is easy for our all-too-rational minds to protest against these stories with the observation that our clinging to the world is perhaps never completely interrupted – that no matter how deeply we detach from select aspects of our lives, other aspects, perhaps deeply hidden ones, still manifest a tight cling.

But the omnipresence of such clinging does not negate the possibility of dying to our temporal lives, including our own deaths. This results in a state of being that is beyond death, beyond the cosmos, beyond time. And this astonishing state of being can then manifest here on Earth as a force in real human history. We do not properly understand and honor heroic persons like Martin Luther King Jr. unless we see in their living this profound detachment being manifest. Indeed, King may have had hope for living a long and celebrated life, such as the one granted to Nelson Mandela, yet both of these men knew that they might not enter the Promised Land for which they were risking their lives. Fannie Lou Hamer, Ella Baker, Sojourner Truth, Elizabeth Cady Stanton, Susan B. Anthony and millions of other women and men of all races, cultures, places, and times have manifested this eschatological-detachment style in their everyday temporal living. We can never be sure who is and who is not manifesting such saintly living. We can, however, suspect the presence of such a life even in the accessible, modest, humble, but premier scholar Rudolf Bultmann who lived rather happily and honored until a ripe old age of 92. He certainly described the eschatological life thoroughly enough to make it likely that he knew what he was talking about.

Whatever be the best description of eschatological living, we can assume that Christian ethics is about viewing historical time from the perspective of Eternity, understanding that our mission as the People of God means being "sent from Eternity to planet Earth."

The Eternal Mission to Planet Earth

Being a Contrarian Presence

The lifestyle and the work of People of God is inherently contrary to the majority views and trends of living. History includes awakenings of judgment upon the obsolete and evil practices in which the majority are enmeshed. History includes rivers of new life being forged by courageous and creative people in all sorts of unlikely places. All of us who rejoice in these realistic judgments and in these rivers of creative newness – all of us who seek to join them, will experience ourselves as a contrarian presence. We may be surprised at the transformation toward realism that can take place in response to us. And we may also be surprised at the extent of the stubborn opposition that can rise against us. But in general we need not be surprised. This is the way it has been and will continue to be. Contrarian Presence is the long-haul experience of the People of God.

I have long been enamored with the last chapter of the Gospel of John in which Peter and some other disciples, having experienced the crucifixion of Jesus, decide to return to fishing. But their fishing is not going well. Then the resurrected Jesus appears on the beach and called out them to throw their nets on the other side of boat. They do, and the fish caught are so numerous that they cannot pull the net on board. They have to drag it to shore. Peter cries out, "It's Him!" and jumps in the water and swims to shore. As Peter is sitting next to the resurrected Jesus eating fish, Jesus asks him if he loves him. Peter insists that he does, but Jesus responds, "Then feed my sheep." This same conversation is repeated two more times, and Peter is getting upset over being asked three times. Then the gospel writer makes plain what "feeding my sheep" entails. The food entailed is Peter's own body and blood. Peter still resists with a question about John's longevity. Jesus responds, "If it should be my will that he should wait until I come, what is that to you? Follow me." Then the gospel writer with his characteristic humor adds this parenthesis:

(That saying of Jesus became current in the brotherhood, and was taken to mean that that disciple would not die. But in fact Jesus did not say that he would not die; he only said, "If it should be my will that he should wait until I come, what is that to you?")[14]

The tradition has been that Peter did die rather early and that John lived to an old age. This reminds me of Martin Luther King dying early and Nelson Mandela living to a very old age. We never know what our destiny will be when we choose to "feed sheep" in the sense meant by this clever story.

Thinking Comprehensively

One of the contrarian aspects of a true Christian life is thinking outside the boxes in which most people comfortably dwell. There is a universal craving to keep life as simple as possible. But our lives in real history are not simple. Any picture we attempt to draw about the real challenges we face is a simplification. Nevertheless, we can move toward comprehensive thinking. On the following page I am sharing a chart about how to save the planet and humanity from the horrors of a decaying imperial civilization and usher in a viable and flourishing humanity on this planet. Preposterous as that may sound, that is exactly what comprehensive thinking means.

The background for this chart is a model of all the essential social processes that make up any whole human society. Each society institutionalizes these social processes differently, but must give some measure of attention to all these basic topics. Obviously, this is a model, and all models can be improved. Nevertheless, this is a pretty good model, certainly the best one I have drawn in my lifetime. Earlier, I used a model built by members of the Order:Ecumenical that had the cultural processes on top. I inverted that model because I now believe that the cultural processes are better pictured as the depth of a society rather than its top.

---

[14] John 21:23, The New English Bible

The Eternal Mission to Planet Earth

Then upon this general model I have picked out seven specific arenas of social process where our contemporary societies are most open to radical change. I have used the metaphor of *"whistle points"* that can cause an *"avalanche of change."* Perhaps you recall how an avalanche can start on a mountainside of gathered snow by the mere sounding of the relevant tone. A few flakes begin to vibrate, setting in motion other flakes that continue this exponential growth of disturbance until a huge flow of snow is happening. On the following chart I have listed seven places where skillful "whistling" has avalanche potential for social change.

Obviously, this chart is complex, raising hundreds of questions that an entire book could not fully settle. My intent here is to signal what I mean by "comprehensive thinking." My intent is to overwhelm both you and myself with considerations that we could spend a life time in further understanding. But I also intend this challenge to be utterly serious: these are possibilities that a comprehensive openness to 21st century history reveals.

The Eternal Mission to Planet Earth

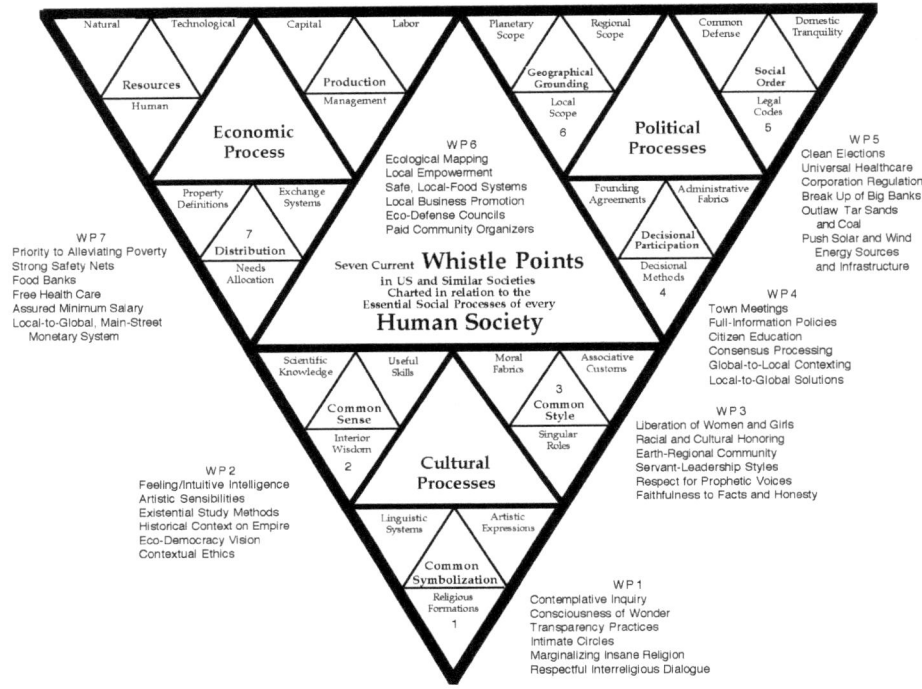

A large version of this chart is available:
Email jgmarshall@cableone.com

Organizing our Local Parish

The global, continental, and national perspectives, inherent in the chart just cited, is not the end of the story. We also face selecting tactical actions in our local places. Below is another chart that gives a sense of the sort of comprehensive ethical imagination local expressions of the People of God need to consider in order to manifest love for the local place where they live.

This chart assumes that the Christian Resurgence Circles mentioned in the last chapter are one of many organizations that we could create in our local places or Parishes. I am using the word "Parish" in the sense of the mission area of a specific body of

Christian servants. I am enamored with the concept of *"Interfaith Parish,"* the meaning of which is that we are not talking about Christians caring for Christians or Muslims caring for Muslims, but all the Awed Ones in the Parish caring for everyone who lives there. I am also enamored with the concept of the *"Bioregional Parish"* – by which I mean defining my area of local service as a specific piece of the planet defined by planetary features – land and water shapes, animals, plants, and humans. The service to be done in that Parish is service not only to humans, but also to all the species of life that live there and all the inanimate features and resources that make living possible and fruitful.

Also, the following chart suggests that we have two types of tactics to carry out. One set has to do with the more secular fundamentals and the second set has to do with organizations that are more inward or "religious" in focus. The Christian Resurgence Circle is one such religious organization, but there are others that members of that Circle might promote. Obviously, this specific list of things is incomplete and may not apply to every Parish. This chart is aimed at expanding our minds relative to thinking through comprehensively what local Christian service includes.

I am suggesting that members of a CRC think of themselves as *community organizers.* In his first run for president, Barack Obama suffered ridicule for his "credentials" as a community organizer. I am suggesting that CRC members wear *"community organizer"* as a badge of honor.

The Eternal Mission to Planet Earth

	Suggested Tactics for Local Community Action		
	Cultural	Political	Economic
Some Local Community Tactics	Local Theater House Concerts Ecological Celebrations Womens' Support Group Men's Support Group Social Ethics Courses Imaginative E-magazine Newspaper Items Communal Nodes	Democratic Party Enhancement Social & Ecological Education & Lobbying Key Protests on behalf of the 99%	Organic Gardens Community Gardens Food Cooperatives Energy Efficient Architecture, Equipment, & Transport Innovative Businesses
Some Next Christianity Tactics	Theological Courses Church School Classes Meditation Circles Spirit-Life Groups	Christian Resurgence Circles	A Christian Resurgence Service Fund

Transforming our Home Continent

Our local "Parish" work is a lifetime operation and is so demanding that we will be tempted to think that it is all we are called to do. But local parish work will be without final success if that is all that we the People of God do. We are also called to do our Parish work in the context of serving the continent and the globe. We are called to put forth direct energy toward actions that are directed toward national and continental issues that are happening in the planetary context. This includes electoral politics on a local, state, national, and global level of concern. This includes protest marches, demonstrations, and pioneering actions that turn tides of change on various widespread issues. Obviously, each of us cannot do everything; we will end up choosing specific things that we are, or feel we are, most qualified or passionate about. BUT ALL THESE TOPICS ARE ON OUR PLATES. Such topics spell out the Demand of God upon our lives. Any topics we choose are to be chosen in the context of serving everything that needs serving. What we don't do still needs doing, and we are responsible for inspiring or encouraging someone to do it. The People of God respond to God, and God's Demand is inclusive. We are called to love all our neighbors in all parts of the planet as we love ourselves. We are not called to love only people like ourselves, or people that we like, or people that we think we can help. All neighbors are the responsibility of the People of God. The impossibility of this Demand is its Eternal quality. There is boundless forgiveness available to make up for our failure to fully respond to this inclusive Demand. So, we have no need to cut down the Demand to some supposed human size.

Inviting Others into Eternity

Also the Demand includes a depth dimension as well as an expansive dimension. We are called to invite others into this state of Eternity in which we, the People of God, are functioning. This is the essence of the witnessing love described earlier. We are out to release other people from their Earth-bound clinging and assist them to also hear the Call to a return to Earth for the demanding service described above. Actually, massive and radical social changes only come about when millions of people hear this Eternal Call and obey it.

Rebuilding the Cities of Judea

This cryptic heading refers to creating the new institutions of the People of God – in this case a Next Christianity. That was what was happening when some of the Judeans exiled in Babylon answered the call to return to Judea and rebuild the institutions of peoplehood that could house and sustain the mission to humanity that they knew themselves called to be. This was not a pretty calling. Almost everything in Palestine was in ruins or decaying, and the people living there were not entirely agreeable to the "rebuilding" that these returnees had in mind. A desert had to be crossed, a livelihood invented, and unwelcome work commenced and carried out with little or no clarity about what the final consequences would be. This should sound familiar to those of us who have already begun to build a Next Christianity.

Looking back we can give thanks to those who rebuilt the Cities of Judea, for without their hard work there may not have been a Jesus, a Paul, an Augustine, a Mohammed, and so on. As we look forward, we do not know if there will be generations of humans in the far future who will give thanks to us. But we do not need to know. We only need to do what we are called to do. We can count on God to work out the consequences in whatever way it all must come to pass. Our fragmentary deeds are forgiven before they are done or even conceived. Such confidence in Reality rather than in ourselves is the power that bends history into something that may one day be called "progress."

The Cost of Discipleship

We know that the humanity that we are inviting to join us in Eternity-style living and in Eternity's tasks are in dread *flight* from such realism. Some are in an angry *fight* with such realism. They may be willing to defend their *flight/fight* pattern to the death, perhaps our death rather than their death. But we know that what they are defending is an illusionary substitute for Reality, and that Reality is an unavoidable wrath toward all such substitutes. All we "substituters" for Reality are headed toward the hell of despair. The most unfortunate among us are those who make it to their deaths without experiencing our inherent despair. Despair is a doorway to life. We (some of us) know that because we have been there. If so, we also know that our mission to this Planet may cost us our lives at the hands of the still despairing. At the same time we know that our integrity, our realism, and our "Eternal" quality of life is preferable to the despair of returning to the qualities of fallen humanity, among whom we dwell and with whom we still participate as a daily grievous discovery of the extent of our own estrangements. So the final cost of discipleship is the Demand to stay awake and press on toward the full stature of our primal hero, Jesus, the Anointed One – the Awed One who knew personally the Awesome and was filled with Awe.

And we can maintain this hope because we see the potential in every human being that we are discovering in ourselves. Every human being is, beneath all his or her flight, fight, and unconsciousness, the profound humanness of Jesus. So our hope is to be Jesus, to call out the Jesus in others, and together with millions of others to live out this Eternal mission to planet Earth.

Appendix:
The Realistic Living League
of Next Christianity Organizers

The "RLL" or "League" for short
League: an organization of persons sharing a common interest or purpose.

The Realistic Living League is a proposal for meeting the need for leadership for organizing a Next Christianity. Each region of the North American Continent and each local Circle of group practice needs leadership that is well versed in this specific experiment in Next Christianity. These five pages are intended to define this project:

Members

The Realistic Living League is composed of members who make these three commitments:

I. To meet at least weekly with at least two other League members who are open to the Spirit Journey implied in accessing profound humanness through the mediation of a vital Next Christian religious practice, and who are committed to this and the next two commitments.

II. To create and do a daily practice of solitary exercises and study aimed at the Spirit maturity needed for leadership in organizing a workable expression of this Next Christianity.

III. To commit to read the basic books in the following mini-library that define the core understandings of this particular movement in Christian resurgence. Many other books have contributed and need to contribute to this movement, but the first books listed on the next page form a backbone of commonality that will allow us to know and say who we are as this movement and this exploration.

Realistic Living League of Next Christianity Organizers

Other books for further enrichment reading are also listed on the following page. These are optional relative to this study commitment.

The books and manuals listed on the next pages provide the resources for developing a curriculum for a home-conducted, seminary-level, leadership-training program for this movement. Finding a way to encourage this reading is a key reason for launching the **Realistic Living League of Next Christian Organizers**. We need leadership who enjoy a significant degree of commonality, enabling them to work together successfully across the North American continent and beyond. On the third, fourth, and fifth pages is an outline for a curriculum of study spread over three years.

PS: Many more people than these league members will be involved in the overall experiment of a Next Christianity. This program of further training for a self-selected leadership role is not intended to negate our operating principle that all members of the Next Christianity are asked to **lead** in the various ways that are appropriate to each person. Also, we want to extend and deepen the principle of the priesthood of all believers. We have no desire to create a new clergy-laity stratification in the Next Christianity.

Realistic Living League of Next Christianity Organizers

A Mini-Library for the Realistic Living League of Next Christianity Organizers

Basic Books in Classic Post-Kierkegaardian Theology
Søren Kierkegaard -- *The Sickness Unto Death*
H. Richard Niebuhr -- *Radical Monotheism and Western Culture*
Paul Tillich -- *The Shaking of the Foundations*
Dietrich Bonhoeffer -- *Life Together*
Rudolf Bultmann -- *Primitive Christianity in its Contemporary Setting*
Simone Weil -- *Waiting for God*
Joseph Mathews -- *Bending History:* Talks of Joseph Wesley Mathews **Vol. I**
    editor John Epps *with:* John Cock, George Holcombe, Betty Pesek, & George Walters
  Bending History: Talks of Joseph W. Mathews, **Vol. II**, *toward a New Social Vehicle*
    editor John Epps *with:* James Campbell, James Wiegel, Clarence Mann,
        Marilyn Crocker, and George Holcombe

Key Symposium-Inspired Works in Theology and Mission

The following were composed to enable a 21st Century social vision, theological clarification, and journey practices rooted in decade-long discussions and writing projects related to the Research Symposium on Christian Resurgence:

The Road from Empire to Eco-Democracy by Gene Marshall, Ben Ball, Marsha Buck,
        Ken Kreutziger, and Alan Richard

  Also by Gene Marshall with help from Joyce Marshall, Marsha Buck, Alan Richard, & others:
The Call of the Awe: Rediscovering Christian Profundity in an Interreligious Era
*Great Paragraphs of Protestant Theology: A Commentary on the 20th Century
        Theological Revolution*
Jacob's Dream: A Christian Inquiry into Spirit Realization
The Enigma of Consciousness: A Philosophy of Profound Humanness & Religion
*The Love of History and the Future of Christianity: Toward a Manifesto for
        a Next Christianity*

Key Methods Resources
Brian Stanfield -- *The Art of Focused Conversation: 100 Ways to Access Group Wisdom in
        the Workplace*
    -- *The Workshop Book: From Individual Creativity to Group Action*
    -- *The Courage to Lead: Transform Self, Transform Society*
Joyce Marshall -- *Solitary Exercise Manuals*
Priscilla Wilson - Kathleen Harnish & Joel Wright *The Facilitative Way: Leadership that
        Makes the Difference*

Realistic Living League of Next Christianity Organizers

The above are Basic Readings,
The following are Important Enrichments:

Readings in Christianity and Ecology
Thomas Berry -- *The Dream of the Earth* and *The Great Work: Our Way into the Future*
Charlene Spretnak -- *The Resurgence of the Real: Body, Nature, and Place in a Hypermodern World*
-- *Relational Reality: New Discoveries of Interrelationship . . .*
Wes Jackson -- *Altars of Unhewn Stone: Science and the Earth*

Readings in Liberation Theology and Feminism
Mary Daly -- *Beyond God the Father: Toward a Philosophy of Women's Liberation*
-- *Amazon Grace: Re-calling the Courage to Sin Big*
Charlene Spretnak -- *States of Grace: The Recovery of Meaning in the Postmodern Age*
Gustavo Gutierrez -- *A Theology of Liberation: History, Politics and Salvation*
James Cone -- *The Risks of Faith: The Emergence of a Black Theology of Liberation*

Further Witnesses in the Wake of the Joe Mathews Inspiration
John Baggett -- *Seeing Through the Eyes of Jesus: His Revolutionary View of Reality & . . . Significance for Faith*
John Cock -- *The Transparent Event: Post-Modern Christ Images*
-- *Our Universal Spirit Journey: Reflection and Verse for Creation's Sake*
Richard Elliot -- *Falling in Love with Mystery: We Don't Have to Pretend Anymore*
Wesley Lachman -- *The Shortest Way Home: A Contemplative Path to God*

Also helpful are the following biographies
of the seven luminary figures listed in group one above:
Søren Kierkegaard -- *The Moment Before God* by Martin J. Heinechen
H. Richard Niebuhr -- *H. Richard Niebuhr: A Lifetime of Reflections on Church&World* by Jon Diefenthaler
Paul Tillich -- *Paul Tillich: His Life and Thought* by Wilhelm & Marion Pauck
Dietrich Bonhoeffer -- *Dietrich Bonhoeffer: a Biography* by Eberhard Bethge
Rudolf Bultmann -- *Rudolf Bultmann: a Biography* by Konrad Hammann
Simone Weil -- *Beyond Power: Simone Weil and the Notion of Authority* by Desmond Avery
Joseph Mathews -- *Brother Joe: A 20th Century Apostle* by James K. Mathews

Realistic Living League of Next Christianity Organizers

A Year-One Study Program for the Realistic Living League of Next Christianity Organizers

The idea here is that in the first year of this home-conducted, seminary-level curriculum, each of the following six books are studied or restudied to the extent appropriate for representing the whole movement in these breakthrough insights. Two considerations have predominated in choosing these selections for the first year: (1) accessibility to a wide range of persons, and (2) the most urgently needed insights with which to begin the encompassing this overall curriculum.

Basic Books in Classic Post-Kierkegaardian Theology

H. Richard Niebuhr -- *Radical Monotheism and Western Culture*
Paul Tillich -- *The Shaking of the Foundations*

Key Symposium-Inspired Works in Theology and Mission

Great Paragraphs of Protestant Theology: A Commentary on the 20th Century Theological Revolution
The Love of History and the Future of Christianity: Toward a Manifesto for a Next Christianity

Key Methods Resources

Brian Stanfield -- *The Art of Focused Conversation: 100 Ways to Access Group Wisdom in the Workplace*
Joyce Marshall -- *Solitary Exercise Manuals* (Using one or more of these manuals on solitary practice)

*Also choose one or more from
the enrichment list
outlined above*

A Year-Two Study Program for the Realistic Living League of Next Christianity Organizers

In the second year of this home-conducted, seminary-level curriculum, each of the following seven books are studied or restudied to the extent appropriate for representing the whole movement in these breakthrough insights. The selections are considered to be: (1) somewhat more difficult than the first-year selections, and (2) somewhat dependent upon the insights of the first-year selections.

Basic Books in Classic Post-Kierkegaardian Theology
Dietrich Bonhoeffer -- *Life Together*
Joseph Mathews -- *Bending History: Talks of Joseph Wesley Mathews* **Vol I**
 Bending History: Talks of Joseph W. Mathews, **Vol. II,** *toward a New Social Vehicle*

Key Symposium-Inspired Works in Theology and Mission
The Road from Empire to Eco-Democracy
The Call of the Awe: Rediscovering Christian Profundity in an Interreligious Era

Key Methods Resources
Brian Stanfield -- *The Workshop Book: From Individual Creativity to Group Action*
Joyce Marshall -- *Solitary Exercise Manuals* (Using one or more of these manuals on solitary practice)

*Also choose one or more from
the enrichment list
outlined above*

A Year-Three Study Program for the Realistic Living League of Next Christianity Organizers

In the third year of this home-conducted, seminary-level curriculum, each of the following seven books are studied or restudied to the extent appropriate for representing the whole movement in these breakthrough insights. These selections are considered to be (1) the most challenging of their respective lists and (2) somewhat dependent upon the insights of the first and second year selections.

Basic Books in Classic Post-Kierkegaardian Theology
Søren Kierkegaard -- *The Sickness Unto Death*
Rudolf Bultmann -- *Primitive Christianity in its Contemporary Setting*
Simone Weil -- *Waiting for God*

Key Symposium-Inspired Works in Theology and Mission
Jacob's Dream: A Christian Inquiry into Spirit Realization
The Enigma of Consciousness: A Philosophy of Profound Humanness & Religion

Key Methods Resources
Brian Stanfield -- *The Courage to Lead: Transform Self, Transform Society*
Joyce Marshall -- *Solitary Exercise Manuals* (Using one or more of these manuals on solitary practice)
Priscilla Wilson - Kathleen Harnish & Joel Wright *The Facilitative Way: Leadership that Makes the Difference*

*Also choose one or more from
the enrichment list
outlined above*

Table of Figures:

The Wedge of History and the God of History	160
How the Awesome Occasions Awe	190
The Wedge of History and the Almighty of History	197
Whistle Points for Change in Society	256
Tactics for Local Community Action	258

Publisher's Comments

Resurgence Publishing Corporation is pleased to present *The Love of History and the Future of Christianity: Toward a Manifesto for a Next Christianity,* by Gene W. Marshall with a Foreword by John L Epps. Gene Marshall's groundbreaking efforts to call for a realistic living approach to being a 21st century Christian echoes Joseph Wesley Mathews Legacy represented in other Resurgence Publishing Corporation books such as the "Bending History" Series and the "Transforming the Legacy" Series. By rooting this call in the journey of Christendom and the Christian Church history, Gene gives the reader both depth and perspective for his quest for a manifesto.

If you enjoy this publication by Gene you may enjoy other works he has written over the years:

The Road from Empire to Eco-Democracy (coauthor)
ISBN: 978-1-46208364-0, 287 pages

Jacob's Dream: *A Christian Inquiry into Spirit Realization*
ISBN: 978-1-4401-1355-0, 289 pages

Great Paragraphs of Protestant Theology: *A Commentary on the 20th Century Theological Revolution*
ISBN: 1089045-08-0, 79 pages (8 1/2 X 11)

The Call of the Awe: *Rediscovering Christian Profundity in an Interreligious Era*
ISBN: 0-595-26353-4, 317 pages

To Be or Not to be a Christian: *Meditations and Essays on Authentic Christian Community*
ISBN: 0-9611552-3-X, 321 pages

The Reign of Reality: *A Fresh Start for the Earth*
ISBN: 0-961155-2-1, 261 pages

For more information on Gene's publications please visit his website at www.RealisticLiving.org.

Also please visit the Resurgence Publishing Corporation website for publications by other authors, many of which are noted in this publication.

Resurgence Publishing Corporation (RPC) is a not-for-profit corporation founded in the state of Florida by M. George Walters, John P. Cock, and Betty C. Pesek. Its primary purpose is to promote the utilization of the archives of Joseph Wesley Mathews for research and publications that further the spiritual and social tasks that are Joe's legacy. In collaboration with the heirs of Joseph Wesley Mathews, the Institute of Cultural Affairs, Chicago, and the sponsorship of Wesley Theological Seminary, Washington, D.C., Joseph Wesley Mathews Archives where placed at the Seminary December 19, 2009 and are available for academic and public research.

M. George Walters, Corporate Secretary
Resurgence Publishing Corporation
www.ResurgencePublishing.com

CPSIA information can be obtained
at www.ICGtesting.com
Printed in the USA
LVHW011124161119
637567LV00034B/832/P